Careers in Information Technology

Careers in Information Technology

Editor
Michael Shally-Jensen, Ph.D.

SALEM PRESS
A Division of EBSCO Information Services, Inc.
Ipswich, Massachusetts

GREY HOUSE PUBLISHING

Publisher's Cataloging-In-Publication Data
(Prepared by The Donohue Group, Inc.)

Names: Shally-Jensen, Michael, editor.
Title: Careers in information technology / editor, Michael Shally-Jensen, Ph.D.
Other Titles: Careers in--
Description: [First edition]. | Ipswich, Massachusetts : Salem Press, a division of EBSCO
        Information Services, Inc. ; [Amenia, New York] : Grey House Publishing,
        [2016] | Includes bibliographical references and index.
Identifiers: ISBN 978-1-68217-148-6 (hardcover)
Subjects: LCSH: Information technology--Vocational guidance--United States. |
        Computer science--Vocational guidance--United States.
Classification: LCC T58.5 .C375 2016 | DDC 004.023--dc23

First Printing

PRINTED IN THE UNITED STATES OF AMERICA

CONTENTS

PUBLISHER'S NOTE

Careers in Information Technology contains twenty-three alphabetically arranged chapters describing specific fields of interest in this field. Merging scholarship with occupational development, this single comprehensive guidebook provides information technology students with the necessary insight into potential careers, and provides instruction on what job seekers can expect in terms of training, advancement, earnings, job prospects, working conditions, relevant associations, and more. *Careers in Information Technology* is specifically designed for a high school and undergraduate audience and is edited to align with secondary or high school curriculum standards.

Scope of Coverage

Understanding the wide net of jobs in information technology is important for anyone preparing for a career within that field. *Careers in Information Technology* comprises twenty-three lengthy chapters on a broad range of occupations including jobs such as computer systems analyst, web administrator, and computer support specialist, as well as in-demand jobs including game developer, robotic technician, and UX designer. This excellent reference also presents possible career paths and occupations within high-growth and emerging fields in this field.

Careers in Information Technology is enhanced with numerous charts and tables, including projections from the US Bureau of Labor Statistics, and median annual salaries or wages for those occupations profiled. Each chapter also notes those skills that can be applied across broad occupation categories. Interesting enhancements, like **Fun Facts**, **Famous Firsts**, and dozens of photos, add depth to the discussion. A highlight of most chapters is **Conversation With** — a two-page interview with a professional working in a related job. The respondents share their personal career paths, detail potential for career advancement, offer advice for students, and include a "try this" for those interested in embarking on a career in their profession.

Essay Length and Format

Each chapter ranges in length from 3,500 to 4,500 words and begins with a Snapshot of the occupation that includes career clusters, interests, earnings and employment outlook. This is followed by these major categories:

- **Overview** includes detailed discussions on: Sphere of Work; Work Environment; Occupation Interest; A Day in the Life. Also included here is a Profile that outlines working conditions, educational needs, and physical abilities. You will also find the occupation's Holland Interest Score, which matches up character and personality traits with specific jobs.
- **Occupational Specialties** lists specific jobs that are related in some way, like software developer, librarian, multimedia artist and animator, and chief science officer. Duties and Responsibilities are also included.

- **Work Environment** details the physical, human, and technological environment of the occupation profiled.
- **Education, Training, and Advancement** outlines how to prepare for this field while in high school, and what college courses to take, including licenses and certifications needed. A section is devoted to the Adult Job Seeker, and there is a list of skills and abilities needed to succeed in the job profiled.
- **Earnings and Advancements** offers specific salary ranges, and includes a chart of metropolitan areas that have the highest concentration of the profession.
- **Employment and Outlook** discusses employment trends, and projects growth to 2020. This section also lists related occupations.
- **Selected Schools** list those prominent learning institutions that offer specific courses in the profiles occupations.
- **More Information** includes associations that the reader can contact for more information.

Special Features

Several features continue to distinguish this reference series from other career-oriented reference works. The back matter includes:
- Appendix A: Guide to Holland Code. This discusses John Holland's theory that people and work environments can be classified into six different groups: Realistic; Investigative; Artistic; Social; Enterprising; and Conventional. See if the job you want is right for you!
- Appendix B: General Bibliography. This is a collection of suggested readings, organized into major categories.
- Subject Index: Includes people, concepts, technologies, terms, principles, and all specific occupations discussed in the occupational profile chapters.

Acknowledgments

Thanks to editor Michael Shally-Jensen, who played a principal role in shaping this work with current, comprehensive, and valuable material. Thanks are also due to Vanessa Parks, who took the lead in developing "Conversations With," with help from Allison Blake, and to the professionals who communicated their work experience through interview questionnaires. Their frank and honest responses provide immeasurable value to *Careers in Information Technology*. The contributions of all are gratefully acknowledged.

EDITOR'S INTRODUCTION

Introduction

We all use information technology of one type or another throughout the day to perform our jobs, keep up-to-date on the latest news, stay connected with friends and family, or just to explore and have fun. With the wide variety of computers, smartphones, tablets and other high-tech devices on which we depend, not to mention all of the software programs we load onto them, our society depends on skilled professionals in information technology to keep things running and keep us moving into the future. The Labor Department predicts that IT, or tech, jobs will grow faster than the average for all jobs, at a rate of 12 percent over the next decade. In fact, tech occupations are expected to add a half million new jobs over the decade, owing to the continuing growth of cloud computing, the collection and storage of "big data," the ongoing demand for mobile computing, increased cybersecurity needs, and the coming of the "Internet of Things," whereby more home and office appliances and other items are becoming connected to the internet and learning to communicate with each other, often without any human involvement. In 2015, the median annual wage for IT occupations was $81,430, considerably higher than the median annual wage for all occupations, which was $36,200.

The IT Industry and Career Opportunities

Providing a firm overview of the state of the information technology industry is difficult because new innovations and new trends develop at a rapid pace. Yet, this is also one reason why working in the IT makes it fascinating for those involved in the field. IT professionals need not only a broad understanding of modern technology but also a future-oriented perspective, to enable them to appreciate where technology is headed. This means keeping up-to-date on the latest devices and applications while also seeing how current products and services could be improved with the addition of further knowledge, creativity, or skill.

The current major industry growth areas include the following:

Big Data and Big Analytics. Cloud computing means greatly increased storage capacity and also a sharp rise in services providing free storage in order to have access to users' personal data (or, in most cases, metadata). Google, Microsoft, Amazon, and many other companies are all interested in storing user data and performing analytics in connection with websites visited, files stored, and so on. This has created many new career opportunities in data storage/analytics.

Cybersecurity. As the amount of data linked to the internet continues to grow, so too does the number of cyber-criminals in pursuit of that data in order to use it to their advantage. The fact that organizations and individuals use multiple platforms over the course of a day to carry out their business only compounds the problem of security. Companies must ramp up their security measures to protect their systems and proprietary data. Technologies able to detect unwanted activities and target their sources will continue to provide career opportunities for those interested in the IT field.

Internet Traffic Management. With recent court rulings placing a halt on "net neutrality" and permitting a two-tiered approach to the internet, companies like Netflix will continue to work with vendors to provide "preferred" versus standard streaming services to customers. One result is that broadband expertise and related skills are likely to be in demand as workers ensure "quality of service" for different users. Other technologies in this area include Voice-over IP, remote access, and conferencing/live streaming.

Internet of Things. Although still in its early stages, the Internet of Things (IoT), or communication between machines including household and office appliances and devices, is expected to be a significant growth area in the coming years. Homeowners can already access home security systems remotely, and such applications are likely to continue to expand in the near future.

Business Services. Companies continue to change how they deliver their offerings, shifting toward more flexible consumption models that allow customers to consume and pay for products and services based on need and usage. As more and more businesses begin to think about adapting their business models and operations to the new reality, more opportunities will arise for tech services groups to apply their expertise in the business services sector.

An Ever Changing Landscape

Regardless of the specific industry segment, IT professionals are tasked with continuously monitoring and responding to rapidly developing trends. Many of the trends one sees today in IT share a common theme, namely, that industries and consumers are adopting new technologies faster today than ever before. (Admittedly, this has been said often; and yet it is very true!) Upgrading software and obtaining "next generation" technology has become so commonplace that consumers expect to be notified by manufacturers as soon as new versions become available.

In the early years of the tech industry, new developments usually originated in the public sector—in the military, for example—before being adapted for private corporate and consumer use. Today, in contrast, many developments are driven above all by consumer demand. In the coming years, there will be an ongoing need for IT talent to design and develop new user-friendly, "experience-rich" technologies. As always, this will also include a need for experienced customer support personnel to assist users with their new products.

Two other developments are worth noting here. First: There will be an increasing number of devices and systems, both for organizations and consumers, that will be interconnected via the Internet of Things and related network technologies.

The growing need to develop both software and hardware with capabilities for advanced connectivity, as well as to manage these integrated systems, will create or expand opportunities for those with skills and experience in this area. Second: We will continue to see a sharp increase in the number of apps, along with increased connectivity, and that will result in an increased demand for even more apps. Business organizations will need app specialists to streamline how they offer services to their customers.

On the business side, increased automation will continue to drive a shift in overall business operations, and increase the need for tech-savvy workers in all types of operations. At the same time that automation reduces the number of low-level jobs, it also increases demand for mid-level professionals who are capable of overseeing production processes. Employers will need to hire workers with an IT background, or who have at least trained on IT equipment, to perform these functions and drive their businesses into the future.

Tech Education

Although many if not most careers in technology require a four-year college degree, that is not always the case. Some occupations, such as Web Developer and Customer Support Technician, require only an associate's degree, as do various maintenance, repair, and production-related positions. At the opposite end of the scale, high-level computer engineer positions usually require a doctorate or professional degree. While the majority of technology jobs call for a bachelor's degree or, at minimum, some college or specialized vocational training, many companies offer qualified employees on-the-job training and/or programs leading to certification in new technologies. In truth, education never really ends for those in technology careers because there is always something new to learn.

—M. Shally-Jensen, Ph.D.

Sources

Bureau of Labor Statistics. "Computer and Information Technology Occupations." Bls.gov

Galindo, Sergio. "IT Industry Trends for 2015." Techrader.com

Kelly Service. "2016 Industry Trends for IT Talent." Kellyservices.us

Sallomi, Paul. "2016 Technology Industry Outlook: An Interview." Deloitte.com

Chief Information Officer / Chief Technology Officer

Snapshot

Career Cluster(s): InformationTechnology

Interests: Computer technology, communication, logistics, management, problem solving

Earnings (Yearly Average): $131,600

Employment & Outlook: Much faster than average growth expected

OVERVIEW

Sphere of Work

Chief Information Officers (CIO) and Chief Technology Officers (CTO) are executives responsible for computer-related or technology-related aspects of an organization's operation. CIOs and CTOs are executive management, and are typically answerable to an organization' Chief Financial Officer (CFO) or Chief Executive Officer (CEO). While CTO/CIO positions are interchangeable in some

organizations, in other situations CIOs and CTOs fulfill different roles. CIOs are usually responsible for managing the implementation of existing technology to meet the needs of the organization, and are also typically responsible for creating an organization's technological strategy. CTOs, by contrast, are more often responsible for overseeing the development or implementation of new technology. While most CTOs therefore have training or experience in engineering and technology, CIOs more often have a background in business and management.

Work Environment

CIO/CTOs work in office environments and most work full time. CIO/CTOs may spend much of their time in meetings, either meeting directly with employees and/or other managers or conducting meetings via email and telephone. CIO/CTOs are also typically responsible for a variety of management tasks, including meeting with personnel and planning work for other members of the IT staff. In some companies, CIO/CTOs may also be asked to negotiate purchases with vendors or arrange meetings with clients/customers.

Profile

Working Conditions: Work Indoors
Physical Strength: Light Work
Education Needs: Bachelor's Degree, Master's Degree
Licensure/Certification: Not Required
Opportunities For Experience: Work in a Related Occupation, Deputy CIO/CTO Experience
Holland Interest Score*: ECI

* See Appendix A

Occupation Interest

Individuals looking to become CIOs or CTOs should have a strong interest in technology as well as management and business. Most CIO/CTOs are primarily managers and so need strong interpersonal communication skills, reasoning ability, and considerable organizational skills for planning and scheduling. IT positions tend to be investigative, as individuals in CIO/CTO roles are often asked to solve organizational problems with technological solutions. Individuals looking to become CIO/CTOs should also be achievement oriented as individuals often spend considerable time working through an organization to achieve sufficient credentials to warrant consideration for executive IT positions.

A Day in the Life—Duties and Responsibilities

The daily tasks for a CIO/CTO will differ markedly depending on the nature of the organization. Typically, a CIO/CTO may spend part of each day in meetings with staff, other executives, clients, or vendors. CIO/CTOs may spend time evaluating the daily operations of the IT department, or developing new projects with members of their staff. CIO/CTOs may also spend time evaluating the work completed by their department or by members of the IT staff. In addition, CIO/CTOs may spend time on a typical day receiving status and/or project updates from staff regarding ongoing projects.

CTOs may part of their time directly involved in the design and production process, or supervising a team assigned to develop new technology. Both CTOs and CIOs also spend time researching new technology, which may include attending seminars or listening to presentations from vendors. CIOs may be responsible for all data management within an organization or may handle a specific aspect of an organization's operation, such as customer service data systems or electronic data processing.

Duties and Responsibilities

- Evaluate an organization's tech infrastructure
- Work with designers, project managers, and other executives
- Establish and develop key goals for the IT department
- Supervise and/or recruit staff
- Research or evaluate new technology for use in the organization
- Plan work for other professionals
- Meet with or negotiate with vendors for a company's supply needs
- Complete budget and/or financial planning for the IT department or entire organization

OCCUPATION SPECIALTIES

Virtual CIO

Virtual CIOs (vCIOs) are contractors that work, either temporarily or over longer terms, for organizations without the infrastructure to support a permanent CIO position.

Chief Infrastructure Officer

A Chief Infrastructure Officer is in charge of managing a company or organization's infrastructure needs, including technology investment but also investment in other physical infrastructure.

Chief Science Officer

A Chief Science Officer is the lead executive of a scientific research program at an organization. CSOs are the equivalent of CTOs for scientific development or research organizations.

Chief Medical Information Officer

A CMIO is a Chief Information Officer for a hospital or medical research organization. CMIOs are responsible for managing a hospital's IT resources, budget, and must be able to understand the specific needs of doctors and other medical professionals.

Federal Chief Information Officer

The Federal Chief Information Officer is the head of the U.S. Office of Electronic Government, a position created under the 2002 E-Government Act. The FCIO is responsible for managing federal IT policy and overseeing government investment in technology development.

WORK ENVIRONMENT

Physical Environment

CIOs and CTOs spend most of their time in an office environment, though CTOs, depending on their field, may also spend time in a computer lab or engineering lab. CIOs and CTOs may be asked to travel to attend conferences or to meet with representatives of other companies or vendors. In some organizations, a CIO or CTO may divide their time between two or more facilities.

Relevant Skills and Abilities

Communication Skills
- Writing effectively
- Communicating in meetings and via electronic mail

Interpersonal/Social Skills
- Being able to create and work within groups

Organization & Management Skills
- Coordinating teams of IT professionals
- Managing people/groups
- Developing broad overviews of IT use and needs

Research & Planning Skills
- Creating proposals for IT development or budgeting
- Researching emerging technology

Technical Skills
- Performing technical work
- Working with computers, programming languages, and hardware

Human Environment

As executive managers, CIO/CTOs often spend time meeting with clients, other managers/executives, and employees. CIO/CTOs should be comfortable working with a team or work group and most professionals in the field report that face-to-face contact with employees, colleagues, and/or clients is a daily part of the job.

Technological Environment

CIOs and CTOs work with computer and data technology daily and must continually learn about new developments in IT systems. Professionals in the field may need to learn to use database management software like NoSQL, Oracle PL/SQL, or Apache. Some positions may require individuals to be familiar with programming languages like C, C++, Python, etc. In some cases, individuals may need to be familiar with web development software like Apache Tomcat, JavaScript, or Pages ASP. Most positions in the field require professionals to research emerging technology, which may include attending conferences and seminars on software and hardware developments.

EDUCATION, TRAINING, AND ADVANCEMENT

High School/Secondary

High school students interested in becoming CIOs should focus on obtaining an education in business and/or marketing. Those interested in pursuing work as CTOs may want to focus on obtaining a technological education focused on computer science and engineering. For all professionals in the field, a diverse education is recommended, including taking classes in mathematics, history, English, industrial arts, and graphic arts. Most professionals in the field have at least a Bachelor's Degree and so high school students should take college preparatory classes to help prepare them to enter college after graduation.

Suggested High School Subjects
- Algebra
- Introduction to Computers
- Sociology
- History
- English
- Introduction to Business
- Industrial Arts
- Graphic Arts/Graphic Design
- Computer Programming
- Public Speaking
- Applied Mathematics
- Engineering
- Physics
- World Languages

Famous First

Bank of America executive Alfred R. Zipf, credited with designing the first computer system used specifically by the banking industry, was a pioneer in the CIO field. Zipf began with Bank of America as a transit clerk in 1936 and rose through the ranks to management. Working with the Stanford Research Institute, Zipf helped to design and create ERMA (Electronic Recording Method of Accounting) in the 1950s, the first computer system designed for the banking industry. Bank of America created a new position, Chief Information Officer, for Zipf, making him the first American to hold the CIO title.

College/Postsecondary

Most individuals seeking to become CTOs should have a strong background in IT and might consider pursuing college degrees in computer or information science. Such degrees typically introduce students to computer programming, mathematics, engineering, and software/hardware development. Individuals seeking to become CIOs might obtain Bachelor's degrees in business administration or marketing. Those with advanced degrees, such as MBAs (Masters of Business Administration) may have an advantage in applying for CIO positions.

Related College Majors
- Business Administration
- Marketing
- Finance
- Telecommunications Management
- Applied Technology Management
- Computer Networking & Security
- Electronics

Adult Job Seekers

Typically, CIOs/CTOs work towards upper management from subordinate IT or lower management positions. Individuals with bachelor's degrees or higher can apply for entry level management or IT positions and attempt to work their way up to upper management.

Professional Certification and Licensure

Currently there are no general licensing requirements for individuals working as CIOs or CTOs. In some fields, individuals may need to obtain licensing or certificates of achievement in specific types of technology. In a computer sciences or web development company, for instance, individuals seeking CIO or CTO positions may need certification in various programming languages or types of hardware/software systems.

Additional Requirements

Whether or not a CIO or CTO is directly involved in the development of IT technology, professionals in the field benefit from a strong understanding of modern computer and information systems. Those with experience or familiarity with a wide variety of computer programming languages, hardware systems, operating systems, and software tools may have an advantage on the job market.

Fun Fact

Jason Goldman—the first person to hold the job of Chief Digital Officer at the White House— actually majored in astrophysics because he wanted to work at a planetarium when he was a kid. In an interview on www.whitehouse.gov, he said one of most interesting people he'd ever met was Puff Daddy

Source: https://www.whitehouse.gov/blog/2015/04/13/qa-first-ever-white-house-chief-digital-officer-people-purpose-puff-daddy-and-hulk

EARNINGS AND ADVANCEMENT

Salaries for CIO/CTOs vary widely by industry, geographic location, and industry. The Bureau of Labor Statistics (BLS) estimated a median salary of $131,600 in 2015, for individuals working as either CIOs or CTOs. Those at the lowest 10 percent of the field earned around $80,160, while those at the upper end of the spectrum earned salaries in excess of $187,200. As CIO/CTO positions are considered "executive management," applicants are unlikely to qualify for open positions without first accruing significant experience in IT management or development. Individuals should therefore plan on spending 5 to 10 years working in the field before expecting to warrant consideration for executive management.

Metropolitan Areas with the Highest Employment Level in this Occupation

Metropolitan area	Employment	Employment per thousand jobs	Hourly mean wage
New York-Jersey City-White Plains, NY-NJ	23,690	3.66	$84.99
Washington-Arlington-Alexandria, DC-VA-MD-WV	14,320	5.93	$78.14
San Jose-Sunnyvale-Santa Clara, CA	13,830	13.66	$91.44
Boston-Cambridge-Newton, MA	11,140	6.33	$71.28
Chicago-Naperville-Arlington Heights, IL	10,300	2.89	$63.74
Atlanta-Sandy Springs-Roswell, GA	9,750	3.93	$65.36
Los Angeles-Long Beach-Glendale, CA	8,800	2.14	$73.47
Minneapolis-St. Paul-Bloomington, MN-WI	8,520	4.53	$65.65
Seattle-Bellevue-Everett, WA	8,040	5.23	$73.66
San Francisco-Redwood City-South San Francisco, CA	7,270	7.13	$88.60

Source: Bureau of Labor Statistics

EMPLOYMENT AND OUTLOOK

According to the BLS there were approximately 349,000 individuals employed as CIOs, CTOs, and IT managers in 2014. Due to the continuing expansion of IT into nearly every facet of business and finance, the IT field is growing at 14 to 15 percent per year, which is far faster than the average of 7 percent for all occupations. The digitization of finance and healthcare have provided a wealth of new opportunities in the field. In addition, the introduction of cloud computing and the integration of cloud technology into a variety of businesses are expected to create IT opportunities for those with experience in cloud computing.

Related Occupations
- Computer and Information Research Scientists
- Computer Hardware Engineers
- Computer Programmers
- Information Security Analysts
- Web Developers
- Network and Computer Systems Administrators
- Software Developers
- Database Administrators

Related Military Occupations
- Army CIO

Conversation With . . .
SREE SREENIVASAN

Chief Digital Officer, City of New York, New York
CDO professional for 4 years

1. What was your individual career path in terms of education/training, entry-level job, or other significant opportunity?

I studied history at St. Stephen's College in Delhi and was a professional journalist in India. Eventually, I moved to the U.S. and taught journalism at Columbia University for 20 years. In 2012, I became the first Chief Digital Officer of Columbia University and, about a year later, became the first CDO of the Metropolitan Museum of Art, which I did for three years before being hired by the City of New York almost a year ago.

Along the way, I founded social media educational programs Social Media One-Night Stand and Social Media Weekend. I was part of the founding team at DNAinfo.com, named one of the six hottest startups of 2010 by Business Insider. My podcast on CBS Radio's PlayIt is the "@Sree Show: Talking tech, culture, entrepreneurship."

My job at Chief Digital Officer is to help make New York City the most tech-savvy, the most transparent, and the most digitally equitable city in the world. That's what the mayor tweeted when I was hired.

Digital technology has already changed the world and will continue to change the world.

2. What are the most important skills and/or qualities for someone in your profession?

A Chief Digital Officer (CDO) is different from a Chief Technology Officer (CTO). A CDO usually deals with public engagement, whereas a CTO mainly deals with infrastructure and planning and wires and wireless and computers and devices. The CDO works more on the overall strategy of connecting with the public. The CDO role is relatively new. It's still being created and adapted, so it's different in different industries. It requires a deep understanding of technology, a deep understanding of the potential of specific platforms, and a deep understanding of the problems and pitfalls of those platforms. You also need an understanding of how technology has evolved and where consumers and industries are going.

3. What do you wish you had known going into this profession?

I wish I had known how big the internet was going to be. I understood a little bit, but not the scale and how it would transform the world. I would have understood and been able to do a lot more with the technology. Hey, I would have invested in some of these things. I might have joined one of these companies.

4. Are there many job opportunities in your profession? In what specific areas?

Lots and lots of companies are excited about getting a CDO into their company. But while there are a lot of opportunities, it's not like there are a lot of CDO jobs; every company will have only one CDO. But getting on that path is really important. That means figuring out where things are going, where technology is changing, so that you can understand and prepare for the changes that are coming.

5. How do you see your profession changing in the next five years? What role will technology play in those changes, and what skills will be required?

I believe that all the changes we've seen in the last 10 years, we're going to see even more in the next 10 years—faster, more deep and more meaningful changes. And that's hard to believe because we've had so many changes already.

One of the ways things are going to change is that the expertise of the folks who are in this role is going to get more complicated. I'm lucky that I entered when I did. The next generation is going to have to know a lot more technology, a lot more hands-on technology.

6. What do you enjoy most about your job? What do you enjoy least about your job?

What I enjoy most is the ability to work with people. You help people every day and make their lives better. That's what you do every morning—you think of how you can reduce red tape, make things better, faster, easier for people. Reduce aggravation. That's a wonderful thing. The hardest thing about being a CDO is you have to work very closely with lots of different people, which is exciting, but also means you don't have full control. It's not like you're the CEO. You have to depend on other people to execute a lot of the things you want to do.

7. Can you suggest a valuable "try this" for students considering a career in your profession?

What they can try is internships at big organizations that have CDOs. Or working with a company that doesn't have a CDO, but working with the Chief Technology Officer or Chief Information Officer and thinking about occasions where if somebody's priority was not technology, where they would have benefited by having a digital strategy. By the time you get into your career, there's a good chance there'll be a CDO for that company. There are hundreds and hundreds and soon thousands of CDOs. I would also read all the archives of www.cdosummit.com. I think that'll help.

MORE INFORMATION

IEEE Computer Society
2001 L Street NW, Suite 700
Washington, DC 20036-4928
202-371-0101
www.computer.org

CompTIA
3500 Lacey Road, Suite 100
Downers Grove, IL, 60515
866-835-8020
www.comptia.org

Computer Research Association
1828 L Street, NW, Suite 800
Washington, D.C. 20036-4632
202-234-2111
www.cra.org

Association for Computing Machinery (ACM)
2 Penn Plaza, Suite 701
New York, NY 10121-0701
800-342-6626
www.acm.org

Telecommunications Industry Association (TIA)
1320 North Courthouse Road
Suite 200
Arlington, VA 22201
703-907-7700
www.tiaonline.org

Micah Issitt/Editor

Computer & Information Systems Manager

Snapshot

Career Cluster(s): Business Administration; Information Technology; Science, Technology, Engineering & Mathematics

Interests: Computer systems, analyzing data, solving problems, communicating with others

Earnings (Yearly Average): $131,600

Employment & Outlook: Faster than average growth expected

OVERVIEW

Sphere of Work

Computer and information systems managers, also known as information technology (IT) managers, are responsible for organizing, directing, and coordinating operations in a variety of computer-related fields, such as electronic data processing, network security, and systems analysis. They help to establish the IT goals of a company and are in charge of implementing computer systems to successfully meet these goals. IT managers consult with technology users, vendors,

and technicians to help assess a company's IT needs and system requirements.

Work Environment

Computer and information systems managers typically work within an office environment. A majority of managers work directly for computer-systems design and IT services firms. Other managers work for financial firms, manufacturing firms, or government offices on a federal, state, or local level. As communications technologies improve, it is not uncommon for computer and information systems managers to telecommute. Most managers work full time during the week. Some overtime may be required.

Profile

Working Conditions: Work Indoors
Physical Strength: Light Work
Education Needs: Bachelor's Degree, Master's Degree
Licensure/Certification: Recommended
Opportunities For Experience: Military Service, Volunteer Work, Part Time Work
Holland Interest Score*: ECI

* See Appendix A

Occupation Interest

The computer and information systems profession normally appeals to people who have strong analytical and problem-solving skills and a solid background in computer systems. New innovations in computer systems mean that an IT manager must stay on top of the latest technologies in order to remain competitive. The profession tends to attract people who enjoy collaborating with others to solve problems. Most managers enter the profession with a computer-science or business degree, but many others come from diverse career backgrounds.

A Day in the Life—Duties and Responsibilities

Computer and information systems managers apply their knowledge and problem-solving skills to improve the computer systems of an organization. They must be able to collaborate with employees and others in the IT field. The workday of a computer and information systems manager can vary, depending on the organization's specific field. Meetings with other managers, technology vendors, and IT personnel are common.

Throughout the day, a manager helps plan, organize, and direct the installation and upgrading of the organization's computer hardware and software. They work with others in IT to make sure the organization's network and electronic data are secure. Part of their daily routine usually entails assigning and reviewing the work of others in IT, including systems analysts and programmers. Before a new or modified computer system or program is implemented, a manager must review and approve it. During all of these activities, managers adhere to their organization's operational budget; in order to maintain this budget, they need to negotiate with technology vendors.

It is rare for one manager to perform all of these duties. Most managers have a specialty position and work in a specific IT team of an organization. For example, a chief technology officer (CTO) will assess new technologies and determine if they will be a benefit to an organization, while a chief information officer (CIO) is in charge of directing the organization's overall technology strategy. If an organization does not have a CIO, then the CTO typically handles those responsibilities.

Duties and Responsibilities

- Managing all organizational computing systems
- Meeting with management team, department heads and vendors to jointly cooperate and solve problems
- Consulting with management and other organization members to determine computing needs
- Reviewing and coordinating project schedules
- Providing organization members with technical support
- Developing information resources that deal with issues in data security and disaster recovery
- Creating and understanding organization goals and procedures
- Training and supervising technical staff
- Staying up to date with the latest technology

OCCUPATION SPECIALTIES

Chief Technology Officers

Chief Technology Officers evaluate the newest and most innovative technologies and determine how these can help their organization.

Information Technology Directors

Information Technology Directors manage the computer resources for their organization.

Project Managers

Project Managers develop requirements, budgets and schedules for their organization's information technology projects.

WORK ENVIRONMENT

Transferable Skills and Abilities

Research & Planning Skills
- Identifying problems
- Solving problems

Technical Skills
- Performing scientific, mathematical and technical work
- Using technology to process information
- Understanding which technology is appropriate for a task
- Applying the technology to a task
- Maintaining and repairing technology

Physical Environment

Computer and information systems managers spend the majority of their workday in well-lit office environments. The specifics of the environment vary depending on the organization that employs them.

Human Environment

Collaboration and communication are essential to the job of a computer and information systems manager. In order to accurately

- Working with machines, tools or other objects

Communication Skills
- Speaking effectively
- Writing concisely
- Listening attentively
- Reading well

Interpersonal/Social Skills
- Motivating others
- Cooperating with others
- Asserting oneself
- Being able to work independently

Organization & Management Skills
- Paying attention to and handling details
- Performing duties that change frequently
- Managing people/groups
- Managing time
- Managing equipment
- Demonstrating leadership
- Making decisions
- Meeting goals and deadlines
- Working quickly when necessary

Research & Planning Skills
- Analyzing information
- Developing evaluation strategies
- Using logical reasoning
- Setting goals and deadlines
- Defining needs

assess the needs and goals of an organization's system, a manager has to collaborate with IT personnel, systems analysts, and technology vendors. Managers usually have to negotiate prices with technology vendors.

Technological Environment

Computer and information systems managers work with a large assortment of computer systems, hardware, and software. Each system is different, depending on the organization's field. If a manager is telecommuting, a variety of communication technologies can be used, including a laptop or smartphone.

EDUCATION, TRAINING, AND ADVANCEMENT

High School/Secondary

Employers typically require applicants to have at least a high school diploma or an equivalent degree, although most positions in the field require a bachelor's degree or higher. High schools normally offer an assortment of classes that an individual interested in the profession could benefit from. Any courses in computer science, mathematics, and business management would help an aspiring IT manager develop a good background for the profession. Some high schools even offer extracurricular computer clubs, where the fundamentals of computer systems can be learned.

Suggested High School Subjects
- Algebra
- Applied Communication
- Applied Math
- Business & Computer Technology
- Business Data Processing
- Calculus
- College Preparatory
- Computer Programming
- Computer Science
- English
- Geometry
- Keyboarding
- Mathematics
- Statistics
- Trigonometry

Famous First

The first era in computer and information systems management began with IBM mainframe computers of the late 1950s and early 1960s. These machines often took up entire rooms in business facilities and required teams of specialists to maintain them. In later decades, as microprocessors and client/server systems came to dominate, the need to share and manage information grew exponentially.

College/Postsecondary

Typically, a computer and information systems manager must have at least a bachelor's degree. While managers enter the field from a variety of different educational backgrounds, the majority of them have degrees in computer science, information science, or a related field. Most managers have taken courses in computer programming, advanced mathematics, and software development. Because of the various business aspects of the profession, many managers also have completed business-related courses.

Some employers require that a manager have a graduate degree. A common graduate degree for a manager is a master of business administration (MBA), which typically takes two years to complete. It is common for people pursuing their MBAs to take these classes in the evenings, after work, thereby gaining work experience while also completing their graduate studies.

Most technical schools offer computer science or programming programs. Usually these programs last from six months to a year. Students are given formal classroom instruction as well as hands-on training. Technical schools are a great place for an individual to network with more experienced people in the field. Many of these schools also offer job-placement programs.

Because new developments in computer technology are occurring regularly, managers should be willing to pursue professional-development courses throughout their career in order to stay competitive and relevant.

Adult Job Seekers

Anyone interested in a career as a computer and information systems manager should be aware that it takes years of experience and training in order to attain a managerial position. For instance, CTOs may need up ten to fifteen years of IT experience before being considered for the position. A strong background in computer and information systems is required, so an individual entering the field should be sure he or she has the necessary experience. If an individual has no experience in the field, he or she should consider enrolling in a college or technical school that offers a relevant program.

Professional Certification and Licensure

Although it is usually not required, a manager can choose to become certified as a specialist in a number of different IT applications. Managers with professional certification are more likely to advance into higher-paying positions. Professional certification is a way for an individual to demonstrate his or her skill and expertise in the profession. Managers can attain certification through independent certifying agencies or technology vendors.

Additional Requirements

Computer and information systems management demands great collaborative and communication skills. Managers must also be good at solving problems and managing budgets and be able to think independently and creatively. The job requires strong analytical skills in order to assess the best way to solve an IT-related problem.

Fun Fact

The Information Superhighway may need a traffic cop. Every second, about 6,000 tweets, more than 40,000 Google queries, and more than 2 million emails travel its lanes, according to Internet Live Stats.

Source: http://www.livescience.com/54094-how-big-is-the-internet.html

EARNINGS AND ADVANCEMENT

Earnings depend on level of responsibility and specialty. Median annual earnings of computer and information systems managers were $131,600 in 2014. The lowest ten percent earned less than $80,160, and the highest ten percent earned more than $200,000.

Computer and information systems managers may receive paid
vacations, holidays and sick days; life and health insurance; and
retirement benefits. These are usually paid for by the employer. At
higher levels of management, they can also receive benefits such as
expense accounts, stock options and bonuses.

Metropolitan Areas with the Highest Employment Level in this Occupation

Metropolitan area	Employment	Employment per thousand jobs	Annual mean wage
New York-Jersey City-White Plains, NY-NJ	23,690	3.66	$176,780
Washington-Arlington-Alexandria, DC-VA-MD-WV	14,320	5.93	$162,530
San Jose-Sunnyvale-Santa Clara, CA	13,830	13.66	$190,190
Boston-Cambridge-Newton, MA	11,140	6.33	$148,260
Chicago-Naperville-Arlington Heights, IL	10,300	2.89	$132,570
Atlanta-Sandy Springs-Roswell, GA	9,750	3.93	$135,950
Los Angeles-Long Beach-Glendale, CA	8,800	2.14	$152,820
Minneapolis-St. Paul-Bloomington, MN-WI	8,520	4.53	$136,560
Seattle-Bellevue-Everett, WA	8,040	5.23	$153,220
San Francisco-Redwood City-South San Francisco, CA	7,270	7.13	$184,290

Source: Bureau of Labor Statistics

EMPLOYMENT AND OUTLOOK

Computer and information systems managers held about 350,000 jobs nationally in 2014. Employment of computer and information systems managers is expected to grow faster than the average for all occupations through the year 2024, which means employment is projected to increase 10 percent to 19 percent. Almost every organization in today's workforce needs to keep a computer network running smoothly and secure from hackers, viruses and other attacks. The growth of security as a main concern for organizations will help to fuel the growth of computer and information systems managers.

In addition, the demand for organizations to have newer, faster and more mobile networks; the growth of the use of information technology in the healthcare field; and the growth of e-commerce will continue to create new jobs for computer and information systems managers. Those who have experience in internet technologies and web applications will be in especially high demand.

Employment Trend, Projected 2014–24

Computer and information systems managers: 15%

Operations specialties managers: 7%

Total, all occupations: 7%

Note: "All Occupations" includes all occupations in the U.S. Economy. Source: U.S. Bureau of Labor Statistics, Employment Projections Program

Related Occupations
- Computer Engineer
- Computer Network Architect
- Computer Programmer
- Computer Support Specialist
- Computer Systems Analyst
- Database Administrator
- General Manager & Top Executive
- Information Security Analyst

- Information Technology
  Project Manager
- Librarian
- Medical Records
  Administrator
- Network & Computer Systems
  Administrator
- Operations Research Analyst

- Software Developer
- Web Administrator
- Web Developer

Related Military Occupations

- Computer Programmer
- Computer Systems Officer
- Computer Systems Specialist

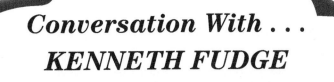

Conversation With . . .

KENNETH FUDGE

Director of Information Technology
Harbor Health Services, Boston, Massachusetts
IT professional, 25 years

1. What was your individual career path in terms of education/training, entry-level job, or other significant opportunity?

My career path took several turns before landing as Director of Information Technology. In my junior year at a vocational technical high school, I began working for a small medical software firm as an applications developer, writing code, creating financial reports, etc. I began college as a computer science major, but soon realized that I had a knack for business and changed my major to information systems. It was through my college experience that I began to understand that IT could drive the success or failure of an organization.

After college, I worked at several small start-ups where I designed, implemented and managed the computing infrastructures, usually as the sole IT person. The start-ups included medical services and device manufacturing (lasers optics and building fiber optical cables). Each company came with new rules, challenges and expectations. But I learned from every company I worked at and I was able to build a portfolio of skills that I continue to grow today. Look at every job as an opportunity to grow your knowledge, skills and contacts.

2. What are the most important skills and/or qualities for someone in your profession?

It's important to know the customer your company is seeking and to know who the user of your computer system is. You need to understand business and should learn all aspects of whatever business you're in. That's the only way to fully understand the needs of your users and of the company's customers.

The ability to think outside the box is a great quality for an IT director. Businesses look to IT to solve problems. Be the person that finds a workable solution.

With the tools we provide to staff to do their jobs well, IT can drive a business' success or failure. Provide the right tools for the user and you'll have success.

People skills are important, because we interact with every employee, from entry level to executive. You need the ability to look beyond the four walls of your company to see how other companies are implementing technology and how you can use the same technology.

3. What do you wish you had known going into this profession?

IT has evolved into a 24/7 job. When I started working in IT—before the internet—businesses ran mostly Monday to Friday, 9 to 5. Today businesses run 24/7. This translates into working late nights, weekends and holidays. Someone from IT is always on call. Finding the right life balance is important. You need to be careful to not burn out.

Also, I recommend that you seek out an executive level mentor at every organization you work for, but preferably not the Chief Information Officer (CIO). My best mentors have been CEOs and CFOs. They will help guide you throughout your career.

4. Are there many job opportunities in your profession? In what specific areas?

Yes. Every company needs IT. Figure out what part of IT you're good at: support, networking, wireless, database administration, mail … the list is huge. Then find an industry that excites you. Do you like big or small companies? Do you want to give back and work for a non-profit? Figure out what you're passionate about and look for jobs there.

5. How do you see your profession changing in the next five years? What role will technology play in those changes, and what skills will be required?

Technology moves at lightning pace, but most businesses do not—and for good reason. Understanding both the positive and negative impact of emerging technologies will help your organization keep pace with trends and opportunities that will help it grow and prosper. Part of your job is to guide the organization through the myriad of technology, extracting the hype from the possible.

6. What do you enjoy most about your job? What do you enjoy least about your job?

I enjoy seeing the business succeed. In the 11 years I've been in my current position, we've have added new service areas, built four new facilities and grown the budget by almost 200 percent. I enjoy seeing my co-workers excel in their careers. The biggest challenge today is security, but it's also an opportunity. I spend 20 percent of my time protecting the company from external and internal threats. The risks and penalties associated with a data breach are great, so I need to be proactive. But I view this as an opportunity to increase my skills by learning the technology to protect my organization.

7. Can you suggest a valuable "try this" for students considering a career in your profession?

IT is more than technical support; we are business leaders who help determine strategic goals and implement technology to achieve them. Reach out to a CIO or someone at the director level and talk to them about what they feel is important in IT. You'll either love it or hate it by the time you are done.

MORE INFORMATION

Association for Computing Machinery
2 Penn Plaza, Suite 701
New York, NY 10121-0701
800.342.6626
www.acm.org

Association of Information Technology Professionals
401 North Michigan Avenue
Suite 2400
Chicago, IL 60611
800.224.9371
www.aitp.org

Computing Research Association
1828 L Street NW, Suite 800
Washington, DC 20036
202.234.2111
www.cra.org

Institute for the Certification of Computer Professionals
2400 East Devon Avenue, Suite 281
Des Plaines, IL 60018
800.843.8227
www.iccp.org

Institute of Electrical and Electronics Engineers Computer Society
2001 L Street NW, Suite 700
Washington, DC 20036-4928
202.371.0101
www.computer.org

Patrick Cooper/Editor

Computer-Control Machine Tool Operator

Snapshot

Career Cluster: Manufacturing; Production

Interests: Machinery, computer programming, mechanical problem solving, design

Earnings (Yearly Average): $36,440

Employment & Outlook: Slower than Average Growth Expected

OVERVIEW

Sphere of Work

Computer-control machine tool operators are responsible for the setup and operation of computer numerical controlled (CNC) machines, including lathes, mills, and turning machines. They operate machines that form, shape, and cut metal and plastic materials used in factories. Operators are responsible for monitoring machines and adjusting them as needed. Computer-control machine tool operators work in a wide range of industries, from automotive manufacturing to machinery and plastics production.

Work Environment

Computer-control machine tool operators work in machine shops. As these shops present a number of safety hazards, operators must wear earplugs for protection from work noise, safety goggles to protect eyes from flying particles, and reinforced boots to protect feet from heavy equipment. Operators are expected to adhere to strict quality control and safety standards. Most computer-control machine tool operators stand throughout the day, but movement is limited and repetitive.

Profile

Working Conditions: Work Indoors
Physical Strength: Medium Work
Education Needs: On-The-Job Training, High School Diploma or G.E.D., High School Diploma with Technical Education, Junior/Technical/Community College, Apprenticeship
Licensure/Certification: Recommended
Opportunities For Experience: Apprenticeship, Part-Time Work
Holland Interest Score*: REI

* See Appendix A

Occupation Interest

Individuals drawn to the profession tend to be independent workers who are interested in complex machinery. They should be able to perform routine tasks without losing attention to detail. Operators are invested in accuracy and precision and interested in mechanical problem solving. Although they work independently, operators must cooperate regularly with colleagues. Individuals interested in the computer-control machine field must be knowledgeable about computer programming, design templates, and computer software. They must work well under pressure and be able to remain focused for long periods.

A Day in the Life—Duties and Responsibilities

The daily duties of a computer-control machine tool operator include inspecting machines for wear and damage before beginning machine operation. Once a machine is in operation, the operator calculates how best to lift and feed materials through the machine and monitors the size and shape of cuts. Some operators may use cranes or lifts to maneuver large pieces. Operators listen for sounds that may indicate worn or faulty components and check for changes in machine vibration and temperature that might indicate a problem. Lubricants and cooling systems are employed to ensure proper machine operation. On occasion, an operator may stop a machine to make minor repairs or to modify or adjust processing according to preset machining sequences

Computer-control machine tool operators use precision tools to install, align, or replace bits and cutting heads. They prepare materials for processing while the machine is in operation, ensuring smooth workflow. They also inspect and measure finished pieces with gauges and calipers to ensure correct machine operation and may work with production lines that include hoists and conveyor belts. Operators are also responsible for cleaning their machines and performing closing inspections at the end of the workday.

Operators are not often required to write, but they must be able to follow complex written instructions. They are often responsible for the input of production data and sometimes the creation of reports. Computer-control machine tool operators may confer with programmers and supervisors to identify problems with machining programs.

Duties and Responsibilities

- Reviewing set-up sheet and specifications to determine operational sequences
- Bolting fixtures to machine bed
- Positioning metal stock in fixture and securing work piece in place
- Assembling cutting tools in tool holders and positioning tools in spindles

OCCUPATION SPECIALTIES

Numerical Control Router Set-Up Operators

Numerical Control Router Set-Up Operators set up and operate multi-axis, numerically controlled routing machines to cut and shape metallic and non-metallic workpieces.

Numerical Control Milling-Machine Operators

Numerical Control Milling-Machine Operators set up and operate multi-axis, numerically controlled milling machines to mill surfaces on metallic and non-metallic workpieces.

Numerical Control Drill-Press Operators

Numerical Control Drill-Press Operators set up and operate numerically controlled drill presses that automatically perform machining operations such as drilling, reaming, counter-sinking, spot-facing and tapping of holes in metal workpieces.

Numerical Control Jig-Boring Machine Operators

Numerical Control Jig-Boring Machine Operators set up and operate numerically controlled jig-boring machines to perform such jigging operations as boring, drilling and counter-sinking holes in metal workpieces.

WORK ENVIRONMENT

Physical Environment

Most computer-control machine tool operators work in machine shops contained within larger factories. Some operators work with very large pieces of material, such as aerospace components, and must use hoists, cranes, and other lifting devices. Machine shops may contain contaminants such as particulates and hazardous fumes, and operators must wear protective clothing and masks to reduce exposure.

Transferable Skills and Abilities

Organization & Management Skills
- Making decisions
- Paying attention to and handling details

Research & Planning Skills
- Developing evaluation strategies

Technical Skills
- Performing scientific, mathematical and technical work
- Working with machines, tools or other objects
- Working with your hands

Human Environment

Although computer-control machine tool operators carry out their daily tasks independently, they usually work in a team setting, so physical proximity to other workers is common. Noise and vibration make routine communication difficult. Periodic contact may be made with others to ask advice or receive instructions.

Technological Environment

Computer-control machine tool operators must have some knowledge of computer-aided design (CAD) programs, as they may be required to perform basic programming functions. They sometimes use industrial control software that monitors workflow and inventory and enter data into spreadsheets for reporting purposes.

EDUCATION, TRAINING, AND ADVANCEMENT

High School/Secondary

Students interested in the field of computer-control machine tool operation should study mathematics and mechanics and take any available classes in basic engineering, design, and drafting. Courses in shop math and geometry are also beneficial to those interested in the field.

Suggested High School Subjects
- Algebra
- Applied Math
- Applied Physics
- Blueprint Reading
- Computer Science
- Drafting
- English
- Geometry
- Machining Technology
- Shop Math
- Trigonometry

Famous First

The first computer-aided design (CAD) software was developed jointly in 1964 by General Motors and IBM. The system was first used to design the trunk lids of Cadillac automobiles (a GM brand).

Postsecondary

Although postsecondary education is typically not required, aspiring computer-control machine tool operators may benefit from certified training programs available at many community colleges and technical and vocational schools. Training for the field is also available in the military. Professional organizations such as the National Institute for Metalworking Skills (NIMS) provide resources for those interested in pursuing certified training, including lists of accredited programs. Courses in CAD programs and industrial design may also be helpful.

Related College Majors
- Machine Technologist

Adult Job Seekers

Most adult job seekers in this field will increase their chances of finding work by earning certification prior to applying for positions. Training and certification is available through the NIMS Competency Based Apprenticeship System. Adult job seekers may benefit from the on-the-job experience and flexible training schedules that these apprenticeships provide.

Professional Certification and Licensure

Though certification and licensure are not required, some employers may prefer candidates who have earned credentials in various key metalworking skills. NIMS offers fifty-two credentials based on performance and theory tests and also accredits training programs at technical high schools and colleges throughout the United States.

Additional Requirements

Computer-control machine tool operators usually work forty hours per week. They are typically paid overtime if additional work is required. Physical strength is required to work with the materials involved in industrial production. Good stamina is necessary in order to be able to stand for long periods, and attention to detail is crucial.

Fun Fact

These precise and programmable machines are used for dying, jewelry making, drilling, metal molding, and cutting and shaping.
Source: http://www.slideshare.net/elvistaylormark/interesting-facts-about-cnc-machining

EARNINGS AND ADVANCEMENT

Earnings of computer-control machine tool operators depend on the type of machine operated, and the size, geographic location, and extent of unionization of the employer. Median annual earnings of computer-control machine tool operators were $36,440 in 2014.

Computer-control machine tool operators may receive paid vacations, holidays, and sick days; life and health insurance; and retirement benefits. These are usually paid by the employer. In some cases, employers and employees may contribute jointly to union trust funds used to pay for certain additional fringe benefits.

Metropolitan Areas with the Highest Employment Level in this Occupation

Metropolitan area	Employment	Employment per thousand jobs	Annual mean wage
Houston-Sugar Land-Baytown, TX	5,400	1.90	$39,750
Milwaukee-Waukesha-West Allis, WI	4,010	4.88	$40,790
Chicago-Joliet-Naperville, IL	3,980	1.06	$38,390
Los Angeles-Long Beach-Glendale, CA	3,630	0.89	$37,750
Minneapolis-St. Paul-Bloomington, MN-WI	3,080	1.69	$40,230
Cleveland-Elyria-Mentor, OH	3,080	3.04	$36,950
Warren-Troy-Farmington Hills, MI	2,950	2.58	$40,530
Cincinnati-Middletown, OH-KY-IN	2,250	2.22	$36,640
Philadelphia, PA	2,200	1.18	$41,560
Santa Ana-Anaheim-Irvine, CA	1,770	1.19	$38,110

Source: Bureau of Labor Statistics

EMPLOYMENT AND OUTLOOK

Computer-control machine tool operators held about 120,000 jobs nationally in 2014. Most worked in machine shops, plastics products manufacturing, machinery manufacturing or transportation equipment manufacturing, making mostly aerospace and automobile parts. Employment of computer-control machine tool operators is expected to grow slower than the average for all occupations through the year 2024, which means employment is projected to increase 2 percent to 7 percent. Most jobs will be to replace workers who retire or transfer to other occupations.

Employment Trend, Projected 2014–24

Industrial trades workers: 9%

Total, all occupations: 7%

Computer-Controlled Machine Tool Operators: 4%

Note: "All Occupations" includes all occupations in the U.S. Economy. Source: U.S. Bureau of Labor Statistics, Employment Projections Program

Related Occupations
- Machinist
- Metal/Plastic Working Machine Operator
- Millwright
- Robotics Technician
- Sheet Metal Worker
- Textile Machinery Operator
- Tool & Die Maker

Conversation With . . .
KIDIA TYLER

Instructor, CNC Technology
Gateway Technical College, Racine, Wisconsin
CNC field, 19 years

1. What was your individual career path in terms of education/training, entry-level job, or other significant opportunity?

My mother was a punch-press operator and used to bring her tools, like a dial caliper, home. I was fascinated, but she wouldn't let me play with them. She would tell me: "When you get a little older, you can learn how to use them." So when I got older, I took a blueprint reading class and a gauging class, and learned to read calipers. I told her I was ready and she gave me that caliper. From that point on, I took computer numerical control (CNC) and manual machine classes and graduated in 1997 with a technical diploma in numerical control from Gateway Technical College in Racine, Wisconsin.

I started out setting up manual lathes and mills for a couple of years and then I transferred to my company's CNC department. Over the years, I worked for companies that made parts for the automotive, agricultural, and appliance industries. I worked on horizontal and vertical CNC machines.

I switched to teaching CNC technology because of my family. I have four daughters and a son; as they got older, one of my daughters said: "You're never here. You work twelve-hour days, seven days." She was right. I'm a single mother and I worked a lot of overtime and holidays. Also, I was getting tired of carrying heavy tools and getting in and out of machines. I started taking night classes in criminal justice, then saw an opening for this job. I applied and got it, and am now teaching my second semester.

2. What are the most important skills and/or qualities for someone in your profession?

To be a CNC operator, you need to have some math skills. You need to read routings—job instructions on how to complete the process of machining parts—fill out paperwork, follow your work order. You need to pay attention to details.

To work with the machines, you need to know how to operate them, their programs, and how to stop that machine if it's doing something you know it's not supposed to be doing. You'll learn tool offsets, and how to load and unload the offset programs. And you need to know safety on the job. You've got to make sure you are paying attention to your machine and are focused on the job. You have got to be able to look at a part you've made and tell if something's wrong with it.

3. What do you wish you had known going into this profession?

It's not easy to be an African American woman working in a field with predominantly Caucasian men. It was hard to fit in and let them know I could pull my weight. It seems like it's more challenging with skilled work—when you know more than they do. That's when problems came in.

4. Are there many job opportunities in your profession? In what specific areas?

There are lots of CNC jobs within fifty miles of Racine. A lot of employers say they can't get qualified, knowledgeable operators and machinists. They have people coming in who haven't paid their dues and want to make more than $30 an hour in their first machinist job.

5. How do you see your profession changing in the next five years, what role will technology play in those changes, and what skills will be required?

Times are changing and the machines are changing. When I started, you had to make your own programs and blueprints. Now, you go to software for that. I think operators will need to know more programming and how to make blueprints.

6. What do you enjoy most about your job? What do you enjoy least about your job?

I enjoyed working with my hands and figuring out complex blueprints and I loved being a CNC machinist for the 18 years I did it. However, it got to the point I couldn't do it physically, mentally, or spiritually. When you're a CNC machinist you work a lot of overtime and I needed to make a change to spend more time with my family.

What I love about teaching is training students, and teaching them what I know and what to expect in industry. I love when a student stays in contact, goes out, gets a job, and comes back to say, "Oh, you were right." I like hearing about their successes.

But, I'd never taught before so I've had to learn how to teach from a book when I'm used to doing things hands-on. It's taken some time to learn how to hit competencies, or give tests and homework.

7. Can you suggest a valuable "try this" for students considering a career in your profession?

Take courses in manual and CNC machines. And take tours of manufacturers, talk with supervisors, and watch how a CNC machine works.

MORE INFORMATION

National Institute for Metalworking Skills
10565 Fairfax Boulevard, Suite 203
Fairfax, VA 22030
703.352.4971
www.nims-skills.org

National Tooling and Machining Association
1357 Rockside Road
Cleveland, OH 44134
800.248.6862
www.ntma.org

Precision Machined Products Association
6700 West Snowville Road
Brecksville, OH 44141
440.526.0300
www.pmpa.org

Precision Metalforming Association Educational Foundation
6363 Oak Tree Boulevard
Independence, Ohio 44131-2500
216.901.8800
www.pmaef.org

Bethany Groff/Editor

Computer Engineer

Snapshot

Career Cluster: Information Technology; Science, Technology, Engineering & Mathematics

Interests: Computer science, solving problems, collaborating with others

Earnings (Yearly Average): $110,650

Employment & Outlook: Average Growth Expected

OVERVIEW

Sphere of Work

Computer hardware engineers plan, design, and test computer components for use in a variety of industries. These components include computer chips, circuit boards, routers, and more. Computer engineers are involved in each stage of the development process, including designing blueprints, testing the components, and analyzing the results. They are also involved in the manufacturing process. Engineers sometimes work with computer software developers to make sure that the hardware and software components work together correctly.

Work Environment

Computer engineers typically work in research laboratories, where they build and test an assortment of computer models. The environments of these laboratories can vary; the majority of them are located in metropolitan areas. Manufacturing, design, or research-and-development firms commonly employ computer engineers. As communication technology improves, some engineers may be able to telecommute. While they typically work full time—forty hours per week—the work may require overtime on occasion.

Profile

Working Conditions: Work Indoors
Physical Strength: Light Work
Education Needs: Bachelor's Degree, Master's Degree
Licensure/Certification: Usually Not Required
Opportunities For Experience: Military Service, Part-time Work
Holland Interest Score*: IRE

* See Appendix A

Occupation Interest

The computer engineer profession tends to attract individuals with a strong background in computer science and hardware. Most have a degree in computer engineering from an Accreditation Board for Engineering and Technology (ABET)–accredited school. Computer engineers are problem solvers who enjoy figuring out the best solution to computer-related problems. They should also be able to communicate and collaborate with others in the field. Engineers should be interested in the latest technology and be willing to continue their education throughout their career.

A Day in the Life—Duties and Responsibilities

Computer engineers use their education and skills to design, develop, and test new computer hardware and components. These include computer systems, computer chips, and the physical parts of computers. Engineers are also involved in the design and development of new routers, printers, and keyboards. Their daily responsibilities vary depending on the project they are working on. Meetings may be held throughout the day with other engineers, technology vendors, and various other employees.

Computer engineers are normally involved in the entire process of product development and implementation. This includes the manufacturing process. Throughout the day, an engineer will provide technical support to other employees, including designers, the marketing department, and technology vendors. As computer technology is developed and created, engineers will perform tests and ensure that everything meets specifications and requirements. This testing process usually involves analyzing test data, product prototypes, or theoretical models. As new hardware is implemented, an engineer will monitor how it is functioning and make any modifications necessary so that it performs according to specifications. Engineers also make recommendations for additional hardware, such as keyboards, routers, and printers.

When new components are designed and manufactured, engineers have to make sure that the hardware is compatible with software developments. Because of this, hardware engineers collaborate closely with software developers throughout the process.

Duties and Responsibilities

- Designing new computer hardware and overseeing its manufacture
- Analyzing and testing computer hardware
- Modifying hardware to ensure its compatibility with new software and other technologies

WORK ENVIRONMENT

Physical Environment

Research laboratories predominate. At these laboratories, computer engineers design, develop, and build a broad range of computer models, both physical and theoretical. This is also where they test the models. These laboratories are often well lit, very clean, and well ventilated.

Relevant Skills and Abilities

Communication Skills
- Speaking effectively
- Writing concisely

Interpersonal/Social Skills
- Working as a member of a team

Research & Planning Skills
- Solving problems
- Using logical reasoning

Technical Skills
- Performing scientific, mathematical and technical work

Human Environment

Throughout the day, computer engineers will communicate and collaborate with a variety of other professionals in the field, including software developers, sales departments, technology vendors, manufacturers, and other engineers.

Technological Environment

Computer engineers work with a wide variety of computer-related technologies, including systems, hardware, and software. They also work with both physical and theoretical computer models. During the design and manufacturing process, blueprints and specifications are used. Servers that store massive amounts of data are also implemented

EDUCATION, TRAINING, AND ADVANCEMENT

High School/Secondary

Normally employers require applicants to have a high school diploma or an equivalent GED certificate. There are several basic and advanced high school courses that will greatly benefit a student interested in becoming a computer engineer. Courses in computer science, mathematics, and engineering will give a student a good background in the fundamentals of the profession. Extracurricular computer clubs are sometimes available; such a club would also benefit those interested in computer engineering.

Suggested High School Subjects
- Algebra
- Applied Communication
- Applied Math
- Applied Physics
- Calculus
- Computer Programming
- Computer Science
- English
- Geometry
- Mathematics
- Trigonometry

Famous First

The first commercially successful minicomputer was the Digital Equipment Corporation's PDP-8, introduced in 1965. Smaller and less expensive than a mainframe computer, but almost as powerful, the PDP-8 was priced at $18,000 and sold more than 50,000 units. Today, a specimen is on display at the Smithsonian's National Museum of American History in Washington, D.C.

College/Postsecondary

Employers typically require a computer engineer to have at least a bachelor's degree in a related field. Some employers require that an engineer have a degree from an ABET-accredited school. The majority of entry-level professionals have a degree in computer engineering, but employers usually accept electrical-engineering degrees as well. Students should make sure they take the appropriate postsecondary courses that give them a strong background in math and science.

Some technical schools offer programs in computer and electronics technology, which typically include instruction in circuits, systems, and specialized techniques used in the field. Students are given formal classroom instruction as well as the opportunity for practical application in a laboratory setting. Many of these technical schools offer job-placement programs, and they are a great place to network with more experienced professionals.

Since computer engineers work closely with computer software systems, professionals need a solid background in computer programming as well. Most computer-engineering curricula include computer-science courses that can give a student experience with programming.

Specialized jobs in computer engineering and some large firms may require a master's degree. These degrees commonly take two years to complete. Many computer engineers take graduate courses after work, which allows them to acquire work experience while pursuing their master's degree

Related College Majors
- Computer Engineering
- Computer Engineering Technology
- Computer Maintenance Technology
- Computer Programming
- Computer Science
- Information Sciences & Systems

Adult Job Seekers

Because computer technology is always developing, it should be understood that computer engineers must continue their education throughout their careers. If an individual does not have any experience in computer engineering or related fields, he or she should enroll in a college or a technical school that offers a relevant program.

Professional Certification and Licensure

Although it is not normally required, the Institute of Electrical and Electronics Engineers (IEEE) Computer Society can certify computer engineers. Attaining certification helps engineers verify their skills and knowledge of the field's practices. Engineers who have completed a certification program are more likely to achieve higher-paying positions.

Additional Requirements

A computer engineer must possess great analytical skills in order to properly examine complex computer equipment. Problem-solving skills are needed to figure out the best way to improve upon computer hardware. Computer engineers need to be able to think critically in order to identify problems and determine solutions. They should also be willing to continue their education throughout their career in order to keep their knowledge up to date and relevant.

Fun Fact

In 1947, computer engineers traced an error in the Mark II computer at Harvard University to a moth trapped in a relay. They taped the insect to a log and wrote, "First actual case of bug being found." But Thomas Edison used the term "bug" in a similar context decades earlier.

Source: http://americanhistory.si.edu/collections/search/object/nmah_334663

EARNINGS AND ADVANCEMENT

Computer engineers may be promoted after several years of experience. According to a salary survey by the National Association of Colleges and Employers, the starting salary offer for graduates with a bachelor's degree in computer engineering was $67,463 in 2012.

Mean annual earnings of computer hardware engineers were $110,650 in 2014. The lowest ten percent earned less than $66,070, and the highest ten percent earned more than $160,610.

Mean annual earnings of computer software developers were $106,050 in 2014. The lowest ten percent earned less than $63,250, and the highest ten percent earned more than $154,800.

Computer engineers may receive paid vacations, holidays, and sick days; life and health insurance; and retirement benefits. These are usually paid by the employer.

Metropolitan Areas with the Highest
Employment Level in this Occupation (Hardware)

Metropolitan area	Employment [1]	Employment per thousand jobs	Annual mean wage
San Jose-Sunnyvale-Santa Clara, CA	11,620	11.94	$136,220
San Diego-Carlsbad-San Mar-cos, CA	3,820	2.89	$99,050
Dallas-Plano-Irving, TX	3,110	1.39	$101,310
San Francisco-San Mateo-Redwood City, CA	2,630	2.42	$130,470
Austin-Round Rock-San Marcos, TX	2,610	2.95	$106,220
Washington-Arlington-Alexandria, DC-VA-MD-WV	2,550	1.07	$117,180
Santa Ana-Anaheim-Irvine, CA	2,510	1.69	$120,280
Baltimore-Towson, MD	2,260	1.75	$123,020
Los Angeles-Long Beach-Glendale, CA	2,060	0.51	$109,030
Boston-Cambridge-Quincy, MA NECTA Division	1,990	1.11	$115,660

[1]Does not include self-employed. Source: Bureau of Labor Statistics

Metropolitan Areas with the Highest Employment Level in this Occupation (Software)

Metropolitan area	Employment [1]	Employment per thousand jobs	Annual mean wage
San Jose-Sunnyvale-Santa Clara, CA	27,080	27.82	$138,410
Washington-Arlington-Alexandria, DC-VA-MD-WV	24,720	10.39	$110,780
Boston-Cambridge-Quincy, MA	18,600	10.36	$116,270
Dallas-Plano-Irving, TX	13,280	5.93	$99,060
San Francisco-San Mateo-Redwood City, CA	11,360	10.45	$120,400
Los Angeles-Long Beach-Glendale, CA	11,190	2.76	$120,690
New York-White Plains-Wayne, NY-NJ	11,140	2.07	$113,700
Houston-Sugar Land-Baytown, TX	10,670	3.75	$106,090
Atlanta-Sandy Springs-Marietta, GA	10,160	4.26	$96,320
Seattle-Bellevue-Everett, WA	8,730	5.85	$115,800

[1]Does not include self-employed. Source: Bureau of Labor Statistics

EMPLOYMENT AND OUTLOOK

Computer hardware engineers held about 83,300 jobs nationally in 2012. Employment is expected to grow about as fast as the average for all occupations through the year 2022, which means employment is projected to increase 5 percent to 9 percent. Although the use of information technology continues to expand rapidly, the manufacture of computer hardware is expected to be adversely affected by intense foreign competition.

Computer software developers held about 1,020,000 jobs nationally in 2012. Employment is expected to grow much faster than the average for all occupations through the year 2022, which means employment is projected to increase 20 percent or more. This is a result of businesses and other organizations adopting and integrating new technologies and seeking to maximize the efficiency of their computer systems. Mobile technology, the growing use of software applications in the healthcare industry and concerns over cybersecurity will all contribute to job demand.

Employment Trend, Projected 2012–22

Software developers: 27%

Total, all occupations: 11%

Engineers (all): 9%

Computer hardware engineers: 7%

Note: "All Occupations" includes all occupations in the U.S. Economy. Source: U.S. Bureau of Labor Statistics, Employment Projections Program

Related Occupations
- Computer & Information Systems Manager
- Computer Network Architect
- Computer Programmer
- Computer Support Specialist
- Computer Systems Analyst
- Database Administrator
- Information Security Analyst
- Information Technology Project Manager
- Network & Computer Systems Administrator
- Operations Research Analyst
- Software Developer
- Web Administrator
- Web Developer

Related Occupations
- Computer Systems Officer
- Computer Systems Specialist

Conversation With . . . MARGARET LE

Engineering Manager, Heroku, San Francisco, CA
Computer Engineer, 15 years

1. What was your individual career path in terms of education/training, entry-level job, or other significant opportunity?

In seventh grade, I took a computer programming class and learned to write programs using the programming language Turbo Basic. We learned how to give the computer instructions to make it do things like move a duck across a pond on the screen. In high school, I learned another programming language, Pascal. Back then, not every family had access to a personal computer. I was lucky to go to a school that provided a computer curriculum.

Because I've always been interested in cultures and languages, I majored in Linguistics in college, but continued to take computer science courses. Luckily for me, a lot of the theory behind natural language grammars and syntax can be easily applied to computer languages. In fact, there's an area of linguistics called Computational Linguistics that deals with the computational aspects of human language.

The internet was just becoming popular when I was in college. I got my first computer-related job working part-time helping to develop a website for the Great Lakes Commission, which combined my interests in web development and in the environment and conservation.

After college, I worked for a company that created websites for companies. I talked to customers about the requirements for their sites and developed them using a computer programming language that is no longer used. I continued working as a software developer, learning new programming languages and systems. I eventually gained enough experience creating production software to lead the technical direction for teams on which I was a developer. Several years ago, I transitioned from being a software developer to being an engineering manager. As an engineering manager, I'm responsible for ensuring that my engineering team has all the tools they need to build software.

2. **What are the most important skills and/or qualities for someone in your profession?**

One of the most important skills is to enjoy solving problems. You should have an interest in figuring out how to fix or improve things, whether it's finding the quickest/most scenic/least trafficked route to your favorite store or adding extra pockets to a jacket.

Being adaptable also helps. Software and the technology that runs it are constantly changing, both in terms of new advances and in the ways we interact with them. In order to deftly navigate this rapidly changing landscape, you have to be willing to adjust to new conditions.

3. **What do you wish you had known going into this profession?**

I wish I had known earlier that part of continually learning and developing new skills is a willingness to fail.

4. **Are there many job opportunities in your profession? In what specific areas?**

Opportunities in developing software, running software, and building the infrastructure on which that software runs are plentiful, as are roles like mine, leading teams in software development.

Web pioneer Marc Andreessen said, "Software is eating the world." From booking flights to analyzing health information and creating focused preventative care plans, reliance on software and computers is pervasive. There are myriad opportunities to participate as a designer, developer, or engineer. The options are astounding and offer ways to be creative, scientific, and experimental.

5. **How do you see your profession changing in the next five years? What role will technology play in those changes, and what skills will be required?**

In the next five years, I envision this profession changing dramatically. How and where we apply computer technology will continue to grow. I can see people who specialize in other fields acquiring skills in computer engineering to help solve problems in their particular fields. This means that even in traditionally non-computer related fields, we'll see more and more people using technology and engineering skills in their day-to-day jobs. That said, the fundamental skills of curiosity, adaptability, and a passion for solving problems will allow a good engineer to succeed with these changes.

As networked and connected devices become ever more popular, we're seeing an inordinate amount of potentially invaluable data being passed around. Understanding this and opening our minds to the possibilities will be key for computer engineers.

6. What do you enjoy most about your job? What do you enjoy least about your job?

The thing I enjoy most is solving new problems. Every time I find a path toward a solution, I add new skills to my toolbox, whether it's new algorithms and technological frameworks to utilize myself or to teach to other developers.

The thing I enjoy least is sometimes being paged in the middle of the night to resolve an issue with software. This occurs infrequently, but does sometimes happen.

7. Can you suggest a valuable "try this" for students considering a career in your profession?

As a student, you can start by hopping online and trying out the wealth of coding tutorials. Code.org/learn is a great resource. You can also participate in competitions like Technovation Challenge, which is a technology entrepreneurship competition for girls, or Microsoft's Imagine Cup. Both are awesome introductions to computer engineering and great ways to use your creativity and technology skills to create things.

SELECTED SCHOOLS

Many colleges and universities offer programs in computer science; a variety of them also have concentrations in computer engineering. Some of the more prominent schools in this field are listed below.

Carnegie Mellon University
5000 Forbes Avenue
Pittsburgh, PA 15213-3891
Phone: (412) 268-8525
http://www.cs.cmu.edu

Cornell University
4130 Upson Hall
Ithaca, NY 14853-7501
Phone: (607) 255-7316
http://www.cs.cornell.edu/degreeprogs/grad/index.htm

Georgia Institute of Technology
801 Atlantic Drive
Atlanta, GA 30332-0280
Phone: (404) 894-4267
http://www.cc.gatech.edu

Massachusetts Institute of Technology
77 Massachusetts Avenue
Room 38-401
Cambridge, MA 02139-4307
http://www.eecs.mit.edu/index.html
Phone: (617) 253-4603

Purdue University, West Lafayette
701 W. Stadium Avenue, Suite 3000 ARMS
West Lafayette, IN 47907-2045
https://engineering.purdue.edu/Engr
Phone: (765) 494-5345

Stanford University
353 Serra Mall
Stanford, CA 94305-9025
Phone: (650) 723-2273
http://www.cs.stanford.edu

University of California, Berkeley
205 Cory Hall
Berkeley, CA 94720-1770
Phone: (510) 642-3068
http://www.eecs.berkeley.edu

University of Illinois, Urbana, Champaign
201 N. Goodwin Avenue
Urbana, IL 61801
Phone: (217) 333-3527
http://www.cs.uiuc.edu/graduate

University of Michigan, Ann Arbor
Robert H. Lurie Engineering Center
1221 Beal Avenue
Ann Arbor, MI 48109-2102
Phone (734) 647- 7000
http://www.engin.umich.edu/college

University of Texas, Austin
1 University Station C0500
Austin, TX 78712-1188
Phone: (512) 471-9503
http://www.cs.utexas.edu

MORE INFORMATION

Association for Computing Machinery
2 Penn Plaza, Suite 701
New York, NY 10121-0701
800.342.6626
www.acm.org

Computing Research Association
1828 L Street NW, Suite 800
Washington, DC 20036
202.234.2111
www.cra.org

Institute for the Certification of Computer Professionals
2400 East Devon Avenue, Suite 281
Des Plaines, IL 60018-4610
800.843.8227
www.iccp.org

Institute of Electrical and Electronics Engineers Computer Society
2001 L Street NW, Suite 700
Washington, DC 20036-4928
202.371.0101
www.computer.org

Patrick Cooper /Editor

Computer Network Architect

Snapshot

Career Cluster(s): Information Technology; Science, Technology, Engineering & Mathematics

Interests: Computer Science, engineering, analyzing data, solving problems

Earnings (Yearly Average): $100,240

Employment & Outlook: Average Growth Expected

OVERVIEW

Sphere of Work

Computer network architects, also known as data communications analysts, or network analysts, conceptualize, build, and maintain computer information networks for businesses and organizations. Network architects may be employed as part of an organization's computing staff or by companies who specialize in assisting businesses with setting up, monitoring, and maintaining their computer networks. They work closely with other senior members of a company's computing staff, including network security personnel and systems administrators.

Work Environment

Network architects work almost exclusively in administrative and office settings. Some projects, however, may require off-site work. The majority of network architects are employed by computer companies, educational organizations, governments, and finance companies. They are also employed in manufacturing and telecommunications.

Profile

Working Conditions: Work Indoors
Physical Strength: Light Work
Education Needs: Bachelor's Degree,
Licensure/Certification:
 Recommended
Opportunities For Experience:
 Military Service, Volunteer Work, Part
 Time Work
Holland Interest Score*: ICR

* See Appendix A

Occupation Interest

Network architects have a passion and commitment to computing. The field attracts technologically skilled individuals who enjoy analyzing, dissecting, and developing solutions for complex problems. In addition to significant experience with computers and electronics, most network architects are also well versed in fields such as engineering technology, mathematics, and telecommunications.

A Day in the Life—Duties and Responsibilities

Network systems and data communication analysts traditionally work regular business hours, with some exceptions and lengthier hours required during emergencies or for the completion of large-scale projects.

Network architects are responsible for a diverse workload that can require involvement in different tasks and projects simultaneously. Those who are employed by a singular entity are able to focus on modifications and maintenance of one system; conversely, network architects who are employed by computer firms that work with several business clients often work on multiple systems simultaneously.

Computer network architects who are employed by a singular organization, government agency, or business spend their days making adjustments to network technologies to ensure they meet the organization's necessary capacity or traffic volumes. They also address any errors that arise within network systems and repair them quickly to avoid lapses in productivity or communication.

Network architects employed by telecommunications and computer companies specialize in designing, installing, and maintaining networks that are custom-made for the needs of a specific business or organization. The planning process involves extensive collaboration with administrators and staff members. Insight into a particular company's or organization's production process helps network architects determine the type of system and related technical apparatus that can best suit any data communications needs. Network architects also custom-design systems to cater to the needs of business customers, a task that is particular common in industries such as e-commerce, education, media, and publishing.

Duties and Responsibilities

- Designing, implementing, maintaining and modifying all aspects of network and data communications systems
- Monitoring the performance of network and data communications systems and troubleshooting when required
- Maintaining and creating backups of files on the network server to ensure their safety if network problems occur
- Determining when hardware, software and equipment upgrades are necessary
- Diagnosing and solving data communications problems
- Creating procedures for installing and troubleshooting network and data communications hardware and software
- Performing regular tests to ensure that all security measures are functioning properly
- Training users in the proper application of equipment

WORK ENVIRONMENT

Transferable Skills and Abilities

Communication Skills
- Speaking effectively
- Writing concisely
- Listening attentively
- Reading well

Interpersonal/Social Skills
- Being able to work independently

Organization & Management Skills
- Paying attention to and handling details
- Performing duties that change frequently
- Managing time
- Managing equipment/materials
- Coordinating tasks
- Making decisions
- Handling challenging situations

Research & Planning Skills
- Identifying problems
- Determining alternatives
- Gathering information
- Solving problems
- Defining needs
- Analyzing information
- Developing evaluation strategies

Technical Skills
- Performing scientific, mathematical and technical work
- Working with machines, tools or other objects
- Using technology to process information
- Understanding which technology is appropriate for a task
- Applying the technology to a task
- Maintaining and repairing technology

Physical Environment

Computer network architects work primarily in administrative and office settings.

Human Environment

Much of tasks inherent in the work of a network architect require strong collaboration skills. Network architects are also required to solicit information from coworkers and explain complex processes to colleagues and fellow professionals on a daily basis.

Technological Environment

Data architects traditionally have expert-level knowledge of numerous technological tools and software applications ranging from network management, administration, and transaction security software. They are also experts in computer server systems, network switches, programming languages, and connectivity technologies.

EDUCATION, TRAINING, AND ADVANCEMENT

High School/Secondary

High school students can best prepare for a career in network architecture and data communication analysis by completing courses in algebra, calculus, geometry, trigonometry, desktop publishing, programming, and computer science. Advanced placement classes in mathematics and computer-related subjects are also recommended.

Many high school students take advantage of summer internships and volunteer programs offered by local companies to gain a better understanding of computers and computer networks in everyday applications in the professional world.

Suggested High School Subjects
- Algebra
- Applied Communication
- Applied Math
- Business & Computer Technology
- Business Data Processing
- Calculus
- College Preparatory
- Computer Programming
- Computer Science
- English
- Geometry
- Keyboarding
- Mathematics
- Statistics
- Trigonometry

Famous First

The first wide area network (WAN) was created in 1965 by Thomas Marill and Lawrence G. Roberts. This system was a precursor to ARPANET (Advanced Research Project Agency Network), which was managed by Roberts in the late 1960s and early 1970s and which itself was a predecessor of the internet.

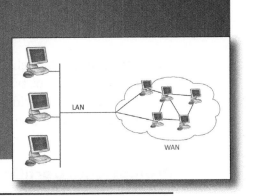

College/Postsecondary

Possession of a bachelor's degree in a computer technology-related field is a commonplace requirement for nearly all employment vacancies in network architecture, particularly those at the entry level. While professionals reach the career path of networks system and data communications architect from numerous academic and professional experiences, network architecture is a distinct field of study at many colleges and universities throughout the United States.

Students enrolled in degree paths related to network design and administration complete coursework in programming, network security, systems analysis and design, technical writing, advanced mathematics, and project management.

Related College Majors
- Computer Engineering
- Computer Engineering Technology
- Computer Maintenance Technology
- Computer Programming
- Computer Science
- Data Processing Technology
- Information Sciences & Systems
- Management Information Systems & Business Data Processing

Adult Job Seekers

Individuals with no background in a related field should enroll in a college or a technical or vocational school that offers a program in network systems data. Technical schools are also a great place for job seekers to network. Communication technologies and standards are always changing, so those making a career transition into the network systems field should be willing to continue learning throughout their career.

Given the amount of technical aptitude required of the position, data communications is not traditionally a field that people seek out when changing careers. Individuals with previous professional experience or academic training in a technological field might find the transition possible.

Professional Certification and Licensure

Dozens of networking certifications are available for professionals in the data communications industry. Network certifications are tailored to specific industries and network communications needs and are available from myriad vendors, associations, and professional organizations that are recognized by professionals in the network communications industry. Additionally, the accumulation of certificates is a common way of illustrating expertise throughout the industry.

Additional Requirements

In addition to excellent technological and computer skills, network architects must possess the patience and resolve to work on complex problems for long periods until the most effective and efficient solution is uncovered. Network professionals must also be willing team players who can work in concert with other computing professionals in a productive manner.

Fun Fact

The first network transmission over the Advanced Research Projects Agency Network (ARPANET) in 1969 was a message sent by a UCLA student to a host computer at Stanford. It was supposed to be the word "login" but only the first two letters were transmitted before the system crashed.

Source: http://www.edn.com/electronics-blogs/edn-moments/4399541/ARPANET-establishes-1st-computer-to-computer-link--October-29--1969

EARNINGS AND ADVANCEMENT

Median annual earnings of computer network architects were
$100,240 in 2014. The lowest ten percent earned less than $56,230,
and the highest ten percent earned more than $155,250.

Computer network architects may receive paid vacations, holidays,
and sick days; life and health insurance and retirement benefits.
These are usually paid by the employer.

Metropolitan Areas with the Highest Employment Level in this Occupation

Metropolitan area	Employment	Employment per thousand jobs	Annual mean wage
Washington-Arlington-Alexandria, DC-VA-MD-WV	8,660	3.58	$113,420
New York-Jersey City-White Plains, NY-NJ	7,220	1.11	$124,320
Dallas-Plano-Irving, TX	4,990	2.14	$105,510
Atlanta-Sandy Springs-Roswell, GA	4,580	1.85	$109,930
Seattle-Bellevue-Everett, WA	3,880	2.53	$107,480
Minneapolis-St. Paul-Bloomington, MN-WI	3,520	1.87	$99,010
Chicago-Naperville-Arlington Heights, IL	3,460	0.97	$113,780
San Jose-Sunnyvale-Santa Clara, CA	3,170	3.14	$144,670
Tampa-St. Petersburg-Clearwater, FL	3,120	2.56	$80,430
Boston-Cambridge-Newton, MA	3,090	1.75	$119,620

Source: Bureau of Labor Statistics

EMPLOYMENT AND OUTLOOK

Computer network architects held about 146,000 jobs nationally in 2014. Employment is expected to about as fast as the average for all occupations through the year 2024, which means employment is projected to increase 5 percent to 10 percent. The increasing reliance on wireless networks will continue to create demand for these workers.

Employment Trend, Projected 2014–24

Computer occupations: 12%

Network and computer systems administrators: 8%

Total, all occupations: 7%

Note: "All Occupations" includes all occupations in the U.S. Economy. Source: U.S. Bureau of Labor Statistics, Employment Projections Program

Related Occupations
- Broadcast Technician
- Computer & Information Systems Manager
- Computer Engineer
- Computer Programmer
- Computer Service Technician
- Computer Support Specialist
- Computer Systems Analyst
- Database Administrator
- Electronic Equipment Repairer
- Information Security Analyst
- Information Technology Project Manager
- Network & Computer Systems Administrator
- Software Developer
- Web Administrator
- Web Developer

Related Occupations
- Computer Programmer
- Computer Systems Officer
- Computer Systems Specialist

Conversation With . . .
RUSS WHITE

Network Architect, LinkedIn
Raleigh, North Carolina
IT professional, 30 years

1. What was your individual career path in terms of education/training, entry-level job, or other significant opportunity?

I have had many lucky breaks. That, combined with a knack for and broad background in engineering—and a lot of hard work—carried my career forward across the years. My background is actually in radio and RADAR systems, which led to discreet electronic systems, and then to computers and programming, and finally to network engineering. The entry level job that most shaped my career was in the Cisco Technical Assistance Center in Research Triangle Park in Raleigh. I joined LinkedIn last year.

2. What are the most important skills and/or qualities for someone in your profession?

It's not so much which skill; it's more a matter of learning to put every skill to some use. From writing to graphic design and tube-based radios, you can translate skills from one area to another, even if they don't seem to relate. There are three key things, however. First, you must learn how to communicate. Writing and speaking are deeply underrated skills in the network engineering world. Second, you must learn to make and keep friends. The real key to success is knowing people, no matter what you do for a living; specifically surrounding yourself with people who are much smarter than you are—not so difficult in my case most of the time! Finally, you must learn to separate principles and ideas from implementation, to understand how things work and why they work that way. You need to move beyond the engineer who knows where to hit the machine to make it work.

3. What do you wish you had known going into this profession?

I wish I'd known more about math, particularly in the realm of algorithms and processes. It's not so much being able to solve problems correctly that counts, but rather the ability to set problems up—to know what method and process you would, or could, use when facing a specific class of problem. This takes a long time to learn, and it seems almost impossible without a lot of straight experience doing it, but if there were one shortcut I wish I'd seen a lot earlier, this would be it.

4. Are there many job opportunities in your profession? In what specific areas?

I would say so, but the field is definitely running in a lot of different directions right now. The most pressing need is for "full stack" engineers, who can work on anything in or connected to the network, at least to some degree. Security is the other big deal right now.

5. How do you see your profession changing in the next five years? What role will technology play in those changes, and what skills will be required?

I hope to see network engineering move out of configuration and automation, and into trying to understand exactly how a network really works, and how it interacts with applications, traffic flows, and the like. Right now we are experiencing the pendulum swings of centralize/decentralize, vendor/not vendor, open source/open standards, and several others. What we need to do is start understanding problems and solutions in a way that allows us to actually engineer a solution, rather than just configuring or specifying our way to a solution. We need to move beyond "just make it work," to "I understand why this works."

I don't see how we can get from where we are to where we need to be, but I do think there are technology, models, and other helpers coming along that might get us over the bar.

6. What do you enjoy most about your job? What do you enjoy least about your job?

I would say what I enjoy most is finding simple ways to solve hard problems. The part I least enjoy is the constant flow of old ideas in new garb. We can only pretend an idea is new so many times. We sip from the firehose while learning very little that's actually new sometimes. This is frustrating.

7. Can you suggest a valuable "try this" for students considering a career in your profession?

There are too many to list, but perhaps the best is to try to walk through open source implementation of a routing protocol and try to understand not only how it works, but why it works that way. Or join an open standards mailing list and follow along, perhaps. There are very few ways to get into this field without actually just getting into it.

MORE INFORMATION

Association for Computing Machinery
2 Penn Plaza, Suite 701
New York, NY 10121-0701
800.342.6626
www.acm.org

Computing Technology Industry Association
1815 S. Meyers Road, Suite 300
Oakbrook Terrace, IL 60181-5228
630.678.8300
www.comptia.org

IEEE Computer Society
2001 L Street, NW, Suite 700
Washington, DC 20036-4928
202.371.0101
www.computer.org

National Workforce Center for Emerging Technologies
Bellevue College
3000 Landerholm Circle SE, N258
Bellevue, WA 98007-6484
425.564.4229
www.nwcet.org

Network Professional Association
1401 Hermes Lane
San Diego, CA 92154
888.672.6720
www.npa.org

John Pritchard/Editor

Computer Programmer

Snapshot

Career Cluster(s): Information Technology; Science, Technology, Engineering & Mathematics

Interests: Computer science, computer technology, solving problems, working alone, working with a team

Earnings (Yearly Average): $79,530

Employment & Outlook: Decline Expected

OVERVIEW

Sphere of Work

Computer programmers are part of the larger information technology (IT) industry. Programmers specialize in creating computer applications and programs. Training for this occupation involves specialized instruction in one or more programming languages, which are sets of codes that instruct computers to perform various functions. Most computer programmers specialize in one or a few programming languages, each of which is used for various types of specialized functions. For instance, there are specific languages used to program 3-D and moving graphics, while

other types of languages are typically used for basic web design and database construction.

Work Environment

Computer programmers work in office environments and typically do most of their work at a desk in front of a computer terminal. Though many programmers work in company offices, some programmers may complete a portion of their work off-site and may work from home, depending on their access to appropriate equipment and networks. Many computer programmers work during regular business hours, though the nature of the work is such that programming may be completed at any time, and many programmers may choose to work irregular hours.

Though some computer programmers work independently, programmers often coordinate with other IT professionals, including project managers, designers, and computer operators. Therefore, computer programmers benefit from skill in both customer service and interpersonal communication. Those who can work well as part of a team will have an advantage finding and maintaining employment in the field.

Computer programmers may work in a variety of organizations, from corporate offices to research facilities. Programmers who work as independent contractors may be hired by a variety of clients, from companies producing web content to film and production studios. Computer programming is at the forefront of technological development and has rapidly become an important facet of commerce, marketing, and communication for hundreds of modern industries.

Profile

Working Conditions: Work Indoors
Physical Strength: Light Work
Education Needs: Junior/ Technical/Community College, Bachelor's Degree
Licensure/Certification: Recommended
Opportunities For Experience: Internship, Military Service, Part Time Work
Holland Interest Score*: IRE

* See Appendix A

Occupation Interest

Those seeking a career in computer programming should be self-motivated and comfortable with tight schedules and deadlines. In addition, programmers must stay abreast of developments in the field and must be comfortable engaging in continuing education to stay informed about the latest evolutions in programming. Those seeking to work as independent contractors will also benefit from learning how to market their services to potential clients and must be motivated enough to pursue work and compete for projects.

A Day in the Life—Duties and Responsibilities

Most computer programmers spend their work hours in either home or work office environments and do most of their work at a desk in front of either a laptop or desktop computer terminal. While a specific project may have a strict deadline, programming work in general can be done at any time of day and can be broken up into numerous separate work periods.

During a typical day on the job, a programmer may write and test code for a certain application and may spend hours refining ongoing projects. In addition, programmers generally work alongside a number of other IT professionals to complete certain projects. A certain amount of time must be dedicated to communicating with colleagues and customers. Part of a workday may also be spent in meetings with designers, project managers, or customers.

Computer programmers working in corporate environments may need to devote more of their time to working with members of a production team, while those working independently may be more able to organize their schedules according to personal preference. In addition, independent contractors must often spend time marketing their work and looking for new jobs. This process may involve sending out queries and applications as well as producing and maintaining a portfolio of work to show potential clients.

Duties and Responsibilities

- Studying problems and determining the steps necessary to solve them
- Documenting the steps involved to create the program
- Testing to make sure the instructions are correct and will produce the desired results
- Rewriting programs if desired results are not produced
- Modifying existing programs to meet new requirements
- Preparing an instruction sheet for use of the program

OCCUPATION SPECIALTIES

Engineering and Scientific Programmers

Engineering and Scientific Programmers write programs to solve engineering or scientific problems by applying a knowledge of advanced mathematics and an understanding of the computer.

WORK ENVIRONMENT

Physical Environment

Computer programmers tend to work in office environments, using a computer terminal to do their work. In large companies with multiple programmers, each programmer may occupy a cubicle, or they may work in shared or private offices, depending on the company. In many cases, programmers are able to complete work on variable schedules, and some may choose to work on certain projects outside of regular business hours. Independent contractors may work from home or from an independent office.

Human Environment

The human environment for a computer programmer can vary considerably according to the industry of employment and whether the individual works as an employee or an independent contractor. In corporate environments, programmers often work alongside designers, technicians, and project managers and function as part of an overall IT team that cooperates to complete projects. Independent contractors work alone most of the time and often work from home.

Whether working as an employee or an independent contractor, computer programmers benefit from strong interpersonal communication skills. Programmers often work to translate ideas produced by designers, project managers, and clients into functional programs. They benefit from strong communication skills and the ability to work with clients, customers, and colleagues.

Transferable Skills and Abilities

Communication Skills
- Speaking effectively
- Writing concisely

Organization & Management Skills
- Following instructions
- Organizing information or materials
- Paying attention to and handling details
- Performing routine work

Research & Planning Skills
- Solving problems
- Using logical reasoning

Technical Skills
- Working with data or numbers

Technological Environment

Computer programming is a rapidly developing field at the forefront of information technology, and programmers must be able to stay abreast of new developments. While the core languages used by programmers may change little from month to month, developers producing software and tools for programmers frequently introduce new products.

In addition, computer programmers must endeavor to remain at the forefront of hardware technology. Computer manufacturing companies frequently introduce new models and new components that provide advancements in speed and processing capability. Computer programmers also benefit from knowledge of computer maintenance and repair, which helps them to prevent hardware and equipment conflicts that can hinder their work.

EDUCATION, TRAINING, AND ADVANCEMENT

High School/Secondary

High school students can prepare for a career in computer programming by taking classes in basic computer science. Some high schools may offer more specific classes in subjects such as web navigation and design, graphic arts, and even basic programming. Students are advised to explore any computer classes offered in order to gain additional experience in basic computer literacy and operation.

Suggested High School Subjects

- Accounting
- Algebra
- Applied Communication
- Applied Math
- Bookkeeping
- Business & Computer Technology
- Business Data Processing
- Calculus
- College Preparatory
- Computer Programming
- Computer Science
- English
- Geometry
- Keyboarding
- Mathematics
- Statistics
- Trigonometry

Famous First

The first regular classes in computer programming were likely those taught in 1960 at the University of Texas. At the time, there were only about two thousand computers in the entire country, virtually all of them IBMs. The main programming language then was Fortran.

College/Postsecondary

Computer programming is a burgeoning field, and most colleges, universities, and technical schools now offer specialized degree and certificate programs in different areas of computer science. Many community colleges and four-year institutions offer classes in computer programming, which generally include one or more separate classes on each programming language.

Postsecondary students can pursue computer programming as a degree focus or as a secondary educational focus. In addition to undergraduate-level programs, several institutions offer graduate-level programs in computer programming for those holding degrees in computer science. Students pursuing degree or certification programs will typically complete assignments that can form the basis of their professional portfolios and can be shown to potential employers. Employers often evaluate potential employees based on the strength of their professional or personal portfolios.

Related College Majors
- Computer Engineering
- Computer Maintenance Technology
- Computer Programming
- Computer Science
- Information Sciences & Systems
- Management Information Systems & Business Data Processing

Adult Job Seekers

Adults seeking to enter the computer programming field are advised to seek out continuing education classes through a community college or technical school. Many institutions offer night and evening classes and online courses, which may or may not be part of a certification program. Adults can also audit classes at universities or community colleges to better assess whether computer programming is of interest as a career path.

Professional Certification and Licensure

There are no certification or licensing standards for computer programmers; however, some individuals may pursue voluntary certification. Such certification programs offer professional proof that a student has completed a certain number of hours working with a specific type of programming or programming language. Computer programmers should consult credible professional associations within the field and follow professional debate as to the relevance and value of any certification program.

Additional Requirements

Computer programmers must be highly self-motivated and detail oriented. Small errors in a program's code can lead to major problems in the final product, and programmers must therefore be capable of carefully checking and rechecking their work to ensure accuracy at every stage of the process.

Fun Fact

The first widely used personal computer, the IBM 5150, was the size of a typewriter and cost $1,565 when it was introduced in 1981.

Source: www-03.ibm.com/ibm/history/exhibits/pc25/pc25_birth.html

EARNINGS AND ADVANCEMENT

Earnings of computer programmers depend on the complexity of the work they do and to some extent on the area of the country in which they work. Earnings tend to be slightly higher in large urban areas. Median annual earnings of computer programmers were $79,530 in 2014. The lowest ten percent earned less than $44,450, and the highest ten percent earned more than $130,800.

Computer programmers may receive paid vacations, holidays, and sick days; life and health insurance; and retirement benefits. These are usually paid by the employer.

Metropolitan Areas with the Highest
Employment Level in this Occupation

Metropolitan area	Employment	Employment per thousand jobs	Annual mean wage
New York-Jersey City-White Plains, NY-NJ	18,460	2.85	$95,690
Chicago-Naperville-Arlington Heights, IL	12,090	3.39	$77,510
Seattle-Bellevue-Everett, WA	11,970	7.79	$123,490
Atlanta-Sandy Springs-Roswell, GA	7,840	3.16	$84,690
Dallas-Plano-Irving, TX	7,680	3.30	$89,490
Los Angeles-Long Beach-Glendale, CA	7,340	1.79	$95,650
Washington-Arlington-Alexandria, DC-VA-MD-WV	7,210	2.98	$98,550
San Jose-Sunnyvale-Santa Clara, CA	6,510	6.43	$93,940
Minneapolis-St. Paul-Bloomington, MN-WI	6,210	3.30	$80,820
San Francisco-Redwood City-South San Francisco, CA	6,110	5.99	$108,070

Source: Bureau of Labor Statistics

EMPLOYMENT AND OUTLOOK

Computer programmers held about 330,000 jobs nationally in 2014. Employment is expected to decline somewhat relative to the average for all occupations through the year 2024, which means employment is projected to decrease by about 8 percent. Factors limiting growth in employment are the ability of many computer users to write their own computer programs, and the outsourcing of computer programming jobs to other countries. Nevertheless, employers will continue to need computer programmers who are skilled in a variety of programming languages.

Employment Trend, Projected 2014–24

Computer occupations: 12%

Total, all occupations: 7%

Computer programmers: -8%

Note: "All Occupations" includes all occupations in the U.S. Economy. Source: U.S. Bureau of Labor Statistics, Employment Projections Program

Related Occupations
- Computer & Information Systems Manager
- Computer Engineer
- Computer Network Architect
- Computer Operator
- Computer Support Specialist
- Computer Systems Analyst
- Computer-Control Tool Programmer
- Database Administrator
- Information Security Analyst
- Mathematician
- Network & Computer Systems Administrator
- Operations Research Analyst
- Software Developer
- Web Administrator
- Web Developer

Related Occupations
- Computer Programmer
- Computer Systems Specialist

Conversation With . . .
WILLIAM P. SMYTH

IT Program Analyst, Federal Government
Washington, D.C.
IT Program Analyst, 31 years

1. **What was your individual career path in terms of education/training, entry-level job, or other significant opportunity?**

I went to Hampton University in Virginia for electrical engineering, but dropped out and joined the U.S. Marine Corps. I ended up doing aviation electronics, which I studied at a community college. I spent six years in the Marines, and played football for the Marine Corps team. NFL teams were scouting me. I went to Atlanta, but wasn't what they were looking for. Then I came to D.C. because the Redskins wanted to see me. However, a motorcycle accident ended my NFL dreams at age 26.

After I healed, I started looking for jobs. At the time, computers were not widespread. I got a downtown D.C. territory repairing electronic typewriters. The law firm Steptoe & Johnson was a client and they had desktop computers. I'd never seen one before, but somebody saw a problem with a cable and asked me to look at it. I traced the cable back, plugged it in, and said, "Try now." That prompted me to get into computers, and I never looked back.

I spent many overnights at law firms setting up networks with little support. It made me really good at my job, even though it could be frustrating. But I'm the kind of person who is persistent and likes to troubleshoot.

Eventually, I moved on to a company called Banctech that built banking machines and computers. I did phone support on networks and was there about five years. The company moved to Texas; I didn't want to go to Texas. So, I found a job as a contractor for a federal agency during Bill Clinton's first term. The agency had no networks or desktop computers, so I was the first one to put in their networks.

After 15 years as a contractor, I was hired eight years ago as a federal employee to support a departmental network and help desk, where I work with a team of 25 people. We handle Freedom of Information requests and run a certification and accreditation program. If someone internally wants to set up a website—for instance, so people can get information from the DOE about solar panels—we review the site and run tests to look for security weaknesses. This is an annual process. In addition, I get pulled in to run projects that are highly technical. For instance, you can't just plug into the internet from our system. Vendors and others who need to do that come to me to find out how.

2. What are the most important skills and/or qualities for someone in your profession?

You really have to understand the theory of computers. If you understand how everything works from the bottom up, you'll be able to troubleshoot. I have to stress that you need a love for this, because things change every six months. If you're not willing to be constantly updated, you'll be far behind pretty quickly.

3. What do you wish you had known going into this profession?

I wish I had known that hacking would become such a big deal. I was on the leading edge when I started, when the internet was DOS-based. I could go onto important websites and there was no protection. Looking back, I could have come up with something to fix vulnerabilities and I wouldn't be working now!

4. Are there many job opportunities in your profession? In what specific areas?

Absolutely. Every day in the news, somebody is getting hacked. However, the security field is intense. You're on the clock 24 hours. Not everybody wants to do that. You can make a lot of money in the security field if you can get those difficult Cisco security certifications. But you can get dismissed real quick, too, if somebody gets into a system you're watching.

5. How do you see your profession changing in the next five years, what role will technology play in those changes, and what skills will be required?

I think it's going to change based on protocols. New protocols—computer languages—are being developed all the time, because every company is trying to stop hackers. And hackers are constantly working on how to get in. You really need to learn programming and protocols.

6. What do you enjoy most about your job? What do you enjoy least about your job?

I most enjoy troubleshooting. When an organization has a problem, I get to figure it out. I least like supporting difficult fellow employees who work in departments other than IT. For instance, I have to approve purchases. If somebody wants a 27-inch monitor, they need to tell me why—and not just assume that they will get it.

7. Can you suggest a valuable "try this" for students considering a career in your profession?

On websites such as http://etherealmind.com or https://learningnetwork.cisco.com/community/learning_center/games, you can play security games, take security tests, or join groups to discuss the topic. You'll find out if you have a real interest in security.

MORE INFORMATION

Association for Computing Machinery
2 Penn Plaza, Suite 701
New York, NY 10121-0701
800.342.6626
www.acm.org

Association of Information Technology Professionals
401 N. Michigan Avenue, Suite 2400
Chicago, IL 60611-4267
800.224.9371
www.aitp.org

IEEE Computer Society
2001 L Street NW, Suite 700
Washington, DC 20036-4928
202.371.0101
www.computer.org

Institute for the Certification of Computer Professionals
2400 East Devon Avenue, Suite 281
Des Plaines, IL 60018-4610
800.843.8227
www.iccp.org

National Association of Programmers
P.O. Box 529
Prairieville, LA 70769
www.napusa.org

Micah Issitt/Editor

Computer Service Technician

Snapshot

Career Cluster(s): Information Technology; Maintenance & Repair
Interests: Computer maintenance and repair, solving problems, working with your hands
Earnings (Yearly Average): $39,517
Employment & Outlook: Decline Expected

OVERVIEW

Sphere of Work

Computer service technicians analyze, maintain, troubleshoot, and repair problems with computer systems. They may specialize in several different areas of computing, from personal computers such as towers, notebooks, and tablets to more complex business systems consisting of multiple servers, network technology, and workstations. Computer service technicians are employed by several different entities. Some work for private computer-repair firms, while others are members of larger organizations. Many service

techs are also employed by retail outlets specializing in computers and electronics.

Work Environment

Computer service technicians work primarily in repair shops, although those employed by large companies may work exclusively in administrative and office settings. Service techs who are employed by retail outlets may work remotely, traveling to businesses and residences in work vans and troubleshooting problems on-site. Computer service technicians who work remotely in homes and businesses must combine their technological savvy with deft customer-service skills to assist clients who are trying to address problems or work with systems they may be unfamiliar with.

Profile

Working Conditions: Work Indoors
Physical Strength: Light Work
Education Needs: On-The-Job Training, High School Diploma or G.E.D
Licensure/Certification: Recommended
Opportunities For Experience: Internship, Volunteer Work, Part Time Work
Holland Interest Score*: RES

* See Appendix A

Occupation Interest

The field of computer service attracts a wide range of technically savvy professionals of all ages. Some are young professionals and students eager to gain experience in computer maintenance while planning a future career in another computer-related field, such as programming, software engineering, or hardware development. Other computer techs are longtime computer hobbyists who have decided to turn their passion for computing into a livelihood.

A Day in the Life—Duties and Responsibilities

Computer service technicians are tasked with a variety of duties and responsibilities each day. Many of their responsibilities vary depending on their particular arena of employment. The multitude of assignments and diverse workload presented to computer repair technicians require deft organization skills and the ability to prioritize and work on multiple projects simultaneously.

Those who are employed as team members in a large institution, such as a business, a university, or a government body, are often responsible for performing a variety of maintenance and upkeep tasks on organizational computer systems, ranging from cleaning out old files to updating antivirus and security software.

Service techs who are employed by computer-repair companies or who are self-employed spend their days evaluating machines in order to diagnose and solve the problems disrupting a computer's normal use. This can involve extensive interactions with customers, who may be contacted to initiate the course of repair best suited to their budget and needs.

Computer service technicians employed by computer stores and other retail electronic outlets perform a variety of tasks outside of maintenance and repair. They may be called upon to set up residential home-computing systems on-site, or they may travel to residences and businesses to assist with computer maintenance and repair.

Duties and Responsibilities

- Keeping maintenance records and repair reports
- Maintaining inventory of parts
- Ordering repair parts and selling supplies
- Advising customers concerning operation, maintenance and programming
- Installing equipment according to manufacturer's specifications
- Repairing equipment and instructing others on service and repair
- Preparing machines for customer use
- Consulting with supervisor to plan layout of equipment
- Running special diagnostic programs through computer equipment to help pinpoint problems

WORK ENVIRONMENT

Physical Environment

Service techs work primarily in office and workshop settings. Computer service technicians may also be required to visit homes and businesses.

Transferable Skills and Abilities

Technical Skills

- Performing scientific, mathematical and technical work
- Working with machines, tools or other objects

Human Environment

Computer repair is both solitary and collaborative. Many computer technicians work individually, while others are required to interact with other professionals and home-computer owners. Technicians who work with clients are often charged with explaining complex concepts in terms novice users can understand.

Technological Environment

Computer service technicians must be very well versed in the common elements of contemporary computer technology, ranging from both personal computer and Mac OS systems to peripherals such as printers, scanners, and mobile technology. Knowledge of networks, system administration, and computer-security apparatuses is also beneficial.

EDUCATION, TRAINING, AND ADVANCEMENT

High School/Secondary

High school students can best prepare for a career in computer service by completing courses in algebra, calculus, geometry, trigonometry, introductory programming, desktop publishing, and introductory computer science. Participation in any available advanced placement (AP) classes in computing and technology are especially recommended, but these courses may not be offered at every school. Science and technology fairs are a good opportunity for students to immerse themselves in computer technology by conceptualizing and creating computer-related projects, while summer volunteer programs and internships at computer-related organizations can provide crucial reinforcement of the fundamentals of computer service.

Suggested High School Subjects
- Algebra
- Applied Communication
- Applied Math
- Blueprint Reading
- Computer Science
- Electricity & Electronics
- English
- Mechanical Drawing
- Shop Mechanics
- Trade/Industrial Education
- Welding

Famous First

The first two-year college to offer a comprehensive computer technician training program to high school graduates may have been Pierce College in Los Angeles, in 1975. As an account in *Computerworld* noted at the time, "the computer industry ... chronically suffers from a critical shortage of skilled, thoroughly trained hardware technicians with 'hands on' experience on today's microprocessors." Hence the need for the Pierce program.

College/Postsecondary

Possession of a postsecondary degree is not a strict requirement for all computer service technician jobs, particularly those at the entry level. Many applicants who have amateur and hobbyist backgrounds in computers and are able to demonstrate their knowledge can often land entry-level positions. Managerial roles in computer service, however, almost exclusively require some kind of postsecondary study in computer science, computer programming, network administration, or the like, as do positions involving work with larger and more complex computer systems, networks, and databases.

Many US colleges and universities offer certification programs in computer technology in addition to more traditional undergraduate-level course work in information technology, computer service, and network administration. Certificate-level course work in computer repair trains students to address all major computer malfunctions and perform routine maintenance, basic hardware upgrades, and systematic troubleshooting.

Related College Majors
- Computer Engineering Technology
- Computer Installation & Repair
- Computer Maintenance Technology

Adult Job Seekers

Computer service is a popular realm of employment for adult job seekers, given its standard hours and localized nature. There is a growing need for technicians as computers and computer-aided technology become more commonplace worldwide. Individuals with personal or professional experience in computer science and technology are traditionally given preference for open positions, particularly when that experience is bolstered by formal education.

Professional Certification and Licensure

Although no specific certification or licensure is required, becoming a certified computer service technician increases an applicant's job opportunities. Membership in one of numerous professional organizations can help computer service technicians stay in tune with emerging trends and technologies related to the field.

Additional Requirements

Computer service technicians must be able to work independently and with little direction or guidance. Service techs must also be willing to regularly update their knowledge of computer hardware and software as the technology evolves.

Fun Fact

Apple trademarked the name "Genius Bar" for its in-store computer support stations, but in 2016, the computer giant began replacing the "bar" with the Genius Grove, a more comfortable, open space complete with ficus trees.
Source: http://www.nytimes.com/2016/05/20/technology/apple-shifts-from-genius-bars-to-genius-groves-hoping-patrons-linger.html?_r=0

EARNINGS AND ADVANCEMENT

Median annual earnings of computer service technicians were $39,517 in 2012. The lowest ten percent earned less than $23,956, and the highest ten percent earned more than $62,137.

Computer service technicians may receive paid vacations, holidays, and sick days; life and health insurance; and retirement benefits. These are usually paid by the employer.

EMPLOYMENT AND OUTLOOK

There were approximately 235,000 computer and electronics service technicians employed nationally in 2014. Employment is expected to decline somewhat relative to the average for all occupations through the year 2024, which means employment is projected to decrease by about 4 percent. Although computer equipment continues to become less expensive and more reliable, malfunctions still occur and can cause severe problems for users, most of whom lack the knowledge to make repairs.

Employment Trend, Projected 2014–24

Computer occupations: 12%

Total, all occupations: 7%

Computer Service Technicians: -4%

Note: "All Occupations" includes all occupations in the U.S. Economy. Source: U.S. Bureau of Labor Statistics, Employment Projections Program

Related Occupations
- Computer Network Architect
- Computer Support Specialist
- Electronic Equipment Repairer
- Home Entertainment Equipment Repairer
- Office Machine Repairer
- Robotics Technician
- Telecommunications Equipment Repairer
- Television & Radio Repairer

Conversation With . . .
CHUCK WHITNEY

Owner, Chipheads Computer Repair
Twin Cities, Minnesota
20-plus years in the computer industry

1. What was your individual career path in terms of education/training, entry-level job, or other significant opportunity?

I got an associate degree and a bachelor's degree in computer science. I sold computers for two years and got my start in repair by doing work for some of my computer-buying customers. I had a general curiosity about computers and enjoyed tinkering with them. I really didn't have a plan and just sort of fell into it. I didn't start the business until I was 32. I just got lucky enough to know 10 percent more than the average person about something that was in high demand and had pretty much zero barriers to entry. Anyone could have done—and still could do—what I did with no formal training at all. There are no licensing or legal barriers to work on computers or networks, except those imposed by some big companies that want certain certifications. But to be a neighborhood computer repair tech, anyone can do it, as long as you can get the results people need.

2. What are the most important skills and/or qualities for someone in your profession?

You need to care about getting results for the people you're helping, each and every day. This is called professionalism, and is difficult to learn if you're not a helpful person.

If you're working with the general public or in a help desk type of situation, communication skills are key. You must be able to understand what people are telling you as well as translate what you are doing to non-technical people.

To run an independent repair business, you need to understand the business part as well as the repair part. You need to be able to actually fix things. General tech skills can be acquired through education, but troubleshooting problems and the ability to keep trying until you find a solution is more of a talent. Most people acquire this skill by tinkering and through trial and error or to satisfy their own curiosity. What was the last thing you fixed yourself, in any situation? If you can't come up with anything, you may not have the troubleshooting gene. If you've fixed your own car for example, you probably have that gene.

You also need time management skills, so that you can fix many things in a reasonable amount of time, and attention to detail.

3. What do you wish you had known going into this profession?

I wish I had understood that a computer service technician's job is to solve a person's problem, not just fix their computer. While often they are the same thing, just as often they are not.

4. Are there many job opportunities in your profession? In what specific areas?

There are opportunities in hardware repair, software configuration, and traditional computer repair, but the growing areas are networking and security. Today, in 2016, I would say don't waste too much time on consumer electronics unless you thoroughly enjoy tinkering. Focus on business networking, network security, or computer forensics.

5. How do you see your profession changing in the next five years? What role will technology play in those changes, and what skills will be required?

Security and privacy protection will be the most important as the hardware itself becomes disposable. Data protection and backup strategies will continue to be important. If you want to be a self-employed tech, focus on what average people want from their tech experience. You'll need to change your focus from a career based on what is wrong with computers to a career based on what's right with them; that is, using computers for peoples' benefit versus fixing broken things.

6. What do you enjoy most about your job? What do you enjoy least about your job?

The best part is appreciative customers. Most people are very appreciative and that's nice. The most frustrating is dealing with issues that are difficult for customers to understand when they're already suspicious of being taken advantage of or becoming victims of online scams. To most people, computers are a magic box. If what you tell them doesn't fit with their mental image of how a computer works (which is almost always wrong), it can be tough for them to accept.

7. Can you suggest a valuable "try this" for students considering a career in your profession?

That's easy … Help as many friends and family solve computer issues and set up secure home networks as you can. Help them create a backup strategy to protect files. Whether they pay you or not doesn't matter—the education you get will be worth it. Tech skills are developed by doing. Build your own computer if you can, especially computers designed for gaming. Tweaking high-end gaming systems will teach you a ton. Branch out into other operating systems besides Windows and Mac. Learning LINUX will teach you a lot about how computers work. Read hardware blogs such as www.tomshardware.com, www.howtogeek.com and slashdot.org.

MORE INFORMATION

Association for Computing Machinery
2 Penn Plaza, Suite 701
New York, NY 10121-0701
800.342.6626
www.acm.org

Association of Computer Repair Business Owners
2215 Jefferson Davis Highway
Suite 201
Fredericksburg, VA 22401
888.710.9006
www.acrbo.com

Computing Technology Industry Association
1815 South Meyers Road
Suite 300
Oakbrook Terrace, IL 60181-5228
630.678.8300
www.comptia.org

Electronics Technicians Association International
5 Depot Street
Greencastle IN 46135
800.288.3824
www.eta-i.org

Information Technology Association of America
601 Pennsylvania Avenue, NW
North Building
Washington, DC 20004
202.682.9110
www.techamerica.org

John Pritchard/Editor

Computer Support Specialist

Snapshot

Career Cluster(s): Information Technology; Science, Technology, Engineering & Mathematics

Interests: Computer technology, solving problems, customer service, communicating with others

Earnings (Yearly Average): $47,660

Employment & Outlook: Faster Than Average Growth Expected

OVERVIEW

Sphere of Work

Computer support specialists provide technical support for computers and a variety of related devices and programs. They may work in an internal support capacity, providing assistance to their fellow employees, or they may provide support to many organizations or individuals as contractors or employees of dedicated technical-support companies. Computer support specialists may specialize in one type of system or software or offer general support. They must be able to offer solutions to complex issues in a high-pressure environment.

Work Environment

Computer support specialists generally work in office facilities, although they may at times be required to provide on-site support in other locations. A specialist may work independently to meet the needs of a small organization or alongside other specialists performing similar tasks in a large help desk facility. Computer support specialists may work more than forty hours per week and may be required to work nights, weekends, and on-call hours as needed.

Profile

Working Conditions: Work Indoors
Physical Strength: Light Work
Education Needs: Junior/
Technical/Community College,
Bachelor's Degree
Licensure/Certification:
Recommended
Opportunities For Experience:
Military Service, Volunteer Work, Part
Time Work
Holland Interest Score*: RIC

* See Appendix A

Occupation Interest

Individuals drawn to the profession of computer support specialist are skilled in computer technology and customer service. They are capable problem solvers interested in understanding complex software and the interactions between various forms of technology. Specialists must be excellent communicators and able to work with customers who are often frustrated or under time constraints.

A Day in the Life—Duties and Responsibilities

The daily duties of a computer support specialist vary according to the organization for which he or she works and the type of support the specialist provides. In general, computer support specialists respond to inquiries or requests for help from clients or fellow employees. They may be responsible for the oversight of all computer systems, or they may specialize in troubleshooting and problem solving for one type of software or computer function.

If they are responsible for organizational systems, computer support specialists may spend their time setting up and programming new computers, repairing and replacing malfunctioning units, installing software , training employees to use the systems in place, and maintaining internal networks and servers. They may also provide help desk services, answering user queries and ensuring that systems function smoothly.

Help desk specialists may receive requests for assistance in person or via phone or e-mail. They often access users' computers remotely. They must be familiar with a variety of operating systems and computer types and be able to identify and understand physical, electronic, and software problems. If the cause of a problem is difficult to identify, a computer support specialist must be able to run diagnostic tests to pinpoint the issue. Specialists reinstall operating systems, remotely clean infected or malfunctioning systems, and work with customers to ensure that problems do not reoccur. They often provide support related to printers, scanners, e-mail, networking and internet access, and word-processing and spreadsheet software.

Computer support specialists must remain up to date regarding advances in computer technology and must be able to explain complex systems in a clear and understandable manner. Because of this, specialists typically undergo a significant amount of ongoing training and may occasionally attend workshops or industry conferences.

Duties and Responsibilities

- Communicating with users, performing diagnostics and reading technical manuals to solve hardware and software problems
- Monitoring overall computer system performance within the organization
- Installing and troubleshooting computer hardware and software for organization members
- Maintaining daily records of actions taken to solve computer hardware and software problems
- Training users in use of computer hardware and software
- Staying up to date with the latest technology

OCCUPATION SPECIALTIES

Technical Support Specialists

Technical Support Specialists respond to questions from their organization's computer users and run diagnostic programs to solve problems.

Help Desk Technicians

Help Desk Technicians answer telephone calls and email messages from customers needing help with computer problems.

WORK ENVIRONMENT

Physical Environment

Computer support specialists typically work in office environments, but the nature of these facilities varies based on industry. A specialist may work in a small office in an individual company or be one of many support specialists housed in a large facility. Though most large support facilities are operated as call centers, some companies have begun to allow employees to work in flexible or shared office spaces or even from their own homes.

Human Environment

Computer support specialists spend their workdays in constant interaction with clients. They may also interact with managers, coworkers, and other support specialists throughout the day. In office support environments, specialists interact regularly with fellow employees.

Transferable Skills and Abilities

Communication Skills
- Speaking effectively
- Writing concisely
- Listening attentively
- Reading well

Interpersonal/Social Skills
- Being able to work independently
- Cooperating with others
- Working as a member of a team
- Being sensitive to others
- Providing support to others
- Teaching others

Organization & Management Skills
- Following instructions
- Organizing information or materials
- Paying attention to and handling details
- Performing duties that change frequently
- Managing conflict
- Making decisions
- Handling challenging situations

Research & Planning Skills
- Gathering information
- Solving problems
- Using logical reasoning
- Determining essential information
- Analyzing information

Technical Skills
- Understanding which technology is appropriate for a task
- Applying the technology to a task
- Maintaining and repairing technology
- Performing scientific, mathematical and technical work
- Working with machines, tools or other objects
- Working with data or numbers

Technological Environment

A computer support specialist must be familiar with all computer technology used by his or her employing organization and should also be able to recommend advances and upgrades to existing systems. A specialist generally must have a thorough knowledge of both hardware and software as well as network systems and other peripheral equipment and accessories.

EDUCATION, TRAINING, AND ADVANCEMENT

High School/Secondary

Students interested in the field of computer support should take courses in computer programming and computer science, as well as algebra and calculus. Business or applied mathematics classes may be useful as well.

Suggested High School Subjects
- Algebra
- Applied Communication
- Applied Math
- Business & Computer Technology
- Business Data Processing
- Calculus
- College Preparatory
- Computer Programming
- Computer Science
- English
- Geometry
- Keyboarding
- Mathematics
- Statistics
- Trigonometry

Famous First

The first video showing what the average day of a computer support specialist is like was posted on YouTube in 2010 in connection with a Department of Labor contest. It was created by Jared Bodine in Tamuning, Guam.

College/Postsecondary

While an associate degree from a technical or two-year college is the minimum educational requirement for computer support specialists in some companies, a four-year degree in computer science is preferred by many employers. A specialist seeking to advance to a specialized, higher-level position may benefit from pursing a master's degree or doctorate, but this level of expertise is generally not needed for a support position.

Related College Majors
- Computer Installation & Repair
- Computer Maintenance Technology
- Computer Programming
- Computer Science
- Data Processing Technology
- Information Sciences & Systems

Adult Job Seekers

Adult job seekers in this field may benefit from the wide variety of computer courses available at vocational, technical, and community colleges. Valuable experience can also be gained in the military, which relies heavily on computer systems.

Professional Certification and Licensure

There is no required certification or licensure for computer support specialists. However, specialists may choose to gain voluntary certification in a number of computer systems, programs, and skills. Such certifications are offered by professional organizations and training centers and may demonstrate to prospective employers that an applicant is well versed in a particular area. Computer support specialists should consult credible professional associations within the field and follow professional debates as to the relevancy and value of any certification program.

Additional Requirements

Computer support specialists must have excellent problem-solving and communication skills. A degree of creativity is also helpful, as specialists may at times be required to devise unusual solutions to problems.

Fun Fact

The most common reason people call help desks is that they've forgotten their password. Password reset tools, like answering a series of questions, can reduce help desk calls by 40 percent, according to Verism Software.

Source: http://www.verismic.com/common-helpdesk-complaints-and-how-to-fix-them/

EARNINGS AND ADVANCEMENT

Median annual earnings of computer support specialists were $47,660 in 2014. The lowest ten percent earned less than $28,980, and the highest ten percent earned more than $81,190.

Computer support specialists may receive paid vacations, holidays and sick days; life and health insurance; and retirement benefits. These are usually paid by the employer.

Metropolitan Areas with the Highest
Employment Level in this Occupation

Metropolitan area	Employment	Employment per thousand jobs	Annual mean wage
New York-Jersey City-White Plains, NY-NJ	27,540	4.25	$59,810
Dallas-Plano-Irving, TX	18,130	7.78	$51,810
Atlanta-Sandy Springs-Roswell, GA	17,610	7.10	$53,810
Chicago-Naperville-Arlington Heights, IL	16,880	4.73	$55,460
Washington-Arlington-Alexandria, DC-VA-MD-WV	16,050	6.64	$61,320
Los Angeles-Long Beach-Glendale, CA	15,590	3.80	$57,320
Houston-The Woodlands-Sugar Land, TX	14,050	4.80	$57,360
Boston-Cambridge-Newton, MA	11,770	6.68	$64,940
Minneapolis-St. Paul-Bloomington, MN-WI	11,170	5.94	$54,640
Phoenix-Mesa-Scottsdale, AZ	10,420	5.56	$50,820

Source: Bureau of Labor Statistics

EMPLOYMENT AND OUTLOOK

Computer support specialists held about 765,000 jobs nationally in 2014. Employment of computer support specialists is expected to grow faster than the average for all occupations through the year 2024, which means employment is projected to increase 10 percent to 15 percent. As computers and software continue to become more complex, demand for computer support specialists to provide technical assistance to individual users and organizations will keep growing, especially in the healthcare industry. However, the outsourcing of some of these jobs overseas will slow growth slightly.

Employment Trend, Projected 2014–24

Computer user support specialists: 13%

Computer occupations: 12%

Computer support specialists: 12%

Computer network support specialists: 8%

Total, all occupations: 7%

Note: "All Occupations" includes all occupations in the U.S. Economy. Source: U.S. Bureau of Labor Statistics, Employment Projections Program

Related Occupations
- Broadcast Technician
- Computer & Information Systems Manager
- Computer Engineer
- Computer Network Architect
- Computer Operator
- Computer Programmer
- Computer Service Technician
- Computer Systems Analyst
- Computer-Control Tool Programmer
- Customer Service Representative
- Database Administrator
- Electronic Equipment Repairer
- Information Security Analyst

- Information Technology Project Manager
- Network & Computer Systems Administrator
- Software Developer
- Web Administrator
- Web Developer

Related Occupations
- Computer Programmer
- Computer Systems Officer
- Computer Systems Specialist

Conversation With . . .
JAMISON JOHNSON

Tier 2 Technical Lead, ActioNet
Washington, D.C.
Computer Support Specialist, 6 years

1. What was your individual career path in terms of education, training, entry-level job, or other significant opportunity?

I went straight into IT based on my high school curriculum and my guidance counselor's advice. I took every single computer class possible; I just liked programming classes! I received a bachelor's degree in computer information systems from Virginia State University. During my senior year, I applied, applied, applied for jobs. About three months after college, I got a consulting job with the U.S. Department of Energy as a "Tier 2" computer support specialist. Now I'm managing that team; 15 to 20 technicians report directly to me and a colleague.

We work on computer issues for the people working in our office. We handle desktop support and network connection issues. We have three tiers of help: Tier 1 Technicians are our first line of troubleshooting; if they're unable to resolve an issue in a timely manner, they escalate to us at Tier 2 to troubleshoot. Above that, Tier 3 is called in to resolve the issue and that may include network administrators, cybersecurity analysts, or website developers.

The cybersecurity threat is always there, and growing as technology advances. I hope to move into that area in the future.

2. What are the most important skills and/or qualities for someone in your profession?

In help desk roles, the key thing is your ability to troubleshoot problems, determine the cause of errors and how to fix them. You need to be an active listener and active learner. There will always be people who have been in your field longer than you; learn from them. You also have to be an instructor, because when your customers have issues, you have to teach them what to do to resolve, for example, a problem that they're causing by the way they use the computer. You need to make good, concise judgment calls.

3. What do you wish you had known going into this profession?

If I'd know that mentors are key in this profession, I would have reached out a long time ago. I try to be that person for students coming out of high school or college. Also, it's imperative to work with your colleagues and collaborate with them. Friendly competition is good, but competing all the time is not healthy.

4. Are there many job opportunities in your profession? In what specific areas?

There are many opportunities in IT, especially here in the D.C. area because of the federal government. Companies will always need people who do what I do. We resolve any customer's situation, and they will always need that support. Information security is booming, and going into this area gives you a good understanding of domestic or international cybersecurity threats. Web developers are always needed; companies will always need to market themselves online and update their websites. Once you go through one of those branches of IT, you can be a manager because somebody must manage these different groups.

5. How do you see your profession changing in the next five years, what role will technology play in those changes, and what skills will be required?

Mobile device payments, such as Apple payments, are an everyday occurrence, and we're going to see that become a norm. In order to process those payments, security needs to increase and those jobs will continue to grow. Everything from a Keurig coffee pot to your television is connected to the internet and will need to be secure. Also in the near future, your phone will have some type of universal translator device so we can bridge language barriers. Finally, we'll see a big push in robotics. If you think about it, we already have vacuum cleaners that are basically robots.

6. What do you enjoy most about your job? What do you enjoy least about your job?

I like that IT offers opportunities. Right now I'm in a help desk role, but if I work hard and network, I have options. I also like that I have early exposure to new technologies. What I least like is the lack of communication between our different operating groups. I've been with a couple of different contracting organizations and that's always an issue. We end up going through a chain of command and it circles around. A direct line of communication would be simpler.

7. Can you suggest a valuable "try this" for students considering a career in your profession?

You can easily Google any job title you want to research, or go on YouTube. A lot of companies offer internships. We've hired people with no prior experience after they interned with us. Also, you can shadow an IT professional to see if it's something you want to study long-term.

MORE INFORMATION

Association of Support Professionals
38954 Proctor Boulevard, #396
Sandy, OR 97055
503.668.9004
www.asponline.com

Computing Technology Industry Association
3500 Lacey Road, Suite 100
Downers Grove, IL 60515
630.678.8300
www.comptia.org

Bethany Groff/Editor

Computer Systems Analyst

Snapshot

Career Cluster(s): Information Technology; Science, Technology, Engineering & Mathematics

Interests: Computer science, solving problems, communicating with others

Earnings (Yearly Average): $85,800

Employment & Outlook: Much Faster Than Average Growth Expected

OVERVIEW

Sphere of Work

Computer systems analysts assist companies in improving their computer systems and processes by analyzing the technology currently in place and suggesting various improvements. They work with the information technology (IT) and business management departments so that both sides can collaborate more effectively and better understand one another's needs. Analysts put together detailed reports of the costs and the positive and negative aspects of a computer system so that management can decide what technologies and applications best suit the needs of their business. Analysts also help design and secure new computer systems and train users.

Work Environment

Computer systems analysts work in a variety of different industries. They may be employed directly by the company they perform analysis for, or they may be contracted by various companies as consultants. Analysts who work as consultants may either be self-employed or work for an IT firm. Communications technologies such as video chat and web conferencing enable some analysts to work remotely, but the majority still travel to clients' locations to work. Office environments predominate.

Profile

Working Conditions: Work Indoors
Physical Strength: Light Work
Education Needs: Bachelor's Degree, Master's Degree
Licensure/Certification: Recommended
Opportunities For Experience: Military Service, Part Time Work
Holland Interest Score*: IER

* See Appendix A

Occupation Interest

Computer systems analysis tends to attract individuals with a strong background in computer science. Analysts must possess excellent problem-solving skills in order to assess flaws and identify areas for improvement in a company's computer system. Communication is essential in order to understand the technological needs of the company and to instruct managers and other workers in how to best use the computer systems being implemented.

A Day in the Life—Duties and Responsibilities

Computer systems analysts spend the majority of their day working with computers. They also spend a great deal of time communicating with other IT employees and the managers of the company they are working for. Analysts use their education and skills to design computer systems, perform information engineering, and set up information systems that allow for greater efficiency and better communication. Analysts who work for a single company tend to specialize in the specific computer systems that company uses. For instance, if an analyst is employed by a financial company, then he or she will most likely specialize in financial computer systems. A contractor analyst is more likely to be experienced in a broad range of computer systems.

Depending on the issues computer systems analysts are called in to address, they may perform a wide variety of tasks. Typically, they begin by going over the existing computer system with IT workers and management. Analysts examine the needs of the company and the role that computer systems play in the business in order to determine the best possible system for the job. An analysis usually entails the preparation of a costs-and-benefits report that helps management decide whether they wish to implement a computer upgrade. Analysts also design and create new systems based on existing hardware and software and oversee the installation of these new systems.

Once the systems are installed, analysts typically run tests to make sure everything is running properly and the network is secure. Then they train employees and managers how to use the system through formal instruction and manuals as needed.

Duties and Responsibilities

- Designing new computer systems
- Adding additional hardware or new software applications
- Preparing cost analysis of new systems
- Determining cause of computer bug and eliminating it from the system

WORK ENVIRONMENT

Physical Environment

Computer systems analysts spend a majority of their time in office environments. These environments vary from job to job. Travel to and from client locations is frequently required, so an analyst should expect to spend time in a car, plane, or other modes of transportation.

Transferable Skills and Abilities

Communication Skills
- Speaking effectively
- Writing concisely

Organization & Management Skills
- Paying attention to and handling details
- Performing duties that change frequently

Research & Planning Skills
- Analyzing information
- Developing evaluation strategies
- Solving problems
- Using logical reasoning

Technical Skills
- Performing scientific, mathematical and technical work
- Using technology to process information
- Working with machines, tools or other objects

Human Environment

To accurately analyze a computer system, an analyst must collaborate closely with a company's IT department and management. He or she may also collaborate with other analysts if further help is needed with a computer system.

Technological Environment

Computer systems analysts work with a broad range of computer software and hardware. The software used varies depending on the type of computer system being analyzed; data-modeling systems are common. Sometimes analysts use communication technologies that allow them to telecommute.

EDUCATION, TRAINING, AND ADVANCEMENT

High School/Secondary

Computer systems analysts are usually required to have a high school diploma or an equivalent certificate. Useful high school courses include computer science, mathematics, and business-related classes. Any advanced computer-related courses will also be a great help.

Suggested High School Subjects

- Accounting
- Algebra
- Applied Communication
- Calculus
- Computer Programming
- Computer Science
- English
- Geometry
- Mathematics
- Statistics
- Trigonometry

Famous First

The first systems analysts predated the computer era and relied on pen and pencil along with ledgers, indexes, and manual spreadsheets to document and improve "systems and procedures" in the workplace. In the 1960s, under the name Management Information Systems (MIS), a marriage between systems analysis and computer technology took place.

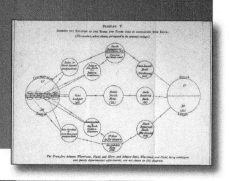

College/Postsecondary

Employers typically require a computer systems analyst to have a bachelor's degree in a computer-related field. However, many analysts enter the field from a variety of different backgrounds, such as economics or business. Most companies prefer a systems analyst who holds a master's degree in information systems or computer science. An advanced degree is not commonly required for entry-level positions but is usually necessary for more advanced positions in the field.

Many technical schools offer computer-science training programs. These programs typically last six months to a year, and they provide students with both hands-on training and formal classroom instruction. These schools are a great place for students to network with others in the profession.

Because each company has special demands for their computer systems, analysts with specific educational backgrounds are needed. For example, an insurance company would need an analyst who has strong knowledge of the needs of that industry. Many analysts begin their careers working in an IT department and gain experience in computer-systems analysis over time.

Because computer technology is always changing, most analysts will continue their education throughout their career in order to stay competitive. An analyst who does not keep up with new and evolving technologies will find their methods quickly become obsolete.

Related College Majors
- Computer Engineering
- Computer Engineering Technology
- Computer Maintenance Technology
- Computer Programming
- Computer Science
- Information Sciences & Systems

Adult Job Seekers

Computer systems analysis requires a deep knowledge of computer systems and their various applications, so interested individuals should be sure that they have the appropriate education and training. An individual with no experience in the field should enroll in a relevant program at a technical school or community college.

Professional Certification and Licensure

Although certification is not usually required by an employer, it is available from system manufacturers, schools, and professional certification organizations. Certificate programs in computer systems analysis are typically engineered for people who already have a strong knowledge of computer systems. Certification is offered for specific types of computer systems as well as for basic knowledge in a range of systems.

Certification is available in a variety of categories, including information systems development, information systems design, and business software development. These certificate programs usually cover fundamental strategies used by analysts.

Additional Requirements

Being a computer systems analyst means analyzing data from a variety of sources and then deciding the best way for a company to move forward. This requires strong analytical and problem-solving skills. An analyst also needs good communication and collaborative skills in order to work effectively with IT personnel and management.

Fun Fact

The percentage of American adults who own computers actually dropped between 2010 and 2015, down from 88 percent to 78 percent. Meanwhile, 86 percent of 18- to 29-year-olds own a smartphone.

Source: www.pewinternet.org/2015/10/29/technology-device-ownership-2015/

EARNINGS AND ADVANCEMENT

Computer systems analysts may increase their advancement opportunities by obtaining additional education. Earnings vary according to the geographic location of the employer, and the computer systems analyst's experience and education.

Median annual earnings of computer systems analysts were $85,800 in 2014. The lowest ten percent earned less than $51,910, and the highest ten percent earned more than $135,450.

Computer systems analysts may receive paid vacations, holidays, and sick days; life and health insurance; and retirement benefits. These are usually paid by the employer.

Metropolitan Areas with the Highest Employment Level in this Occupation

Metropolitan area	Employment	Employment per thousand jobs	Annual mean wage
New York-Jersey City-White Plains, NY-NJ	29,340	4.53	$104,940
Washington-Arlington-Alexandria, DC-VA-MD-WV	22,020	9.11	$103,290
Dallas-Plano-Irving, TX	20,680	8.88	$95,160
Houston-The Woodlands-Sugar Land, TX	18,310	6.25	$102,730
Chicago-Naperville-Arlington Heights, IL	18,250	5.11	$88,230
San Jose-Sunnyvale-Santa Clara, CA	14,240	14.07	$114,790
Atlanta-Sandy Springs-Roswell, GA	13,940	5.62	$87,700
Minneapolis-St. Paul-Bloomington, MN-WI	13,450	7.15	$91,030
Phoenix-Mesa-Scottsdale, AZ	13,110	6.99	$91,460
Los Angeles-Long Beach-Glendale, CA	12,550	3.06	$94,800

Source: Bureau of Labor Statistics

EMPLOYMENT AND OUTLOOK

Computer systems analysts held about 570,000 jobs nationally in 2014. Although they are found in most industries, the greatest concentration of computer systems analysts is in the computer systems design and related services industry. A growing number are employed on a temporary or contract basis or as consultants.

Employment is expected to grow much faster than the average for all occupations through the year 2024, which means employment is projected to increase 20 percent or more. This is a result of organizations continuing to adopt increasingly sophisticated technologies. The demand for "networking" to facilitate the sharing of information, the expansion of client/server environments, and the need for specialists to use their knowledge and skills in a problem solving capacity will be major factors in the rising demand of computer systems analysts.

Employment Trend, Projected 2016–24

Computer systems analysts: 21%

Computer occupations: 12%

Total, all occupations: 7%

Note: "All Occupations" includes all occupations in the U.S. Economy. Source: U.S. Bureau of Labor Statistics, Employment Projections Program

Related Occupations
- Computer & Information Systems Manager
- Computer Engineer
- Computer Network Architect
- Computer Programmer
- Computer Support Specialist
- Database Administrator
- Information Security Analyst
- Information Technology Project Manager
- Management Analyst & Consultant
- Mathematician

- Network & Computer Systems Administrator
- Operations Research Analyst
- Software Developer
- Web Administrator
- Web Developer

Related Occupations
- Computer Programmer
- Computer Systems Officer
- Computer Systems Specialist

Conversation With . . .
RADA KOGAN

Senior Programmer Analyst, Boston College
Boston, Massachusetts
IT professional, 25 years

1. What was your individual career path in terms of education/training, entry-level job, or other significant opportunity?

My path was unconventional. I never got a formal education in information technology. I got my college degree in engineering in what used to be the Soviet Union and became Ukraine. So I came here at 25 with a solid technical background because of the engineering courses and some computer science courses I had taken. It's just that "information technology" in the USSR was an oxymoron—information was controlled and censured! There was no such field as "information technology" because there was no freedom of speech. But when I came here I knew that it was something that I would like to do. I was continually educating myself, taking courses in computer science and IT at Boston University and Brandeis University, but mostly I learned on the job.

My first professional job was as a programmer analyst at Phillips Academy in Andover, MA, but I didn't do much analysis. From there, I went to the Museum of Science in Boston because they had the same system. And from there I moved to the financial sector, working for an investment company. Then I worked at Clean Harbors and later at Cognex, an engineering and manufacturing company in Natick, MA. I started at Boston College almost 10 years ago. I'm a still responsible for code development, but for the last several years, systems analysis has become a large part of my job.

2. What are the most important skills and/or qualities for someone in your profession?

You need creative thinking. You have to be independent and be detail oriented. You need the ability to interpret complex information and concepts, because you're talking to non-technical people and you have to communicate with them in their language. When they want to know why the system can't do this or can't do that, you need to be able to explain systems limitations on their level. And vice versa: you need to translate business requirements to software developers. Analysts are the go-between people. You need to be adaptable, because technology changes rapidly.

You have to possess good communication skills, good presentation skills and good writing skills. Problem solving is important. You have to learn to set priorities and do project management. You need the ability to work under pressure and meet tight deadlines.

3. What do you wish you had known going into this profession?

I was at a disadvantage with limited language skills. I didn't have good writing skills. I was definitely lacking the ability to communicate to non-technical people. It was an issue because I was too technical for them. I had to learn on the job. I wish I had a better understanding of the business side. If I had a degree in information technology, it would have expanded my career choices and definitely would have helped me move up the career ladder. I strongly suggest looking at degree programs in information systems. This is what I didn't get, the business side, how to budget and calculate costs. It's extremely important to enter this field with good fundamental knowledge.

4. Are there many job opportunities in your profession? In what specific areas?

This profession will be in high demand, especially in health care, finance, and education. Every industry uses computer systems. Somebody needs to understand all these processes, how applications connect and integrate, and how information is passed between multiple systems. It's a hot field and it's going to get even hotter.

5. How do you see your profession changing in the next five years? What role will technology play in those changes, and what skills will be required?

We use PeopleSoft, which is a massive business software product. We write programs using a proprietary language; we develop applications within applications. The trend I see is decreased demand for programmers and increased demand for systems analysts. Today, software packages are highly configurable products. As a systems analyst, you need to be able to mold these products to best address the needs of your organization.

6. What do you enjoy most about your job? What do you enjoy least about your job?

I like that I do a variety of things. I interact with people. I do system design work, which I like. I do support. I do development. It's far from being mundane. I like challenges and problem solving. What I like least is the pressure and deadlines, but it's part of the job.

7. **Can you suggest a valuable "try this" for students considering a career in your profession?**

If you like to build diagrams and work with flow charts and you're methodical and curious and really want to understand how processes work, then systems analyst could be a good fit. You're not actually coding anything; you're doing analysis and you're doing graphs. Find an internship. This will tell you, "Oh, I actually hate doing this" or "I do like it." And find a mentor, somebody who will be willing to share their experience.

MORE INFORMATION

Association for Computing Machinery
2 Penn Plaza, Suite 701
New York, NY 10121-0701
800.342.6626
www.acm.org

Association of Information Technology Professionals
401 N. Michigan Avenue, Suite 2400
Chicago, IL 60611-4267
800.224.9371
www.aitp.org

Computing Research Association
1828 L Street NW, Suite 800
Washington, DC 20036
202.234.2111
www.cra.org

Institute for the Certification of Computer Professionals
2400 East Devon Avenue, Suite 281
Des Plaines, IL 60018-4610
800.843.8227
www.iccp.org

Institute of Electrical and Electronics Engineers Computer Society
2001 L Street NW, Suite 700
Washington, DC 20036-4928
202.371.0101
www.computer.org

Patrick Cooper/Editor

Data Entry Keyer / Data Coder

Snapshot

Career Cluster: Business Administration; Health Care; Information Technology

Interests: Computers, typing, paying attention to detail

Earnings (Yearly Average): $29,460

Employment & Outlook: Decline Expected

OVERVIEW

Sphere of Work

Data entry keyers/coders enter information, such as customer or patient records, numbers, lists, and reports, into computers. The position may be part of a multidisciplinary administrative team or a dedicated data entry workforce. Data entry keyers are employed in industries and organizations where large amounts of information entry and processing are needed. These work settings may include banking and finance, health services, energy and mining, business and administration, manufacturing, and government.

Work Environment

Data entry keyers usually work in office environments, although advances in communication technologies are increasing opportunities for off-site or remote work. They spend long hours sitting and working in front of a computer. The position generally requires little interaction with others. Indeed, the job demands the ability to focus on a specific typing task for extended periods without interruption. Most data entry keyers work a forty-hour week during standard office hours, although some may work longer or more flexible hours. Part-time, temporary, and contract work is also often available.

Profile

Working Conditions: Work Indoors
Physical Strength: Light Work
Education Needs: High School Diploma or G.E.D., High School Diploma with Technical Education
Licensure/Certification: Usually Not Required
Opportunities For Experience: Internship, Military Service
Holland Interest Score*: CSR

* See Appendix A

Occupation Interest

This occupation suits individuals who have good typing and general computing skills and who can perform repetitive work over long periods. Data entry may be particularly attractive to those with little formal education who are seeking an entry-level clerical role. Attention to detail, accuracy, and speed are equally important in data entry work. Although no formal qualifications are required for the job, experience using a variety of computing programs and office equipment (such as scanners) is likely to be well regarded by employers.

A Day in the Life—Duties and Responsibilities

A data entry keyer spends most of the workday entering information into computer systems, such as databases and other electronic information repositories. The specific data they work with depends on the type of employer and industry. Data entry keyers may process such data as medical and client records, sales receipts, financial transactions, lists of items, numbers, names, notes, addresses, test results, and equipment details.

The methods of data entry vary as well. Some data entry keyers manually enter information from paper records into an electronic records system using a computer keyboard. Others use a scanner to scan information from hard copies into an electronic system and then check the data for accuracy and missing entries.

Data entry keyers are often required to proofread or check the accuracy of their work or that of others. As they encounter mistakes, introduced either by mechanical or human error, the data entry keyers must correct the data. To rectify some problems, they may need to make adjustments to computer systems or electronic equipment. At times, data entry keyers may also edit or reformat data in existing records.

Beginning data entry keyers often work under greater supervision than those with more experience who may work in virtual solitude or oversee others' work. Tasks given to new data entry keyers tend to be more rote while experienced or more educated employees may receive assignments that are more complex and require some discretionary judgment.

Duties and Responsibilities

- Operating computers or data coding machines
- Setting or adjusting machines for specific operations
- Producing control cards or programs
- Verifying accuracy of data by using a verifier
- Detecting faulty operation of machines

WORK ENVIRONMENT

Physical Environment

Bright, clean office settings predominate. Data entry keyers work at desk stations in front of computers. Some data entry keyers may work in home offices, supported by communication technologies. The repetitiveness of the work can be physically and mentally straining. Like other office workers, data entry keyers are at risk for repetitive strain injuries and chronic postural issues; thus, regular stretching and movement is very important to prevent injury.

Transferable Skills and Abilities

Organization & Management Skills
- Paying attention to and handling details
- Performing routine work

Human Environment

Data entry keyers generally work independently. This occupation demands little interaction or communication with other people, although data entry keyers can expect to have some contact with work colleagues and supervisors. A data entry keyer may be part of multidisciplinary administrative team or a member of a dedicated data entry workforce.

Technological Environment

Daily data entry operations demand the use of a computer, keyboard, and software applications for word processing, spreadsheets, databases, and character recognition. Data entry keyers may also use scanners or other electronic devices. Data entry keyers who perform other administrative or clerical tasks may be required to use other standard office technologies, such as the telephone, e-mail, photocopiers, fax machines, and the internet.

EDUCATION, TRAINING, AND ADVANCEMENT

High School/Secondary

High school students can best prepare for a career as a data entry keyer by taking courses in English and applied communication subjects such as business communication. Computing studies, data processing, and typing would also be highly beneficial. Finding part-time data entry work while still in high school is an excellent way to gain entry-level experience. High school students may secure employment as data entry keyers directly following graduation.

Suggested High School Subjects
- Applied Communication
- Business & Computer Technology
- Business Data Processing
- English
- Keyboarding

Famous First

The first coding technology was in the form of plug boards used with mechanical tabulating equipment to support such things as census counting in the 1900s. With the advent of computers in the mid-20th century, punch cards and punch card sorters performed essentially the same function.

College/Postsecondary

Data entry keyers generally require no formal postsecondary educational qualifications, although the completion of database management, word processing, and typing courses at a technical or community college may be well regarded by employers.

On-the-job experience in data entry is usually considered more important than formal qualifications. Most employers provide on-the-job training to prepare new data entry keyers for using the company's specific programs and systems. Experience across a variety of systems and databases is generally attractive to employers, as is experience using related equipment such as scanners.

Related College Majors
- Administrative Assistant/Secretarial Science, General
- Computer Typography & Composition Equipment Operation
- General Office/Clerical & Typing Services
- Information Processing/Data Entry Technology

Adult Job Seekers

Adults seeking employment in data entry are advised to refresh their typing and computing skills and to update their resume. Experience in specific industries and with particular systems and data entry equipment should be highlighted in the candidate's application. Entry-level opportunities may be available on a part-time, full-time, after-hours, weekend, temporary, or contract basis. Networking, job searching, and interviewing skills are critical. Satisfactory scores on a timed typing test may be a condition of employment for many data entry positions.

Opportunities for career advancement within the data entry field are limited due to the nature of the work. Experienced data entry keyers may be considered for more supervisory roles. Those with more experience or further education may also be considered for allied clerical and administrative positions, such as customer service representatives and administrative assistants.

Professional Certification and Licensure

There are no formal professional certifications or licensure requirements for data entry roles.

Additional Requirements

Data entry keyers should enjoy rote, manual tasks and thrive on solitude. Data entry work may be an ideal occupation for those who desire indoor office work but have little formal education and for those who prefer a flexible schedule to accommodate other commitments, such as students. Further experience and education may be necessary for promotion or salary increase. This occupation is typically viewed as a steppingstone to higher administrative positions or more specialized office work.

Fun Fact

One hundred and sixty three words per minute. That's the world record set by Sean Wrona of Ithaca, NY., during a 2010 competition that required him to type a mix of unintelligible phrases and code using multiple keyboard commands.

Source: http://www.pcmag.com/article2/0,2817,2361604,00.asp

EARNINGS AND ADVANCEMENT

Earnings depend on the industry, the geographic location of the employer, and the employee's experience and seniority. Those employed in the transportation, utilities and manufacturing industries earned more than those employed in trade and the financial and service industries.

Data entry keyers had median annual earnings of $29,460 in 2014.

Data entry keyers may receive paid vacations, holidays, and sick days; life and health insurance; and retirement benefits. These are usually paid by the employer.

Metropolitan Areas with the Highest Employment Level in this Occupation

Metropolitan area	Employment	Employment per thousand jobs	Annual mean wage
New York-Jersey City-White Plains, NY-NJ	10,350	1.60	$35,340
Los Angeles-Long Beach-Glendale, CA	7,610	1.85	$31,050
Chicago-Naperville-Arlington Heights, IL	7,210	2.02	$31,890
Dallas-Plano-Irving, TX	5,210	2.24	$31,300
Houston-The Woodlands-Sugar Land, TX	5,140	1.75	$30,520
Phoenix-Mesa-Scottsdale, AZ	3,780	2.01	$29,480
Tampa-St. Petersburg-Clearwater, FL	3,630	2.98	$28,810
Anaheim-Santa Ana-Irvine, CA	3,510	2.31	$33,080
Atlanta-Sandy Springs-Roswell, GA	3,030	1.22	$30,790
Salt Lake City, UT	2,950	4.49	$32,890

Source: Bureau of Labor Statistics

EMPLOYMENT AND OUTLOOK

Data entry keyers held about 200,000 jobs in 2014, and they were employed in nearly every sector of the economy. Employment is expected to decline through the year 2024, however. This is due to increased productivity brought about by new technologies. Job prospects will be best for those data entry keyers with the best technical skills. In particular, the more computer software packages data entry keyers know or expertise they have in combining word processing with graphics or spreadsheets, the better their job opportunities will be.

Related Occupations
- Computer Operator
- Office Machine Operator
- Secretary
- Word Processor

Conversation With . . .
DAWNA ALPHONSE

Abstracter/Coder
University of Massachusetts Medical Center
Worcester, Massachusetts
Data coder, 10 months

1. What was your individual career path in terms of education/training, entry-level job, or other significant opportunity?

I wanted to be a medical illustrator as a kid. After receiving an associate degree in graphic design, I worked in journalism for many years. I was paginating the business section of a newspaper—designing pages on a computer, copy editing, proofreading and working with editors and pressmen to make back-to-back deadlines. Eventually, the newspaper I worked for, MetroWest Daily News in Framingham, Massachusetts, was sold to a national chain that centralized many jobs at their headquarters in another state. We were given months to prepare for the impending layoffs, so I earned a coding certificate at night school.

After working in the newspaper industry for 38 years, I was detail-oriented, worked well under deadline pressure and knew how to deal with people who are stressed. These are marketable skills, and coding for a hospital trauma registry seemed to be a good place to transfer some of these skills. I took a 15-month course in medical coding at Massachusetts Bay Community College, then spent another six months preparing for the six-hour Certified Professional Coder (CPC) test offered by the American Academy of Professional Coders (AAPC.)

I do abstraction, coding and data entry. Abstracting is recording a set of predetermined data requests from software programs, while coding is applying codes that match the diagnosis in your data. You locate codes from the International Classification of Diseases (ICD-10) book, which is why you need training. Most medical coding is for insurance reimbursement, allowing healthcare providers to communicate with insurance companies regarding payment. But the data/codes that I collect in the trauma registry are used in research.

2. What are the most important skills and/or qualities for someone in your profession?

The most important skills for a coder are the ability to see numbers in their correct sequence and attention to detail. Being a Type A personality helps! You also need a solid familiarity with computers. You need to be curious and willing to ask questions because you'll always be learning. The ICD-10 book is updated annually; in 2016 alone, hundreds of changes were being made. You have to behave professionally under stressful deadlines.

For medical coding, a class in medical terminology is a must. Latin would give you a major jump in learning, and a solid background in English is very helpful as you need to read and understand the nuances in medical files.

3. What do you wish you had known going into this profession?

Knowing CPC test-taking skills would have been beneficial. Preparing for the test is a major undertaking. It involves all the body systems, medical terminology, pathology, immunology, radiology, anatomy and physiology and compliance rules. It's a test of both knowledge and logic.

4. Are there many job opportunities in your profession? In what specific areas?

There are more coding jobs than abstracting/coding jobs. Many companies employ just coders. Having a background in medical terminology will open doors to medical secretary and billing jobs while you work toward your CPC certificate, which is essential to be hired as a coder.

5. How do you see your profession changing in the next five years? What role will technology play in those changes, and what skills will be required?

Software is always changing to keep up with a company's needs. You need to be able to change with it. The health care industry is only going to grow as people age and live longer.

6. What do you enjoy most about your job? What do you enjoy least about your job?

I'm never bored, not for a minute. I enjoy bringing data from three different software programs together to be entered into hospital, state and federal databases. These statistics paint a picture of how trauma occurs. By examining this data, researchers devise ways to prevent or reduce trauma. Many people and organizations use the data in their research and the research is as varied as the people doing it. Besides the trauma registry, there are registries for blood, cancer, etc. I enjoy being part of that.

I haven't been doing it long enough to know what I like least. I truly enjoy learning, but I imagine the need to constantly update your knowledge might deter some people.

7. Can you suggest a valuable "try this" for students considering a career in your profession?

Volunteering in a hospital or in a physician's office would be a good experience. State workforce centers, also known as unemployment offices, can help you match your personality traits with a career. I took the Myers Briggs personality test. Medical coding was the best fit for my personality. You don't need to be unemployed to use the workforce center. Use it. Your taxes are paying for it!

MORE INFORMATION

International Association of Administrative Professionals
P.O. Box 20404
Kansas City, MO 64195
816.891.6600
www.iaap-hq.org

National Business Education Association
1914 Association Drive
Reston, VA 20191-1596
703.860.8300
www.nbea.org

Kylie Hughes/Editor

Database Administrator

Snapshot

Career Cluster(s): Business Administration; Information Technology

Interests: Computer technology, solving problems, detail-oriented work, numbers

Earnings (Yearly Average): $81,710

Employment & Outlook: Faster Than Average Growth Expected

OVERVIEW

Sphere of Work

Database administrators manage computer databases and networks for businesses, government agencies, hospitals, universities, and other organizations. They set up computer networks according to the needs of the client, integrate data from old systems into new networks, and perform troubleshooting activities as needed. Their responsibilities include organizing, accessing, and increasing storage space for data, adding and deleting users, and purging outdated programs. They are also charged with the security of the networks on which they work, periodically installing and updating firewalls and virus protection software. Database administrators train

employees on new systems and communicate with employees on any changes to or issues with the network.

Work Environment

Database administrators work in offices, computer labs, and similar environments. These facilities are generally clean, well lit, and well ventilated. Many administrators' offices are large rooms that contain a company's central server as well as work stations. In some cases, telecommuting may be an option. Database administrators typically work a standard forty-hour week, although those hours may be increased when major issues occur in the company's network or a new network is brought on line. Some administrators work longer hours also because they are on call, standing by outside of business hours in case any problems with the network arise.

Profile

Working Conditions: Work Indoors
Physical Strength: Light Work
Education Needs: Bachelor's Degree,
Licensure/Certification: Required
Opportunities For Experience:
 Internship, Military Service, Part Time
 Work
Holland Interest Score*: IRE

* See Appendix A

Occupation Interest

Somebody interested in database administration should be good at problem solving, pay close attention to detail, and find satisfaction in working independently. Database administrators are in high demand, a trend that is expected to continue. Even during challenging economic times, businesses are less likely to lay off their database administrators in light of the major roles they play in operations. Database administrators are needed in virtually every industry, giving graduates a wide range of professional environments in which to seek employment.

A Day in the Life—Duties and Responsibilities

Database administrators are in charge of storing and managing a business's computer networks and maintaining up-to-date internet security programs. Administrators meet with key employees to determine their needs. Based on the information provided, they design new systems, write new code, upgrade existing networks and programs, install new programs, and remove outdated files and software to free up space and improve speed. Database administrators run periodic tests on programs and networks in order to monitor efficiency and processing speed, check for problems, or locate both full and unused data files. Administrators frequently train new employees on the systems and, when bringing a new feature or database online, train current employees as well. Administrators may be asked to man a help desk to resolve any individual user issues or be on call after business hours to safeguard against network failures or crashes.

In addition to managing the database, administrators must develop and install firewalls that prevent the spread of viruses, spam, and other internet based problems. Database administrators must research the most effective virus protection software, write code that blocks unwanted entry into e-mail systems, and keep abreast of new viruses and hacker tactics.

Duties and Responsibilities

- Working with clients to determine the types of databases needed
- Designing and creating database tables
- Defining data relationships between tables
- Designing application interfaces and data entry systems
- Writing the code that allows comparing and cross-referencing of data
- Testing to make sure steps are correct and will produce the desired results
- Debugging and rewriting programs if unexpected results are received

WORK ENVIRONMENT

Physical Environment

Database administrators work in computer labs, offices, and similar professional environments. These areas are generally clean, well lit, and well ventilated. Depending on the company, some database administrators may be able to work from home. There is not very much physical activity involved with these positions, although administrators may be asked to move hard drives, monitors, and other hardware over short distances.

Transferable Skills and Abilities

Communication Skills
- Speaking effectively
- Writing concisely

Interpersonal/Social Skills
- Being able to work independently

Organization & Management Skills
- Organizing information or materials
- Paying attention to and handling details
- Performing routine work

Research & Planning Skills
- Identifying problems
- Solving problems
- Using logical reasoning

Human Environment

Database administrators work with all levels and types of employees within their respective organizations, including executives, managers, entry-level employees, administrative personnel, and salespeople. They also interact with external software and hardware vendors as well as off-site network administrators.

Technological Environment

Database administrators must be skilled with both desktop and laptop computer hardware (including printers, disk drives, and external hard drives), servers and data storage systems, and other devices. They should also be capable of using a wide range of computer software, including virus prevention, archival, database management, metadata (which provides information about the data collected by a network), and other programs.

EDUCATION, TRAINING, AND ADVANCEMENT

High School/Secondary

High school students should study computer science and mathematics such as algebra, calculus, geometry, and trigonometry. Additionally, business and accounting courses will help database administrators understand the particular companies for which they will work, as well as how business is conducted in general.

Suggested High School Subjects
- Accounting
- Algebra
- Applied Communication
- Applied Math
- Bookkeeping
- Business & Computer Technology
- Business Data Processing
- Calculus
- College Preparatory
- Computer Programming
- Computer Science
- English
- Geometry
- Keyboarding
- Mathematics
- Statistics
- Trigonometry

Famous First

"The first on-line, real-time, interactive database system," according to management consultant Tim Bryce, "was double-entry bookkeeping which was developed by the merchants of Venice in 1200 A.D." The modern computerized database is a more sophisticated version of the same.

College/Postsecondary

Most database administrators complete a two-year associate degree or a four-year bachelor's degree in computer science, management information systems (MIS), or similar fields. The bachelor's degree is preferred in a competitive job market. A master's degree in business administration with a focus on information systems, though not necessary, will provide even more of an advantage. Postsecondary students are encouraged to seek internships at professional organizations.

Related College Majors

- Computer Engineering
- Computer Engineering Technology
- Computer Maintenance Technology
- Computer Programming
- Computer Science
- Data Processing Technology
- Information Sciences & Systems
- Management Information Systems & Business Data Processing

Adult Job Seekers

Individuals with limited experience as database administrators are encouraged to start out as computer programmers, software developers, and help desk technicians in order to gain more experience, which can lead to internal promotion to the position of database administrator. Qualified and experienced database administrators should apply directly to companies, government agencies, and other organizations. Additionally, there are a number of job placement agencies that specialize in placing information systems professionals such as database administrators in open positions.

Professional Certification and Licensure

Many software companies and universities provide certification programs for database administrators. Microsoft, for example, offers an intensive certification course on usage of their SQL (structured query language) databases. Some companies require such certification; even when this is not the case, being certified will certainly enhance a candidate's competitiveness regarding open positions.

Additional Requirements

Database administrators must be able to analyze complex systems and address intricate issues. They should have strong research skills, which are critical in monitoring new developments in viruses, hacker attacks, and programs that can block these threats. Because the technology changes so often, database administrators should be prepared to take occasional classes in order to stay up to date. They must also have excellent communications skills, with the ability not only to help others with system problems but also to train them in how to maximize their use of the network.

Fun Fact

Big data is not just for government and big business. The website makeuseof.com's list of "15 Massive Online Databases You Should Know About" includes databases dedicated to airliners, the Human Genome Project, graves, and guitars.

Source: http://www.makeuseof.com/tag/15-massive-online-databases-know/

EARNINGS AND ADVANCEMENT

Earnings depend on the size and location of the employer and the education and experience of the employee. Median annual earnings of database administrators were $81,710 in 2014. The lowest ten percent earned less than $45,460, and the highest ten percent earned more than $127,080.

Database administrators may receive paid vacations, holidays, and sick days; life and health insurance; and retirement benefits. These are usually paid by the employer.

Metropolitan Areas with the Highest Employment Level in this Occupation

Metropolitan area	Employment	Hourly mean wage	Annual mean wage
New York-Jersey City-White Plains, NY-NJ	5,580	$46.77	$97,290
Washington-Arlington-Alexandria, DC-VA-MD-WV	4,800	$47.64	$99,100
Atlanta-Sandy Springs-Roswell, GA	4,250	$41.06	$85,400
Chicago-Naperville-Arlington Heights, IL	3,350	$40.57	$84,390
Houston-The Woodlands-Sugar Land, TX	3,260	$38.15	$79,350
Dallas-Plano-Irving, TX	3,210	$41.91	$87,180
Phoenix-Mesa-Scottsdale, AZ	2,610	$39.71	$82,600
Los Angeles-Long Beach-Glendale, CA	2,560	$45.93	$95,540
Boston-Cambridge-Newton, MA	2,390	$40.68	$84,600
Minneapolis-St. Paul-Bloomington, MN-WI	2,380	$43.46	$90,400

Source: Bureau of Labor Statistics

EMPLOYMENT AND OUTLOOK

There were about 120,000 database administrators employed nationally in 2014. Many database administrators were employed by internet service providers; web search portals; and data processing, hosting, and related services firms. Others work for government, manufacturers of computer and electronic products, insurance companies, financial institutions, and universities.

Employment of database administrators is expected to grow faster than the average for all occupations through the year 2024, which means employment is projected to increase 10 percent or more. Growth in the computer systems design industry, the demand for networking services, the expansion of client-server environments and the development of new technologies will all contribute to the growing need for database administrators. Opportunities will be best for those who stay current with the latest database applications and technical advancements.

Employment Trend, Projected 2014–24

Computer occupations: 12%

Database administrators: 11%

Total, all occupations: 7%

Note: "All Occupations" includes all occupations in the U.S. Economy. Source: U.S. Bureau of Labor Statistics, Employment Projections Program

Related Occupations
- Computer & Information Systems Manager
- Computer Engineer
- Computer Network Architect
- Computer Operator
- Computer Programmer
- Computer Support Specialist
- Computer Systems Analyst
- Computer-Control Tool Programmer
- Information Security Analyst

- Information Technology
  Project Manager
- Network & Computer Systems
  Administrator
- Web Administrator

Related Occupations
- Computer Programmer
- Computer Systems Specialist

Conversation With . . .
LEONORA GIOVANANGELO

Executive Office of Labor & Workforce Development
Commonwealth of Massachusetts
IT professional, 29 years
Database Management, 16 years

1. What was your individual career path in terms of education/training, entry-level job, or other significant opportunity?

I was studying accounting at Bentley College in Massachusetts and I was not passionate about it. We had to take an IT class as a requirement. I just fell in love with programming because I'm a very black-and-white person. I love math because to me, there's one right answer. I have a very mathematical mind. It's very easy for me to figure out if I've done something well. I have a passion for IT. After college, I started out in my first job as a programmer, which I did for three or four years. Then an opportunity come up to be a database administrator (DBA) and I jumped on it.

A database is a collection of information; it's basically where the information is held. It's almost like a big Excel spreadsheet. A lot of being a database administrator is just making sure that everything is put together as efficiently as possible, so that the information can be accessed efficiently. It's all about relationships between the data. I've been working for the state of Massachusetts since 2002. Before that, I was a database administrator for Boston University. Working for the state and working for private enterprise are very different. The pace is very different. Things get done more quickly in the private sector. In the private sector one can expect to put in extra hours, whereas in the public sector, due to union rules, your days typically have a specific start and end time.

2. What are the most important skills and/or qualities for someone in your profession?

Attention to detail is big, and the ability to solve problems. You also need to be able to think outside the box. Often when programmers and developers have a problem, their first line of defense will be to talk to the DBA. I see myself as being a business analyst. Data warehousing is for reporting information. You have to meet with users and understand their terminology and really, really understand what they do and then report back to the developers. A DBA is like a middleman between business and IT. Being able to speak both sides is critical. If you don't understand the business side, you're not going to get the right answers. You need to be able to ask the right questions—and that goes for IT in general. You need to be able to think quickly. Communication skills and the ability to get along with other people is key, in any job. If you don't have that, you're in trouble.

3. What do you wish you had known going into this profession?

How demanding it can be. You're on call on the time. I've been on call 24 hours a day, 7 days a week, 365 days a year. I missed out on a lot of things when I was over at BU. You have to be flexible, that's for sure. Some DBA jobs don't require that, because they don't have off-hours support. Sometimes when you're on call, you can handle it without going into the office. It depends on how serious it is. A representative from each group might have to come in and be onsite. When I was younger, I thought that was exciting. Also, when you're younger, you have a lot f energy. But now my priorities have changed. It's about quality of life.

4. Are there many job opportunities in your profession? In what specific areas?

Yes, there are. Database administration is always gong to be hot. Every company needs a database administrator—at least one DBA. We have several here. Other big areas are security, software engineering, software developer, project management and web developer.

5. How do you see your profession changing in the next five years? What role will technology play in those changes, and what skills will be required?

Security is huge. It's a server environment here and every week the help desk sends out emails about some sort of security concern. Working in IT, you have to keep a pulse on what's out there and keep yourself current, or you can really be left behind.

6. What do you enjoy most about your job? What do you enjoy least about your job?

What I enjoy most is solving problems. I'm a real problem solver. I really enjoy getting out from behind the desk staring at my computer and talking to people. There are people in IT who thrive on that, because they can't deal with people. But as time goes on, I'm realizing that I really enjoy interacting with other people.

What I like least is being on call.

7. **Can you suggest a valuable "try this" for students considering a career in your profession?**

A fantastic resource is YouTube. There's a lot of information there to help you figure out whether or not you like something. On coursera.org you can take free courses from top universities. Microsoft Virtual Academy (mva.microsoft.com) offers free online training, including a section for students. If working on a spreadsheet is something that catches your attention, then, yes, database management might be a good option for you.

MORE INFORMATION

Association for Computing Machinery
2 Penn Plaza, Suite 701
New York, NY 10121-0701
800.342.6626
www.acm.org

Data Management Association International
19239 N. Dale Mabry Highway, #132
Lutz, FL 33548
813.778.5495
www.dama.org

IEEE Computer Society
2001 L Street, NW, Suite 700
Washington, DC 20036-4928
202.371.0101
www.computer.org

Institute for the Certification of Computer Professionals
2400 East Devon Avenue, Suite 281
Des Plaines, IL 60018-4610
800.843.8227
www.iccp.org

League of Professional System Administrators
P.O. Box 5161
Trenton, NJ 08638
www.lopsa.org

Network Professional Association
1401 Hermes Lane
San Diego, CA 92154
888.672.6720
www.npa.org

Professional Association for SQL Server
203 North LaSalle, Suite 2100
Chicago, IL 60601
425.967.8000
www.sqlpass.org

Michael Auerbach/Editor

Desktop Publisher

Snapshot

Career Cluster: Arts, Computer Systems/Technology, Media & Communications

Interests: Art, Graphic Design, Printing, Writing

Earnings (Yearly Average): $38,804

Employment & Outlook: Decline Expected

OVERVIEW

Sphere of Work

Desktop publishers use digital word-processing and design software to arrange and prepare design layouts for newspapers, books, magazines, and other materials for print or online publication. Desktop publishers may also work as graphic designers, creating and modifying graphics for publication. Desktop publishers typically work closely with editors, designers, graphic artists, and computer programmers in the design of web-based or printed publications. Depending on their area of employment, desktop publishers may spend time editing and writing text for publication in addition to supervising layout and design. Desktop publishing is utilized by a variety of companies, from traditional print publishers

to the many businesses that produce web-based publications for advertising and informational purposes.

Work Environment

Desktop publishers work closely with writers, editors, and designers to complete projects for publication. Those who work on web-based publications may work with web designers or computer programmers to create websites for online publication. They may also work with graphic designers to create and refine fonts, images, and other graphics. Desktop publishing can be performed in a standard office, using a desktop or laptop computer. Some desktop-publishing specialists may be able to complete part of their work off-site in a home office.

Profile

Working Conditions: Office Environment

Physical Strength: Light Work

Education Needs: On-The-Job Training Technical/Community College Bachelor's Degree

Licensure/Certification: Usually Not Required

Physical Abilities Not Required: No Heavy Work

Opportunities For Experience: Apprenticeship, Part-Time Work

Holland Interest Score*: CRE, RCE, RCS

* See Appendix A

Occupation Interest

Desktop publishing attracts individuals interested in graphic design, printing, and technical artistry. Many desktop publishers have backgrounds in art or writing. A strong knowledge of both subjects is helpful to anyone interested in the field. Digital design for web publications has become an important facet in the field of publishing, and demand is increasing for desktop-publishing specialists with experience and expertise in web design, digital art, and computer programming.

A Day in the Life—Duties and Responsibilities

The printing process is typically divided into three stages: prepress, printing, and postpress activities. Desktop publishers are generally considered part of the prepress team, and they may also spend time working with professionals during the printing process.

Desktop publishers usually work full time during regular business hours, though overtime or alternate schedules are sometimes necessary during seasonal peak periods or when working on time-sensitive projects. For example, newspapers may require night workers to prepare for early-morning publication. Holidays and special events may also require employees to work extra hours. In some cases, desktop publishers work part-time hours or during varying schedules depending on the deadlines for upcoming projects. Some desktop publishers are able to work from a home office, but this requires frequent communication and collaboration with other individuals involved in various parts of a project.

During a typical day, a desktop publisher communicates with writers, editors, project managers, and designers about ongoing and upcoming projects. They also gather pictures or artwork from various sources and then arrange the images into a cohesive and attractive layout for publication. Desktop publishers write, edit, proofread, and arrange text and work with various typefaces. Desktop publishers also merge files from design and publishing programs and therefore need to have extensive knowledge of a variety of digital design, writing, editing, and image-processing programs.

Duties and Responsibilities

- Placing text and graphics into desktop publishing software programs
- Locating and editing graphics, such as illustrations and photographs
- Working with designers and writers to create printed or online pieces
- Checking layouts for errors and making corrections

WORK ENVIRONMENT

Physical Environment

Offices and workspaces for desktop publishers tend to be quiet, indoor environments comprised of desks and worktables for laying out print samples. Most desktop publishers work at a desk or worktable with a computer, and they also spend time in a printing room or print shop checking on projects.

In some cases, desktop publishers work in offices that are attached to industrial printing presses as is the case with many large-scale magazines, newspapers, and book publishers. Desktop publishers do not typically work in a printing room environment but may visit the printing press to examine printed examples of their projects to ensure that the digital layout transitions well to the printed copy.

Human Environment

Desktop publishers are part of a creative team and work closely with writers, editors, and various design professionals to complete projects. In some cases, companies hire desktop publishers to work on interoffice or professional publications specific to their industry, which often requires publishing professionals to work closely with industry specialists. A pharmaceutical company interested in publishing printed or web-based information about a specific medication, for instance, would expect a desktop publisher to work closely with their in-house sales team as well as with physicians and pharmacists to ensure the information was accurate and clear. In some small companies, there is less interaction between groups since desktop publishers tend to work independently and are responsible for the writing, editing, and graphic design duties in addition to organizing layouts for publication.

Skills and Abilities

Communication Skills
- Writing clearly and concisely

Creative/Artistic Skills
- Having an eye for layout and graphic design elements

Interpersonal/Social Skills
- Being able to work independently as well as on a team

Organization & Management Skills
- Following instructions
- Managing time
- Meeting goals and deadlines
- Paying attention to and handling details

Technical Skills
- Performing technical work using computer software
- Working with text and graphics
- Working with technology/ hardware

Other Skills
- Understanding printing terms and measurements

Technological Environment

Desktop publishers use specific digital publishing software and other computer programs to create and manage their projects. The digital design software programs produced by Adobe Systems have become one of the industry standards in this field, but it is important for desktop publishing professionals to have experience in a variety of digital composition and graphic design software programs. Desktop publishing professionals must also understand computer operation and technical maintenance. Continued education is necessary in order to stay abreast of software changes or new programs relevant to the field. Many of the skills and technologies employed by desktop publishers are made use of in non-print environments such as e-books and other digital formats.

EDUCATION, TRAINING, AND ADVANCEMENT

High School/Secondary

High school students can prepare for a career in desktop publishing by taking classes in journalism, composition, art, and drafting. Some high schools offer graphic design programs and train students in the use of printing and publishing software. In addition, desktop publishers should be knowledgeable about grammar, spelling, and editing procedures, as they typically must check and revise their work prior to printing. Basic English skills developed through a high school education are essential for those pursuing work in the publishing field.

Suggested High School Subjects
- Algebra
- Applied Communication
- Applied Math
- Arts
- Composition
- English
- Graphic Communications
- Keyboarding
- Machining Technology
- Photography

Famous First

The first desktop publishing application, PageMaker, came out in 1985. It was created by Paul Brainerd, co-founder of Aldus Corporation. The software was designed for use with a Macintosh computer linked to an Apple Laser-Writer printer. Brainerd, in fact, coined the term "desktop publishing."

Postsecondary

Community colleges and technical institutes sometimes offer courses and programs in the field of desktop publishing. Typically, desktop publishers hold associate degree in journalism or graphic design.

Individuals can also enter the publishing field by pursuing a bachelor's degree or higher certification in graphic design, graphic arts, or a specific print-oriented program. Journalism and technical writing programs are viable avenues into desktop publishing when supplemented with courses in computers, computer software, and graphic design.

Related College Majors
- Desktop/Electronic Publishing
- Digital Imaging
- Graphic Communications
- Typography & Composition

Adult Job Seekers

Adults interested in pursuing desktop publishing as a career are advised to seek out community college or technical certification programs in their area. Individuals with a background in manual or computer design may have a competitive advantage in transitioning to the desktop publishing field.

Professional Certification and Licensure

Desktop publishers are not legally required to hold a professional certificate or license; however, some employers may require workers to undergo specific training. Some technical institutes, community colleges, and universities offer certification courses in the software programs used in desktop publishing as well as training programs in other aspects of computer-aided programming and design. Desktop publishers typically receive on-the-job training while working under experienced professionals. Some independent desktop publishing specialists work as freelancers or independent contractors and work for several different clients.

Additional Requirements

Desktop publishers must possess attention to detail and the interest and ability to make aesthetic judgments that combine artistic sensibility with technical precision. Because exact measurements are needed, desktop publishers also benefit from experience with basic mathematics and geometry since exact measurements are used when developing and creating projects.

EARNINGS AND ADVANCEMENT

Earnings depend on the type, size, geographic location, and union affiliation of the employer, and the employee's experience and skills. Median annual earnings of desktop publishers were $38,804 in 2012. The lowest ten percent earned less than $23,062, and the highest ten percent earned more than $62,881.

Desktop publishers may receive paid vacations, holidays, and sick days; life and health insurance, and retirement benefits. These are usually paid by the employer.

Metropolitan Areas with the Highest
Concentration of Jobs in this Occupation

Metropolitan area	Employment	Employment per thousand jobs	Hourly mean wage
New York-White Plains-Wayne, NY-NJ	630	0.12	$26.16
Chicago-Joliet-Naperville, IL	600	0.16	$21.37
Boston-Cambridge-Quincy, MA	430	0.25	$21.95
Philadelphia, PA	380	0.21	$21.54
Washington-Arlington-Alexandria, DC-VA-MD-WV	380	0.16	$21.82
St. Louis, MO-IL	370	0.29	$15.90
Los Angeles-Long Beach-Glendale, CA	360	0.09	$20.22
Minneapolis-St. Paul-Bloomington, MN-WI	320	0.18	$23.02

[1] Does not include self-employed. Source: Bureau of Labor Statistics, 2012

EMPLOYMENT AND OUTLOOK

There were approximately 16,000 desktop publishers employed nationally in 2012. Employment is expected to decline through the year 2020. Improvements in printing technology will result in the rising productivity of desktop publishers and the ability for non-printing professionals to create their own printed and online materials, resulting in less demand for these workers.

Employment Trend, Projected 2010–20

Total, All Occupations: 14%

Arts, Designing, Entertainment, Sports and Media Occupations: 13%

Art Directors: 9%

Note: "All Occupations" includes all occupations in the U.S. Economy. Source: U.S. Bureau of Labor Statistics, Employment Projections Program

Related Occupations
- Photoengraver & Lithographer
- Prepress Technician
- Printing Machine Operator

Conversation With . . .
STEPHANIE CHAMBERS

Asset Production Specialist
17 years in the profession

1. What was your individual career path in terms of education, entry-level job, or other significant opportunity?

I graduated with a bachelor of science degree with a major in journalism and a minor in speech communication. I focused on news writing and while I enjoyed that, I didn't really have the personality that you need to go out and interview people and chase stories. While in college, I took graphic design courses, so that's the route I pursued when I left school. My first job out of college was with an insurance company, designing brochures and other internal marketing pieces. From there, I moved onto a marketing job for another company, discovered I didn't like marketing, and went back to desktop publishing, this time working for a company that published industrial catalogs for large retailers, such as Home Depot and Lowe's. My job required that I program code to create, automate, and lay out these catalogs. That's not the usual path into this field. Most people do layouts and design; I ended up in the programming aspect of it. In my current job, I'm the middle person who takes written content and prepares it to go into a content management system. That then goes to the engineering department, which produces the content online.

2. Are there many job opportunities in your profession? In what specific areas?

The publishing industry is evolving so fast it is hard to imagine what is next. Instead of hiring permanent employees, publishing companies are tending to hire temporary and contract help. Hardware and software engineers and project managers are in demand.

3. What do you wish you had known going into this profession?

I wish I had a crystal ball so I could have seen the technological advances that were going to transform the publishing industry. It would have been nice to know that it would become harder to be able to create books and that the internet was going to revolutionize the need for digital content and the reuse of that content to such a variety of platforms.

4. How do you see your profession changing in the next five years?

I think that publishing technology is going to get faster, harder, more complex, and more platforms and devices will emerge. Open source, community-driven efforts are going to continue to revolutionize how publishing companies store, reuse and publish their content. It's very exciting to see how these efforts are providing alternatives to the software programs that have always been the industry standard, such as Adobe's inDesign and Photoshop.

5. What role will technology play in those changes, and what skills will be required?

Technology will be key to changes in the publishing industry. Our layout editors and copy editors have had to learn XML, which stands for extensible markup language. In addition to their regular editing duties, they're responsible for inserting the XML tags that allow the text to be stored, retrieved, and used in different ways for different formats and platforms, such as e-books, smart boards, iPads, and mobile devices. It's a good idea to keep an open mind because the skills that you need for a particular desktop publishing position are likely to grow to include ones that you hadn't even thought of, just because of the need to stay on top of the technological changes

6. Do you have any general advice or additional professional insights to share with someone interested in your profession?

I strongly encourage anyone interested in publishing to also pursue a degree in engineering or computer science. It's important to understand the back-end programs that fuel the content that we see and read. Learn as much as you can about computers and how things work behind the scenes, not just what the end user sees. Ask yourself, what makes this program work this way? Think globally and if something scares you, challenge yourself to figure it out.

7. Can you suggest a valuable "try this" for students considering a career in your profession?

For someone interested in working in publishing technology I would suggest they try to create their own web page using CSS and HTML. A good exercise would be to take a web page, view its source file and figure out how different scripting languages are used to build a web page. Try to improve the web page's functionality and/or learn to add new interactive features. If you think this exercise is fun, you may want to pursue this as a career.

SELECTED SCHOOLS

A variety of colleges and universities offer programs in graphic communications with a concentration in desktop/electronic publishing. This includes many community/technical colleges. Below are listed some of the more prominent institutions in this field.

Black Hills State University
1200 University Street
Spearfish, SD 57799
800.255.2478
www.bhsu.edu

California Polytechnic State University
San Louis Obispo, CA 93407
805.756.1111
www.calpoly.edu

Carroll University
100 N. East Avenue
Waukesha, WI 53186
262.547.1211
www.carroll.edu

Ferris State University
1201 S. State Street
Big Rapids, MI 49307
231.591.2000
www.ferris.edu

Idaho State University
921 S. 8th Street
Pocatello, ID 83209
208.282.0211
www.isu.edu

Rochester Institute of Technology
1 Lomb Memorial Drive
Rochester, NY 14623
585.475.2411
www.rit.edu

St. Mary's University of Minnesota
700 Terrace Heights
Winona, MN 55987
507.457.6987
www.smumn.edu

Texas State University, San Marcos
601 University Drive
San Marcos, TX 78666
512.245.2111
www.txstate.edu

University of Houston
4800 Calhoun Road
Houston, TX 77004
713.743.2255
www.uh.edu

Western Illinois University
1 University Circle
Macomb, IL 61455
309.298.1414
www.wiu.edu

MORE INFORMATION

**Graphic Arts Education and
Research Foundation**
1899 Preston White Drive
Reston, VA 20191
703.264.7200
www.gaerf.org

**National Association of Schools
of Art and Design**
11250 Roger Bacon Drive, Suite 21
Reston, VA 20190-5248
703.437.0700
www.nasad.arts-accredit.org

Printing Industries of America
200 Deer Run Road
Sewickley, PA 15143
800.910.4283
printing@printing.org
www.printing.org

**Society for Technical
Communication**
9401 Lee Highway, Suite 300
Fairfax, VA 22031
703.522.4114
www.stc.org

Type Directors Club
347 W 36th Street, Suite 603
New York, NY 10018
212.633.8943
www.tdc.org

Micah Issitt/Editor

Electronic Commerce Specialist

Snapshot

Career Cluster: Business, Information Technology, Marketing, Sales & Service

Interests: Computers, Internet, advertising, graphic design, sales

Earnings (Yearly Average): $63,490

Employment & Outlook: Faster than Average Growth Expected

OVERVIEW

Sphere of Work

E-commerce (or electronic commerce) specialists help consumers and businesses buy and sell goods and services on the internet and social media. They focus on three types of transactions: business-to-consumer, in which a business sells directly to individuals; business-to-business, in which a business provides other businesses with necessary services or products, such as office supplies; and consumer-to-consumer, in which a consumer resells products to other consumers, often through online auction sites. E-commerce

specialists assess consumer behavior, analyzing markets and customer preferences. Based on their findings, they research, design, and produce websites and advertisements to market client products and services.

Work Environment

E-commerce specialists work in a wide range of environments, as they only need access to the internet to conduct business. Some are based in offices, while others may be based out of private residences. Work hours vary and may be erratic, especially when deadlines approach. The physical demands of e-commerce are limited, but the fast pace and financial stakes of the work can be stressful, and there is a risk of back and repetitive motion conditions associated with long periods of computer use.

Profile

Working Conditions: Work Indoors
Physical Strength: Light Work
Education Needs: Bachelor's Degree
Licensure/Certification: Usually Not
  Required
Opportunities For Experience:
  Volunteer Work, Part-Time Work
Holland Interest Score*: ECA

* See Appendix A

Occupation Interest

Individuals attracted to the position of e-commerce specialist are computer savvy and possess an understanding of effective advertising (such as linking consumer behavior to e-commerce strategy). They frequently enter the field with prior experience in an associated industry such as graphic design, marketing, or sales and apply that knowledge to internet based commerce. Many specialists are independent consultants, so individuals entering that area of the field must be self-motivated and capable of working independently, while those working on teams must have excellent teamwork and communication skills.

A Day in the Life—Duties and Responsibilities

E-commerce specialists coordinate with clients and web design teams to facilitate online business transactions between a business and consumers, a business and other businesses, or a consumer and other consumers. First, specialists consult with clients to identify client pursuits and needs, as well as to determine the market for the product or service. They then research the market, creating business

models, forecasting revenues, analyzing electronic market trends
and performance, and monitoring competitors. In order to gain an
understanding of consumer behavior in regard to the specific product
or service, they analyze search engine patterns, taking into account
keywords and phrases that consumers use to find certain services and
goods. With this data, specialists tailor a client's website to appear
prominently in search engine results for relevant, commonly searched
keywords. In addition, specialists assist in customizing the content and
functionality of the website so that it will attract and retain customers.

When a client's website is up and running, specialists work to promote
it through targeted ad sales and placement, marketing campaigns,
sponsorships, and other promotional activities. They monitor
the success of their strategies through analysis of website traffic,
determining how many individual consumers have viewed the site,
what percentage of these visitors made a purchase, in what region the
site's visitors live, and other sales and demographic data. Specialists
may then modify their marketing strategies or the website itself in
order to attract more or different customers.

Depending on their individual roles and employers, e-commerce
specialists may also track sales, coordinate procurement and inventory
control operations, and update online catalogues. They may generate
online transaction security policies and measures, and they may also
assist clients in tracking and responding to customer comments and
complaints via online and live customer service programs.

Duties and Responsibilities

- Planning and coordinating marketing activities to promote products and services
- Monitoring market trends and developing long-range marketing strategies
- Determining the financial aspects of marketing activities
- Creating content that effectively describes product and service offerings on site
- Completing market research analysis in an effort to increase sales
- Consulting with and supervising marketing, design and technical staff to create design and functionality of site

WORK ENVIRONMENT

Relevant Skills and Abilities

Communication Skills

- Speaking effectively
- Writing concisely
- Listening attentively
- Reading well
- Expressing thoughts and ideas
- Persuading others
- Reporting information
- Editing written information

Interpersonal/Social Skills

- Motivating others
- Cooperating with others
- Working as a member of a team
- Being able to work independently
- Being honest
- Having good judgment

Organization & Management Skills

- Initiating new ideas
- Paying attention to and handling details
- Coordinating tasks
- Managing people/groups
- Managing time
- Managing money
- Managing equipment/materials
- Delegating responsibility
- Demonstrating leadership
- Promoting change
- Selling ideas or products
- Making decisions
- Organizing information or materials
- Meeting goals and deadlines
- Performing duties which change frequently

Physical Environment

E-commerce specialists are typically employed or contracted by corporations, consulting firms, nonprofit organizations, government agencies, and similar groups. Consequently, office settings predominate, although they can range from large spaces in corporations to small home offices.

Human Environment

E-commerce specialists interact and work with a wide range of professionals, private consumers, and clients. These may include salespeople, marketing and advertising executives and professionals, graphic and web designers, webmasters, online editors, warehouse managers, and merchants. Specialists may need to work as part of a team in order to meet client goals, so communication and people skills are essential.

Technological Environment

E-commerce specialists work primarily with computer systems and software. As such, they must be proficient in using hypertext markup language

Research & Planning Skills
- Predicting
- Creating new ideas
- Gathering information
- Identifying problems
- Solving problems
- Setting goals and deadlines
- Defining needs
- Analyzing information
- Developing evaluation strategies

Technical Skills
- Performing scientific, mathematical or technical work
- Working with data or numbers

(HTML), electronic payment systems, spreadsheet programs, and multimedia, graphic design, and computer-aided design (CAD) software.

EDUCATION, TRAINING, AND ADVANCEMENT

High School/Secondary

High school students interested in a career in electronic commerce should study computer science, including business data processing, graphic communications, and other information technology classes that focus on business applications. Business courses themselves are critical, including classes in accounting, economics, and entrepreneurship. Math courses, including algebra and statistics, are also useful. Communications courses such as composition and public speaking help build a student's interpersonal and business presentation skills, while courses in social studies and sociology provide a foundation for the aspiring e-commerce specialist's understanding of consumer behavior.

Suggested High School Subjects
- Accounting
- Algebra
- Applied Communication
- Applied Math

- Arts
- Bookkeeping
- Business
- Business & Computer Technology
- Business Data Processing
- Business English
- Business Law
- Business Math
- College Preparatory
- Composition
- Computer Science
- Economics
- English
- Entrepreneurship
- Geometry
- Graphic Communications
- Keyboarding
- Mathematics
- Merchandising
- Psychology
- Social Studies
- Sociology
- Speech
- Statistics
- Trigonometry

Famous First

The first federal financial transaction over the internet was a 1998 payment by a branch of the U.S. Treasury to GTE Corporation, a predecessor of Verizon Communications. The electronic checking system used in the transaction was developed by the nonprofit Financial Services Technology Consortium. The amount of the GTE payment was $32,000.

College/Postsecondary

E-commerce specialists generally have a minimum of a bachelor's degree in a relevant field. Some hold degrees in information technology, software design, and similar technical areas, while others approach the profession from a business or graphic design background. Internships, whether paid or volunteer, may prove helpful in exposing postsecondary students to the field.

Related College Majors
- Business & Personal Services Marketing Operations
- Business Administration & Management, General
- Business Marketing/Marketing Management
- Marketing Management & Research
- Marketing Research

Adult Job Seekers

Qualified individuals may apply directly to corporations, consulting firms, and other organizations that post openings on their websites or at job fairs. Established specialists may also choose to pursue independent consulting. Professional trade associations dedicated to e-commerce may provide job listings, career resources, and valuable networking opportunities.

Professional Certification and Licensure

Although there are no required licensure or certification requirements for e-commerce specialists, some professionals choose to obtain certification in e-commerce, e-marketing, and other relevant fields. As with any voluntary certification process, it is beneficial to consult credible professional associations within the field and follow professional debate as to the relevancy and value of any certification program.

Additional Requirements

E-commerce specialists must demonstrate proficiency in both business and information technology, with a particular ability to understand how business practices are adapted to the internet. They should also be able to effectively communicate and coordinate with clients, many of whom may not be experienced in web-based commerce. Furthermore, specialists must be creative, flexible, and able to quickly adjust when market forces or client needs shift.

Fun Fact

In 2016, half of all consumers are expected to make online transactions via mobile devices. Mobile sales in 2015 were up 38.7 percent from the prior year, at $104.5 billion.

Source: http://www.entrepreneur.com/article/269933 and https://www.internetretailer.com/mobile500/#!/

EARNINGS AND ADVANCEMENT

Median annual earnings of e-commerce specialists were $63,490 in 2014. The lowest 10 percent earned less than $33,790, and the highest ten percent earned more than $112,680.

E-commerce specialists may receive paid vacations, holidays and sick days; life and health insurance; and retirement benefits. These are usually paid by the employer.

Metropolitan Areas with the Highest
Employment Level in This Occupation

Metropolitan area	Employment	Employment per thousand jobs	Annual mean wage
New York-White Plains-Wayne, NY-NJ	7,140	1.32	$79,900
Los Angeles-Long Beach-Glendale, CA	4,710	1.16	$69,270
Washington-Arlington-Alexandria, DC-VA-MD-WV	4,580	1.93	$84,990
Seattle-Bellevue-Everett, WA	3,850	2.58	$87,520
San Francisco-San Mateo-Redwood City, CA	3,380	3.11	$95,600
Chicago-Joliet-Naperville, IL	3,290	0.88	$67,150
Dallas-Plano-Irving, TX	3,170	1.42	$71,600
Boston-Cambridge-Quincy, MA	2,790	1.55	$79,140
Minneapolis-St. Paul-Bloomington, MN-WI	2,680	1.47	$67,630
San Jose-Sunnyvale-Santa Clara, CA	2,590	2.66	$106,580

Source: Bureau of Labor Statistics

EMPLOYMENT AND OUTLOOK

E-commerce specialists held about 150,000 jobs nationally in 2014. Employment of e-commerce specialists is expected to grow much faster than the average for all occupations through the year 2024, which means employment is projected to increase 25 percent or more. The large number of businesses that are now communicating with their customers and selling their products and services online will continue to create demand in this field for many years to come.

Employment Trend, Projected 2014–24

E-commerce specialists: 27%

Computer occupations: 12%

Total, all occupations: 7%

Note: "All Occupations" includes all occupations in the U.S. Economy. Source: U.S. Bureau of Labor Statistics, Employment Projections Program.

Related Occupations

- Advertising & Marketing Manager
- Advertising Sales Agent
- Copywriter
- Graphic Designer
- Market Research Analyst
- Online Merchant
- Public Relations Specialist
- Statistician
- Web Administrator
- Web Developer
- Writer & Editor

Conversation With . . .
BRENT DURHAM

COO & Founding Partner, iFrog Digital Marketing
Preston, Maryland
E-Commerce specialist, 6 years

1. What was your individual career path in terms of education/training, entry-level job, or other significant opportunity?

Growing up, my good friend's father owned a large car dealership, Preston Automotive Group. Since everybody is going to need a car at some point in life, I picked that as an industry to go into because it covers retail, service, and other skills I could use if automotive didn't work out.

Right out of high school I went to Northwood University in Florida and focused on automotive marketing and business management. I earned a bachelor's in business administration, gained experience working in dealerships, and then went back to Maryland to work at Preston Automotive as an internet marketing manager.

Digital marketing was new. After developing the company's online marketing, internet sales was added to my duties and I became Internet Director. After a year, I decided to get an MBA and moved to Virginia to get my degree from Old Dominion University. My focus was digital marketing with a concentration in global marketing.

I returned to Preston after graduating, and at that point had the knowledge to be an entrepreneur. So, I partnered with Preston's owner, Dave Wilson, and we created a spinoff company—iFrog—to handle internet sales and marketing for our dealership, as well as for non-competing dealerships. Currently, we work with client car dealerships in Cincinnati and the Baltimore-Washington, D.C. area, and we're working our way into Virginia. We also have twenty-two clients (so far) in other types of businesses here in our region.

Everything we do relates to internet commerce and marketing: ads, page searches, social media, and search engine optimization. We manage metadata, content, advertising for mobile devices, and reputation management. We train clients in social media selling. Auto dealership clients like to deal with people who are born and bred in the automotive sales industry and those are the people I've hired for my team.

2. **What are the most important skills and/or qualities for someone in your profession?**

The ability to continually learn is huge. The minute you think you know everything is the minute you get left behind. With the internet, every device constantly changes; we get data from our online traffic and every week we get new data or a new format to advertise to someone. For example, as smartphones became popular, we adapted the way websites, web pages, and displays were viewed by making them "mobile friendly." If you learn code, that will take you far; it's a big portion of this growing field.

Also, you need leadership ability. In high school I actively participated in sports, was student council president, and learned to work with people or a team to accomplish a goal. When we bring on new clients, we are working with a new team. You need to network, too. It doesn't matter what you do in life, there's always somebody who can help you out or give you a leg up.

3. **What do you wish you had known going into this profession?**

HTML!

4. **Are there many job opportunities in your profession? In what specific areas?**

As we grow as a company, I'm noticing a diverse number of job opportunities: video animation, HTML, graphic design, and content writing to optimize Google searches. Social media and marketing are huge and not going anywhere.

You need to analyze data to tell whether a certain advertisement is working, or tweak it to get more return on investment. At iFrog, account managers work with their data analysis team and the graphic design team to develop better calls-to-action—which is ad copy that prompts a viewer to take action, such as "Click Here," or "Shop Now"—design layouts, and advertisement targeting. Also, sales jobs are always growing.

5. **How do you see your profession changing in the next five years, what role will technology play in those changes, and what skills will be required?**

The internet and widespread connectivity is only going to grow. It gives you different advertising channels. Think about how we went from flip phones to smartphones, and now people like bigger screens so that gives me more opportunity to post an ad.

The amount of data we are able to collect on people will grow. Right now, Google and Facebook have the most data, but that will spread to other avenues and spawn new tactics. I see getting to the point where we can basically identify the person who uses a particular IP address and target tailored advertising to them.

6. **What do you enjoy most about your job? What do you enjoy least about your job?**

   I most like working with my whole team to accomplish a goal. It's nice to see a plan come together and get executed. I least like the long hours. My job means I always have to be connected via my smartphone; hopefully I can eventually disconnect for a day or two.

7. **Can you suggest a valuable "try this" for students considering a career in your profession?**

   Use social media to promote something, maybe a change of lifestyle for yourself, like a new workout routine or an event for an organization like a charity. See how big a following you can grow or how many attendees you can draw to your event.

SELECTED SCHOOLS

Many online, technical, and community colleges offer programs leading to either certification (one year) or an associate degree (two years) in web development. Interested students are advised to consult with a school guidance counselor or research area postsecondary schools. For those interested in pursuing a bachelor's degree in marketing and/or e-commerce, there are numerous business schools from which to choose.

MORE INFORMATION

eCommerce Merchants Trade Association
917.388.1698
www.ecmta.org

eMarketing Association
243 Post Road, Suite #129
Westerly, RI 02891
401.315.2194
www.emarketingassociation.com

Women in Ecommerce
P.O. Box 550856
Fort Lauderdale, FL 33355-0856
954.625.6606
www.wecai.org

Michael Auerbach/Editor

Game Designer

Snapshot

Career Cluster(s): Information Technology

Interests: Computer technology, artistic expression, film, media

Earnings (Yearly Average): $63,970

Employment & Outlook: Average Growth Expected

OVERVIEW

Sphere of Work

Game designers are creative professionals involved in the design and production of video games for the digital entertainment market. An emerging field, the game designer position has been described as a hybrid of graphic art and computer programming. There are many different roles within the broader game design and game production field, and while some designers work as writers, storyboarding and writing aspects of the game plot, dialogue, and other written components, other types of designers focus on the aesthetic and graphic aspects of a game. Alternatively, some game designers are also programmers, helping to create the software that enables users to interact with a game environment.

Work Environment

Game designers typically work in office environments or in cubicles within a larger production or development department. Game design is a collaborative discipline and designers working on various aspects of a game, including producers, animators, writers, programmers, and marketing experts, will frequently need to meet and discuss aspects of the process. The Bureau of Labor Statistics (BLS) indicates that nearly 50 percent of visual and graphic artists are self-employed, and some game designers also work remotely while those working for corporations more often work in either offices or cubicles.

Profile

Working Conditions: Work Indoors
Physical Strength: Light Work
Education Needs: Bachelor's Degree
Licensure/Certification: Not Required
Opportunities For Experience: On-the-job training
Holland Interest Score*: AI

* See Appendix A

Occupation Interest

Individuals looking to become game designers should have a background in both art and computer science. Game design also typically involves problem solving, testing, and rigorous evaluation and individuals looking to enter the field should have an interest in investigating complex problems. Game design is also typically collaborative and individuals in the field should therefore have an interest in working as part of a creative team.

A Day in the Life—Duties and Responsibilities

The daily tasks for a game designer differ depending on the designers specific role and the nature of the game being designed. During the preproduction process, writers, artists, and programmers meet to discuss ideas for a game and to map out how the general concept can be turned into a working model. During the production process, designers, animators, writers, and engineers take the models created during preproduction and begin designing the game architecture. Part of this process involves programming and testing the code used in the game. During this stage, a designer may spend most of his or her time working with graphics or animation, or working on programming, while also taking time to meet with producers, managers, and professionals working on other facets of the game. Following the production phase, there is an often lengthy post-production phase in which the game must be tested and refined. It is during this stage that the game is first "played" and that designers, programmers, and artists identify errors and malfunctions that need to be fixed before the game can be released.

Duties and Responsibilities

- Use computer programs to illustrate and design various graphics
- Work with animators, modelers, and software engineers
- Develop concepts and storyboards to map out aspects of the game design
- Work with clients, producers, and directors to ensure project goals are met within specified schedules.
- Research software systems and other technological tools
- Write descriptions of dialogue, plot, and other aspects of the game experience

OCCUPATION SPECIALTIES

Game Mechanic Designer

Game designers specializing in programming or designing specific aspects of gameplay. For instance, in a flight simulation game, mechanics designers will create a detailed plan for the game's flight mechanics.

Level Designer

Level designers work on developing objects and environments within a game. These individuals are responsible for creating a map of the physical locations used within a game and then for determining the way that players interact with in game items and environments.

Lead Designer

A lead designer is a game designer serving in a management role. Lead designers organize teams of designers, oversee various aspects of the design process, and meet with staff from other branches of the company to compare progress and share ideas.

Game Writer

There are a variety of writers involved in the game design process. Some writers are responsible for crafting a plot or story for games that require these elements, while others may work on writing dialogue for characters in the game. Other game writers focus on producing technical information, such as providing instructions to introduce players to the game.

Art Director

An art director is in charge of coordinating all the artis tic aspects of game design. Art directors typically lead an art department which may include concept artists, lead artists, modelers, and animators.

Producers

Producers are administrators who oversee the entire production process. Producers may be responsible for scheduling and overseeing meetings among other members of the design team and for monitoring project budgets for the team.

WORK ENVIRONMENT

Physical Environment

Game designers typically work in office environments. Depending on the company, an individual designer may have an office or may be assigned a cubicle within a design department. Game design companies may also ask designers to work in groups using conference tables or computer labs. Some game designers work freelance or work remotely, thereby allowing professionals in the field to complete some or all of their work from a home office or other location.

Relevant Skills and Abilities

Communication Skills
- Communicating progress via reports and presentations
- Communicating with others in meetings and via digital communication media.

Interpersonal/Social Skills
- Being able work effectively in a group environment

Organization & Management Skills
- Managing people/groups
- Time management and ability to meet deadlines for individual/ group projects

Research & Planning Skills
- Researching developments in the design field
- Maintaining knowledge of design projects produced by competing companies

Technical Skills
- Performing technical work
- Working with computers, programming languages, and hardware
- Skill with drawing, painting, drafting, and modeling

Human Environment

Game design is a collaborative process and prospective designers should be comfortable working in groups and engaging in frequent direct or remote meetings. Individuals in the field report that meetings are a daily part of their activity, including meeting with supervisors or employees, other members of the design, production, or marketing team, or, in some cases, with customers and/or clients.

Technological Environment

Game designers use a wide variety of programming and graphics software. Depending on the specifics of the position, prospective designers might need familiarity with design and drafting programs like Autodesk 3ds Max Design, Autodesk Alias Surface, and Autodesk AutoCAD Civil 3D. For some game projects, designers might need to know how to use action gaming engines like the Unreal Engine. A variety of Adobe Systems programs are used by game designers including Photoshop, Illustrator, AfterEffects, Lightroom, and others. Designing for various systems may also require designers to know how to work with a variety of operating systems, like Microsoft Windows, Apple Macintosh OS, and UNIX. Knowledge of programming languages like Python and Lua is also helpful for professionals in the field. Degree programs for game design typically introduce professionals to software and hardware used in every step of the design process.

EDUCATION, TRAINING, AND ADVANCEMENT

High School/Secondary

High school students looking to become game designers should take classes in computer/digital technology and in visual art and design. Many high schools offer classes in computer science, which includes a general overview of computer technology and basic programming. Mathematics and engineering, specifically electrical engineering, are also helpful for future designers. In addition, because game design is a creative process, classes in creative writing and English will help future professionals to have a better understanding of the writing and scripting process involved in creating some types of video games.

Suggested High School Subjects
- Computer Science
- English
- Introduction to Business
- Industrial Arts
- Graphic Arts/Graphic Design
- Computer Programming
- Applied Mathematics
- Engineering
- Physics
- Creative Writing

Famous First

William "Willy" Higinbotham is famous as the designer of one of the world's first video game precursors. Higinbotham's game, "Tennis for Two," debuted at Brookhaven National Laboratory in October 1958 and used an oscilloscope, a device that allows individuals to view variations in electrical voltage, as a screen. Players, each using separate controllers, competed to bat an illuminated dot back and forth on the screen. Though a number of other electronic games predated Higinbotham's design, Tennis for Two is notable in that the first commercial video game, Pong, was essentially the same game modified to be played on a home system.

College/Postsecondary

A variety of specific college and postsecondary degrees are available for individuals interested in game design. For instance, the University of Southern California offers Bachelor of Arts, Bachelor of Science, and Master's Degree programs in game design where students are introduced to graphic design, 3d design, computer programming, and a variety of other subfields within the game design industry. At USC and a variety of other universities, students are given the opportunity to study game design with professionals in the field as well as to visit studios and private companies working on games for the commercial market.

Related College Majors
- Game and Interactive Media Design
- Computer Animation
- 3D Design
- Computer Programming
- IT Project Management
- Mobile Gaming
- Software Development

Adult Job Seekers

Adults with experience in graphic design or computer programming can apply for jobs as game designers. Those with specific degrees in game design might have a significant advantage over those with backgrounds in either design or programming individually.

Professional Certification and Licensure

There are no specific licensing requirements for game designers, though some learning institutions provide certification for students studying various programming languages used in the field, like Python and Lua. In addition, designers may want to obtain certification in 3D animation, depending on their goals in the industry.

Additional Requirements

Game designers should have a strong understanding of computer technology and visual art. Many game designers are former programmers or graphic artists who transition to the game design field and employers may expect candidates to present a portfolio of their previous programming, design, or artistic projects.

Fun Fact

If you make it to the final level of Diablo 1, the last demonic boss—Diablo himself—says something unintelligible in a creepy voice. But played backwards, it turns out he's saying, in English, "Eat your vegetables and brush after every meal."

Source: http://infinigeek.com/50-epic-video-game-history-facts-you-probably-didnt-know-from-did-you-know-gaming/

EARNINGS AND ADVANCEMENT

Game designers, part of the broader multimedia artists and animators field, earned an average annual wage of $63,970 in May of 2015. Compensation varied significantly by company and region. BLS statistics collected in 2015 indicated that the lowest 10 percent of the field earned less than $36,930, while the highest paid 10 percent earned in excess of $113,600 annually. Depending on the company, game designers may begin their career as an assistant designer or content designer with the opportunity to advance to a lead designer position, which combines programming, design, and management.

Metropolitan Areas with the Highest Employment Level in this Occupation

Metropolitan area	Employment	Employment per thousand jobs	Hourly mean wage
Los Angeles-Long Beach-Glendale, CA	6,660	1.67	$44.58
New York-White Plains-Wayne, NY-NJ	2,560	0.49	$35.78
Seattle-Bellevue-Everett, WA	1,910	1.32	$37.12
Atlanta-Sandy Springs-Marietta, GA	1,260	0.54	$26.66
Bridgeport-Stamford-Norwalk, CT	1,140	2.72	N/A
Chicago-Joliet-Naperville, IL	1,060	0.29	$31.91
Oakland-Fremont-Hayward, CA	910	0.91	$42.70
San Francisco-San Mateo-Redwood City, CA	870	0.83	$40.36
Dallas-Plano-Irving, TX	680	0.32	$26.24
Austin-Round Rock-San Marcos, TX	610	0.71	$23.17

Source: Bureau of Labor Statistics

EMPLOYMENT AND OUTLOOK

According to the BLS, there were 64,400 jobs available for multimedia artists and animators in 2014 and the field was growing at 6 percent per year, indicating average growth compared to jobs in all fields. The debut of new gaming systems and other changes in the field that lead to higher demand for new games can lead to growth in the field. About half of the individuals in the multimedia artists and animators field were self-employed in 2016, though those working in game design specifically are more likely to work for a company.

Employment Trend, Projected 2014–24

Art and design workers: 2%

Multimedia artists and animators: 6%

Total, all occupations: 7%

Note: "All Occupations" includes all occupations in the U.S. Economy. Source: U.S. Bureau of Labor Statistics, Employment Projections Program.

Related Occupations

- Art Directors
- Computer Programmers
- Craft and Fine Arts
- Graphic Designers
- Web Developers

Related Military Occupations

- Army Virtual Training Program Designer

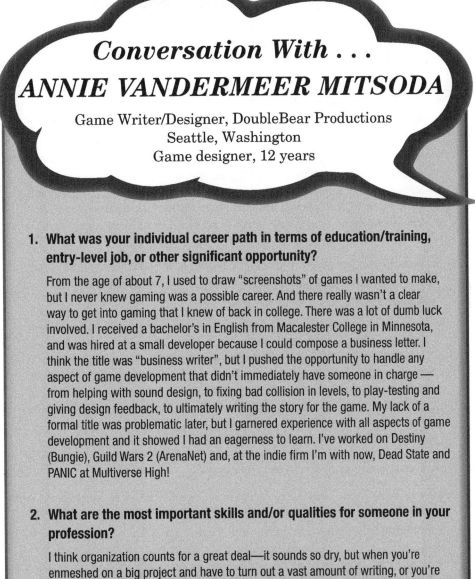

Conversation With . . .
ANNIE VANDERMEER MITSODA

Game Writer/Designer, DoubleBear Productions
Seattle, Washington
Game designer, 12 years

1. **What was your individual career path in terms of education/training, entry-level job, or other significant opportunity?**

From the age of about 7, I used to draw "screenshots" of games I wanted to make, but I never knew gaming was a possible career. And there really wasn't a clear way to get into gaming that I knew of back in college. There was a lot of dumb luck involved. I received a bachelor's in English from Macalester College in Minnesota, and was hired at a small developer because I could compose a business letter. I think the title was "business writer", but I pushed the opportunity to handle any aspect of game development that didn't immediately have someone in charge — from helping with sound design, to fixing bad collision in levels, to play-testing and giving design feedback, to ultimately writing the story for the game. My lack of a formal title was problematic later, but I garnered experience with all aspects of game development and it showed I had an eagerness to learn. I've worked on Destiny (Bungie), Guild Wars 2 (ArenaNet) and, at the indie firm I'm with now, Dead State and PANIC at Multiverse High!

2. **What are the most important skills and/or qualities for someone in your profession?**

I think organization counts for a great deal—it sounds so dry, but when you're enmeshed on a big project and have to turn out a vast amount of writing, or you're designing a massive level with a very precise flow, or involved in countless other tasks … the key thing is you're never doing something by yourself. You've got to make sure others can easily track what you're doing, and most of all that you can. If you can organize stuff so that you can leap right back into a design, you're spending less time trying to get up to speed and more time innovating and polishing.

Beyond that, definitely flexibility. Writers have to branch out into other styles and learn how to tell stories differently. There's a setting genre, like science fiction, and a game genre, like first-person shooter (FPS) or role-playing game (RPG). An RPG in a faster-paced setting genre (like a spy thriller) needs to stick to certain expectations or it will feel "off." A slower thriller can feel plodding; a faster fantasy game can feel confusing. Designers must constantly learn new systems and new tech. Being excited to learn and approaching new problems with patience and persistence is key.

3. What do you wish you had known going into this profession?

It's typical to sigh that it "breaks your heart sometimes," but any profession that relies on creative endeavors draws from a deep emotional well. Also, I wish I'd known to study more scripting languages.

4. Are there many job opportunities in your profession? In what specific areas?

Definitely. I think of game design as a color wheel, with writing, art, and programming as the primary colors. The jobs closest to art are User Interface (UI) designers and level designers; closer to programming are system designers and scripters; and closer to writing are narrative design and content design. Getting to know the needs of a company, and your own inclinations, is a good way to get your foot in the door.

5. How do you see your profession changing in the next five years? What role will technology play in those changes, and what skills will be required?

Mechanically speaking, most work a designer does is within a given toolset, either tied to an engine like Unity or Unreal, or one developed in-house. Structurally speaking, the rise of virtual/augmented reality is becoming more pronounced, as are the demands of multiplayer-focus and mobile development. While core elements of game design are staying the same, I'm seeing writers become more involved with game development, actually implementing their work in the game and collaborating with other team members. I've seen a lot more postings for "narrative designer" than I have for writer, as companies learn the value of having an embedded writer involved with the process of making the game, instead of swooping in and depositing a story awkwardly on top of a bunch of gameplay.

6. What do you enjoy most about your job? What do you enjoy least about your job?

As a kid I loved the idea of creating worlds. Games offer an unparalleled ability to create narratives that you can engage in. The promise of interactivity is something I never tire of.

What I like least are the woes of a creative profession. You never stop working, even if just in your mind.

7. Can you suggest a valuable "try this" for students considering a career in your profession?

When you next play a game, pick out something precise that you enjoy, like a character. Think about the division of labor that made that character: appearance, animations, voice, lines, attacks, etc. Think about how each department contributed to that one part of the game, and then how one department—like writing—contributed across the entire game.

MORE INFORMATION

Entertainment Software Association
575 7th St., NW
Suite 300
Washington, DC 20004
202-371-0101
www.theesa.com

Game Developer Magazine
600 Harrison St.
6th Floor
San Francisco, CA 94107
www.gdmag.com

Graphic Artists Guild
32 Broadway
Suite 1114
New York, NY 10004
212-791-3400
www.graphicartistsguild.org

International Game Developers Association
19 Mantua Road
Mount Royal, NJ 08061
www.igda.org

Micah Issitt/Editor

Information Security Analyst

Snapshot

Career Cluster: Information Technology; Public Safety & Security

Interests: Electronics, computers, analyzing data

Earnings (Yearly Average): $89,290

Employment & Outlook: Faster Than Average Growth Expected

OVERVIEW

Sphere of Work

Information security analysts design and monitor technological systems that shield computer networks from outside threats. They encrypt system data, erect firewalls, and utilize a wide variety of hardware and software tools to ensure that homes, businesses, and government agencies remain protected from criminals, viruses, hackers, and other security threats.

Work Environment

Information security analysts work primarily in administrative and office settings. Analysts work at a variety of locations in and around offices and organizational complexes, most often at their own private workstations. They may also spend time working at the workstations of other employees, servicing their computers or installing equipment. Information security analysts also work in temperature-controlled server housing rooms and may be required to work remotely.

Profile

Working Conditions: Work Indoors
Physical Strength: Light Work
Education Needs: Bachelor's Degree
Licensure/Certification:
Recommended
Physical Abilities Not Required: No
Heavy Labor
Opportunities For Experience:
Internship, Military Service, Volunteer
Work, Part-Time Work
Holland Interest Score*: IRC

* See Appendix A

Occupation Interest

The field of information security attracts critical thinkers with a passion for electronics and computing who enjoy tackling complex problems. Information security analysts often get a tremendous amount of satisfaction from staying ahead of and repeatedly outsmarting security threats. Analysts also possess the patience to scrutinize extremely complicated data.

A Day in the Life—Duties and Responsibilities

Information security analysts handle a wide variety of duties and responsibilities on an everyday basis. Their main responsibility is to see computer systems through cyberattacks from the outside and to prevent such attacks from recurring. They are also tasked with identifying new potential security threats and encrypting archival data.

Data encryption is one of the central tasks of information security analysts. They are also responsible for constructing firewalls to protect organizational information. Some information security analysts are responsible for building, monitoring, and maintaining custom firewall and encryption systems for specific organizations and businesses, while others operate standard network-based firewall applications for a collection of clients.

Information security analysts are constantly on the lookout for security breaches, evidenced by the presence of outside influences on a computer network or traces of past network violations. In the event of a security breach, analysts will alert senior staff members and recommend enhancements to prevent future violations. This constant need for adaptation requires analysts to stay abreast of new developments in computer security technology through ancillary academic coursework, industry publications, annual meetings, and training seminars.

In addition to constantly monitoring the potential security risks that may target their business or organization, information security analysts must also stay informed of legislation and political developments related to digital security, particularly those that affect the rights of business clients and the civil liberties of individuals.

Duties and Responsibilities

- Monitoring the use of data files to protect information from unauthorized access and security violations
- Performing regular systems tests to ensure that all security measures are functioning properly
- Educating users about security issues
- Updating virus protection programs as necessary to combat new threats
- Encrypting data and erecting firewalls to keep information confidential
- Keeping documentation regarding security policies and procedures current
- Keeping abreast of new developments in the field

WORK ENVIRONMENT

Relevant Skills and Abilities

Analytical Skills
- Analyzing data

Communication Skills
- Speaking effectively
- Writing concisely

Organization & Management Skills
- Paying attention to and handling details
- Managing time
- Managing equipment/materials
- Coordinating tasks
- Making decisions
- Handling challenging situations

Research & Planning Skills
- Identifying problems
- Determining alternatives
- Gathering information
- Solving problems
- Defining needs
- Developing evaluation strategies

Technical Skills
- Performing scientific, mathematical, and technical work
- Using technology to process information

Physical Environment

Information security analysts predominantly work in office settings with occasional off-site work. They work in almost every industry, from business and finance to education, government, transportation, communications, and the military.

Human Environment

Many of the tasks of information security analysts are conducted individually. However, the explanation of different security systems to coworkers and clients requires group and one-on-one interactions.

Technological Environment

Information security analysts are highly trained in information technology. They utilize a variety of computer science technologies, including software, hardware, and network technology. They must also be adept at computer programming languages and web communication.

EDUCATION, TRAINING, AND ADVANCEMENT

High School/Secondary

High school students can best prepare for a career as an information security analyst by completing courses in algebra, calculus, geometry, trigonometry, and computer courses such as introductory programming. Exposure to computer systems via internships or volunteer work can also build an important foundation for students interested in being employed in computer science.

Suggested High School Subjects
- Algebra
- Applied Communication
- Applied Math
- Business & Computer Technology
- Business Data Processing
- Calculus
- College Preparatory
- Computer Programming
- Computer Science
- English
- Geometry
- Keyboarding
- Mathematics
- Statistics
- Trigonometry

Famous First

The first convicted computer hacker was a former director of computer security at a Texas insurance firm. In 1985 the man was fired from his job, and three days later company officials discovered that thousands of sales records had been erased from the firm's computer system. The man had used a computer virus of the "worm" type (also known as a "logic bomb") to destroy the files. He was later convicted on third-degree felony charges and sentenced to seven years' probation and a $12,000 fine.

College/Postsecondary

A bachelor's degree is a standard requirement for nearly all employment vacancies in the information security profession. Most candidates arrive to the field after academic training in general computer science, programming or software development, while others prepare for the role by completing degree programs dedicated specifically to computer and network security. Postsecondary students who study information security complete coursework in such topics as network design, intrusion detection, wireless security, system administration, and cryptography. Additional related coursework also includes system administration and architecture and firewall construction.

Related College Majors
- Computer Installation & Repair
- Computer Maintenance Technology
- Computer Programming
- Computer Science
- Data Processing Technology
- Information Sciences & Systems
- Information Security
- Management Information Systems

Adult Job Seekers

The field of information security requires extensive academic and professional training. Individuals with no background in a related field should enroll in a college or a technical or vocational school that offers a program in computer security. Technical schools are also a great place for job seekers to network. Communication technologies and standards are always changing, so information security analysts should be willing to continue learning throughout their career.

Professional Certification and Licensure

There are numerous professional certifications available for information security professionals, each of which expands their frame of reference while making them attractive candidates for professional vacancies. They include Certified Information Systems Security Professional (CISSP), Certified Ethical Hacker (CEH), Certified Information Security Manager (CISM), and Global Information Assurance Certification (GIAC).

Additional Requirements

Information security is a constantly evolving field. Those interested in a career as an information security analyst must possess the patience and professionalism to stay up to date on rapidly emerging developments in a variety of technical disciplines, notably mobile communications, network diagnostics, software development, and hardware design.

Fun Fact

In his 1984 novel *Neuromancer*, William Gibson coined the term "cyberspace" to describe the world of computer networks. As that world has changed, new cyber words have cropped up, too: cyberattack, cybercafe, and cybersecurity.

Source: APStylebook, et al.; http://www.apstylebook.com/online/?do=search_results&search_term=cyber

EARNINGS AND ADVANCEMENT

Mean annual earnings of information security analysts were $89,290 in 2012. The lowest ten percent earned less than $49,960, and the highest ten percent earned more than $135,600.

Information security analysts may receive paid vacations, holidays and sick days; life and health insurance; and retirement benefits. These are usually paid by the employer.

Metropolitan Areas with the Highest Employment Level in this Occupation

Metropolitan area	Employment[1]	Employment per thousand jobs	Hourly mean wage
Washington-Arlington-Alexandria, DC-VA-MD-WV	9,400	4.01	$49.35
New York-White Plains-Wayne, NY-NJ	3,860	0.75	$56.67
Dallas-Plano-Irving, TX	2,450	1.17	$40.52
Boston-Cambridge-Quincy, MA	2,010	1.18	$48.28
Seattle-Bellevue-Everett, WA	1,930	1.37	$46.42
Atlanta-Sandy Springs-Marietta, GA	1,780	0.79	$40.33
Baltimore-Towson, MD	1,670	1.32	$47.87
Houston-Sugar Land-Baytown, TX	1,550	0.59	$45.60

[1]Does not include self-employed. Source: Bureau of Labor Statistics

EMPLOYMENT AND OUTLOOK

Information security analysts held about 75,000 jobs nationally in 2012. Employment is expected to grow much faster than the average for all occupations through the year 2022, which means employment is projected to increase 30 percent or more. Almost every organization in today's workforce needs to keep a computer network running smoothly and secure from hackers, viruses and other attacks. The growth of security as a main concern for organizations will help to fuel the growth of information security analysts.

Employment Trend, Projected 2012–22

Information Security Analysts: 37%

Computer Occupations: 18%

Total, All Occupations: 11%

Note: "All Occupations" includes all occupations in the U.S. Economy. Source: U.S. Bureau of Labor Statistics, Employment Projections Program

Related Occupations

- Computer & Information Systems Manager
- Computer Engineer
- Computer Network Architect
- Computer Programmer
- Computer Support Specialist
- Computer Systems Analyst
- Information Technology Project Manager
- Software Developer

Related Military Occupations

- Computer Programmer
- Computer Systems Officer
- Computer Systems Specialist

Conversation With . . .
RYDER JEFFERSON MOSES

Vice President of Information Security
Electronic Payment Processor, Mid-Atlantic Region
IT, 32 years; Cybersecurity, 5 years

1. What was your individual career path in terms of education/training, entry-level job, or other significant opportunity?

I graduated with a biology degree in 1981 to limited employment opportunities, so I fixed computers and printers because I have good mechanical aptitude. I realized that what really grabbed my attention was networks, data transmission, and telecommunications carrier services between computers. This was before the internet. As my career in network engineering progressed, I experienced, first-hand, the evolution of data transmission protocols for both private and public (internet) networks.

I wound up working as a contractor on government networks, and decided to go back to school so I had the academic credentials to back up the work I'd been doing for 10 years. I got my master's in Telecommunications Management; today I would recommend a degree in information security, which wasn't available at that time.

I went on to work for a company that supports banks in the electronic payment processing industry. As that business grew—dramatically—and credit card processing migrated toward the internet, it became vulnerable to hackers who stole information to produce counterfeit credit cards. This was in the early 2000s, and the increased use of the internet gave rise to new encryption methods for data transmission. As I spent more time implementing encryption methods, I was working closely with people in the developing field of information security.

As encryption grew more sophisticated, the hackers became more sophisticated at uncovering vulnerabilities, which led to the creation of a security standard to force banks, merchants, and processors to improve data protection methods. In my most recent role, I helped explain to merchants the need to implement these measures to meet the Payment Card Industry Data Security Standards. I also helped merchants make changes to support chip-enabled payment cards.

2. What are the most important skills and/or qualities for someone in your profession?

Critical thinking skills, an analytical approach to risk assessment, and a fundamental understanding of cryptography and data transmissions protocols, because you need the ability to do an end-to-end assessment of the data processing environment. Also, you need a clean background check with no arrests and an absolute dedication to integrity. You aren't going to get a join information security if potential employers have any reason to suspect they can't trust you.

3. What do you wish you had known going into this profession?

The fact that you will be on call 24/7, 365 days because you need to drop whatever you're doing and devote all your attention to any kind of data compromise. I once left a company meeting to help decode transaction data in real time after a guy who'd just gotten out of jail for committing credit card fraud stole a dial-up terminal and started doing fraudulent credit card transactions from his house. I was on a conference call with law enforcement sitting in a van across from his house as I manually decoded his fraudulent transactions so they could catch him in the act.

4. Are there many job opportunities in your profession? In what specific areas?

Definitely. Every merchant who accepts credit and debit cards needs technical personnel to assess vulnerabilities and implement measures to protect themselves, the cardholders, and the banks. Many industries face growing information security requirements, including banks, electronic funds processing companies, stock brokerages, hospitals, government agencies, and colleges.

5. How do you see your profession changing in the next five years, and what skills will be required?

In this business, the technology—and the use of technology by the bad guys—evolves at a rapid pace. You have to constantly update your knowledge and skills, and continuously monitor systems and networks for emerging trends in vulnerability exploitation.

6. What do you enjoy most about your job? What do you enjoy least about your job?

I enjoy the satisfaction of knowing I'm helping to protect financial data and reduce the risk of financial losses to cardholders, merchants, and banks. I also enjoy explaining very technical security requirements in terms that everyone can understand. This field pays well, and I enjoy that.

I don't like being on call. I don't like security breaches, and the stress levels associated with protecting the country's commerce infrastructure while knowing that information security is only effective until the bad guys find another vulnerability to exploit.

7. Can you suggest a valuable "try this" for students considering a career in your profession?

Internships are a great way to learn about networks and data transmission technologies. There's also, certainly, a lot of information online. Look into things like Cisco router training. Also, the military is worth considering because they have training opportunities due to the critical requirements for keeping data secure.

SELECTED SCHOOLS

Programs in information security are available at numerous four-year colleges and universities. The student may also gain initial training at a technical or community college. The website of the U.S. National Security Agency's Central Security Service (see below) provides a state-by-state listing of recognized school programs. Below are listed some of the more prominent institutions in this field.

DePaul University
College of Computing and Digital Media
243 S. Wabash Avenue
Chicago, IL 60604
312.362.8381
www.cdm.depaul.edu

George Mason University
Department of Applied Information Technology
5400 Nguyen Engineering Building MS1G8
Fairfax, VA 22030
703.993.4871
ait.gmu.edu

Indiana University, Bloomington School of Informatics and Computing
901 E. 10th Street
Bloomington, IN 47408
812.856.5754
www.soic.indiana.ed

Johns Hopkins University
Department of Computer Science
224 Croft Hall
3400 N. Charles Street
Baltimore, MD 21218
410.516.6134
www.cs.jhu.edu

Northeastern University
College of Computer and Information Science
440 Huntington Avenue
202 W. Village H
Boston, MA 02115
617.373.2462
www.ccs.neu.edu

University of Pittsburgh
School of Information Sciences
135 N. Bellefield Avenue
Pittsburgh, PA 15260
412.624.5230
www.ischool.pitt.edu

University of Maryland, College Park
Department of Computer Science
A.V. Williams Building
College Park, MD 20742
301.405.2662
www.cs.umd.edu

University of Southern California
Computer Science Department
941 Bloom Walk, SAL 300
Los Angeles, CA 90089
213.740.4494
www.cs.usc.edu

University of Texas, San Antonia
Department of Computer Science
One UTSA Circle
San Antonio, TX 78249
210.458.4436
www.cs.utsa.edu

University of Washington
Information School
Mary Gates Hall, Suite 370
P.O. Box 352840
Seattle, WA 98195
206.685.9937
Ischool.uw.edu

MORE INFORMATION

Applied Computer Security Associates
2906 Covington Road
Silver Spring, MD 20910
www.acsac.org

Computer Security Resource Center
National Institute of Standards and Technology
100 Bureau Drive
Mail Stop 8930
Gaithersburg, MD 20899-8930
301.975.6478
csrc.nist.gov

Information Systems Security Association
9220 SW Barbour Boulevard
#119-333
Portland, OR 97219
866.349.5818
www.issa.org

National Security Agency Central Security Service
9800 Savage Road
Fort Meade, MD 20755
301.688.6524
www.nsa.gov

John Pritchard/Editor

Information Technology Project Manager

Snapshot

Career Cluster(s): Business Administration; Information Technology

Interests: Computer science, multi-tasking, communicating with others

Earnings (Yearly Average): $110,000

Employment & Outlook: Faster than Average Growth Expected

OVERVIEW

Sphere of Work

Information technology project managers, often abbreviated as IT project managers, oversee the design and implementation of information technology systems and related infrastructure. The proliferation of computer systems throughout the world has made IT project managers relevant in nearly every type of business and industry. IT project managers work closely with other managers in their organization to understand the company's IT needs. They then direct and supervise the technical staff in implementing

the necessary hardware or software to address those needs, be they data storage, network security, or inventory management. IT project managers are also responsible for ensuring that all IT projects are completed within budget and on schedule.

Work Environment

IT project management professionals work primarily in administrative and office settings, though their exact locations may vary depending on their area of expertise and the type of company that employs them. The work of IT project managers requires extensive interaction with coworkers, outside vendors, and technical staff members. IT project managers must be able to draw out and interpret the specific IT needs of a department or organization and utilize that feedback to develop customized systems. Project managers are also supervisors charged with ensuring that their staff of IT professionals is continually contributing to project advancement in a timely and organized manner.

Profile

Working Conditions: Work Indoors
Physical Strength: Light Work
Education Needs: Bachelor's Degree, Master's Degree
Licensure/Certification: Recommended
Opportunities For Experience: Internship, Military Service, Volunteer Work, Part Time Work
Holland Interest Score*: ECI

* See Appendix A

Occupation Interest

IT project managers are results-oriented multitaskers who thrive in environments where numerous tasks and objectives are active simultaneously. IT project management covers a diverse array of scientific, technical, and managerial knowledge and skills. The majority of IT project management professionals are graduates and professionals who have a strong foundation in mathematics, computer engineering, programming, or computer science. Many IT professionals also possess an academic or professional background in software development, database management, or IT project administration.

Many universities now offer specific undergraduate and postgraduate programs in information technology and project management, but many professionals enter the field with professional and academic backgrounds that span a wide variety of computer-science disciplines.

IT project managers must have strong communication and interpersonal skills as well as excellent management skills.

A Day in the Life—Duties and Responsibilities

A day in the life of an IT project manager involves planning future projects, monitoring the progress of projects that are currently active, and overseeing system maintenance, upkeep, and security tasks. These numerous responsibilities require IT managers to work in close concert with their staff, which can vary in size and scope depending on their organization of employment and particular realm of industry.

In addition to monitoring the progress of active projects, IT project managers also spend a considerable amount of time developing project plans for new initiatives in collaboration with other departmental and organizational staff members. Before work begins on new IT projects, the entire scope of each initiative must be outlined, with specific focus on the systems, schedules, funding, and required staff for each project.

IT project managers hold frequent meetings with subordinates to gauge the progress of active projects. In addition to providing technological and strategic input to resolve project delays or other concerns, IT project managers must also be able to prevent future problems through forethought and a reliance on previous project experience.

IT project managers are often responsible for reporting to executive management in order to outline the successes of previously implemented projects and to address any IT-related concerns relevant to a company or organization as a whole.

Duties and Responsibilities

- Implementing and coordinating project schedules
- Consulting with department heads to create and understand organization needs
- Training and supervising technical staff
- Monitoring the progress of projects to achieve time, budgetary and quality assurance goals
- Meeting with outside consultants, vendors and clients

WORK ENVIRONMENT

Transferable Skills and Abilities

Communication Skills
- Speaking effectively
- Writing concisely
- Listening attentively
- Reading well

Interpersonal/Social Skills
- Motivating others
- Cooperating with others
- Asserting oneself
- Being able to work independently

Organization & Management Skills
- Paying attention to and handling details
- Performing duties that change frequently
- Managing people/groups
- Managing time
- Managing equipment/materials
- Demonstrating leadership
- Making decisions
- Meeting goals and deadlines
- Working quickly when necessary

Research & Planning Skills
- Analyzing information
- Developing evaluation strategies
- Using logical reasoning
- Setting goals and deadlines
- Defining needs
- Identifying problems
- Solving problems

Physical Environment

IT project managers work in a variety of settings across all types of business and industry, including corporate offices, schools, government offices, transportation centers, and industrial or medical settings.

Human Environment

IT project managers must be savvy communicators who can successfully supervise, manage, and coordinate a variety of professionals on a daily basis.

Technological Environment

IT project managers utilize a broad range of technologies, including collaborative operational software, application servers, networking servers, web-development software, and programming languages.

Technical Skills
- Performing scientific, mathematical and technical work
- Using technology to process information
- Understanding which technology is appropriate for a task
- Applying the technology to a task

EDUCATION, TRAINING, AND ADVANCEMENT

High School/Secondary

High school students can prepare for a career in IT project management by completing course work in algebra, calculus, geometry, trigonometry, computer programming, and computer science. Advanced placement (AP) classes in computer-related subjects are especially recommended.

Participation in volunteer work, charities, or team sports can help foster the leadership and managerial skills necessary for large-scale project management. Many IT professionals gain additional experience through summer jobs or internships with computer-related organizations. Supplemental information technology courses offered by universities and community colleges are also helpful.

Suggested High School Subjects
- Accounting
- Algebra
- Applied Communication
- Applied Math
- Business & Computer Technology
- Business Data Processing
- Calculus
- College Preparatory
- Computer Programming

- Computer Science
- English
- Geometry
- Keyboarding
- Mathematics
- Statistics
- Trigonometry

Famous First

The first mainframe-based project management systems that came into wide use were the Nichols N5500, PAC from International Systems, and PC/70 from Atlantic Software, all developed in the early to mid-1970s.

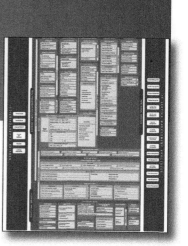

College/Postsecondary

Undergraduate programs related to IT include core course work in UNIX system administration software and programming languages such as Java and C+. In addition to a survey of wireless-network technology and database-management techniques, undergraduate IT students also study business models, network security systems, and infrastructure, as well as information-security management.

Postgraduate and doctoral-level programs in information technology are traditionally dedicated to the exploration and discovery of new strategies and technologies, grounded in a strong foundational knowledge of the history of the field. Graduate students are required to complete a thesis or capstone project related to an emerging trend in information technology; this is often highly specialized work that can be an important precursor for their professional growth and eventual career path.

Related College Majors
- Computer Programming
- Computer Science

- Information Sciences & Systems
- Management Information Systems & Business Data Processing

Adult Job Seekers

Like many supervisory and management professionals, IT project managers work extensive hours. The role often requires evening and weekend work. Due to the vast amount of academic and professional experience required, IT project management is not a traditional choice for those seeking to begin a new career path. The long hours required of the position, particularly in large organizations and corporations, may also pose difficulty for adult professionals eager to achieve a harmonious work-life balance.

Professional Certification and Licensure

Specific certification and licensure is not required for a career as an IT project manager, though numerous national and international professional organizations exist. Voluntarily completing a certification program will give professionals in the field a competitive advantage.

Additional Requirements

IT project managers are talented multi-taskers who can simultaneously execute a wide variety of managerial responsibilities. In addition to being able to monitor all active projects, IT project management professionals must also possess the professional and academic experience necessary to predict and eliminate potential pitfalls before they occur in order to ensure that the systems and infrastructure continue to operate effectively and efficiently.

Fun Fact

The first mouse was called an "X-Y Position Indicator for a Display System," but its inventor, Douglas Engelbart, said the cord coming out the back reminded him of a mouse. The rest is history.

Source: www.computerhope.com/issues/ch001083.htm

EARNINGS AND ADVANCEMENT

According to the Robert Half Technology 2014 Salary Guide, median annual earnings of information technology project managers were $110,000 in 2014. The lowest ten percent earned less than $89,000, and the highest ten percent earned more than $131,000.

Information technology managers may receive paid vacations, holidays and sick days; life and health insurance; and retirement benefits. These are usually paid by the employer.

EMPLOYMENT AND OUTLOOK

Computer and information systems managers, of which information technology project managers are a part, held about 348,000 jobs nationally in 2014. Employment of information technology project managers is expected to grow faster than the average for all occupations through the year 2024, which means employment is projected to increase 10 percent to 19 percent. New and continued uses of technology within organizations will continue to create high demand for these workers, especially those with experience in web applications and internet technologies.

In addition, as organizations rely more and more on technology to grow their revenue, information technology projects managers who have strong communication skills and a good understanding of business practices will have excellent opportunities.

Employment Trend, Projected 2014–24

IT project managers and other computer and information systems managers: 15%

Operations specialties managers: 7%

Total, all occupations: 7%

Note: "All Occupations" includes all occupations in the U.S. Economy. Source: U.S. Bureau of Labor Statistics, Employment Projections Program.

Related Occupations

- Computer & Information Systems Manager
- Computer Engineer
- Computer Network Architect
- Computer Support Specialist
- Computer Systems Analyst
- Database Administrator
- General Manager & Top Executive
- Information Security Analyst
- Medical Records Administrator
- Network & Computer Systems Administrator
- Operations Research Analyst
- Software Developer
- Web Administrator
- Web Developer

Related Military Occupations

- Computer Programmer
- Computer Systems Officer

Conversation With . . .
CHRIS JOHNSON

Director of Strategy and Business Development
Wheelhouse IT, Mount Pleasant, Iowa
IT project management, 17 years

1. What was your individual career path in terms of education/training, entry-level job, or other significant opportunity?

I wanted to be an engineer but as I got into my third year of college, I decided I didn't want to spend three more years in college just to be an engineer, so I changed my major to information systems management. I learned a lot about what goes into infrastructure as it pertains to data schemes. A few months after graduating, I got a job at Graybar. This was the late 1990s, early 2000 and what was huge was vast expanses of infrastructure in the San Francisco Bay area. Companies would order $1 million of CAT 5 cable. Knowing what the cable empowered, I started thinking, "This is pretty cool; maybe this is something I want to get more involved in."

I got a job with a start-up and was lucky because it was in health care, dealing with clinical trials and pharmaceutical companies, so there was a lot of money. The dot com crash didn't really have an impact. They hired me to basically do data collection on quality of life for prostate cancer patients. I had really no experience in IT. They walked me into my new office, I'm 22, and it's probably 1,000 square feet with windows. I've got a $1,000 ergonomic chair and a new laptop. And they said, "We need you to set up all 42 of those computers in the corner and send them to urological practices across the country and in Japan and Australia."

I got the title of Systems Administrator. I had this little orange piece of paper with a toll-free number that I could call if I had problems I couldn't figure out. It was basically trial and error—back then, that's how IT really did work. You found a manual or a textbook and you learned it. Meanwhile, my wife was teaching and I would pick her up after work. I found myself constantly troubleshooting hardware problems at the school and found that I really liked working with computers.

Through hands-on experience, I learned the Apple and Windows operating systems and worked my way up to networking and firewall management. I never took a class until about 2009, when I started my own company, Untangled. I got involved with CompTIA and realized there was actual training. I don't think any other organization provides the kind of education they do the way they do it. It was vendor-neutral. It had a lot of application training where it gave you scenarios but didn't tell you to be an expert in the product; it was more about designing and understanding how the solution should work. A few months ago, I sold the company and joined Wheelhouse.

2. What are the most important skills and/or qualities for someone in your profession?

You have to think logically and think creatively at the same time. Going forward, IT is going to be less and less wrench-turning and more and more coming up with solutions. Obviously, you have to be good at managing projects. You have to be able to keep people on task. It's really easy in IT to get distracted. A project manager tends to pull everyone back in.

3. What do you wish you had known going into this profession?

I wish I had been more focused on developing my skill set. Certifications are really important.

4. Are there many job opportunities in your profession? In what specific areas?

Yes. The IT industry itself is now competing with finance and health care and all the others. Everyone hires IT people. But the bar that you have to climb over to work for an IT company is much lower than in other industries. Getting a job with an IT company is a great place to learn.

5. How do you see your profession changing in the next five years? What role will technology play in those changes, and what skills will be required?

We're going to have to really comply with Payment Card Industry (PCI) and probably National Institute of Standards and Technology (NIST) security standards.

6. What do you enjoy most about your job? What do you enjoy least about your job?

What I enjoy most is solving a problem that those who came before me couldn't. What I enjoy least is having resources and not leveraging them to get the job done. On every project, there are three things to consider—cost, quality and speed. You can't have all three. If you don't want to spend the money, the other two go out the window.

7. Can you suggest a valuable "try this" for students considering a career in your profession?

ITPro.TV, udemy.com and Lynda.com all have decent project management learning tracks. Also, products like Planner, Trello, and Asana all have different philosophies about how to manage time and projects. If you enjoy playing around with them, then maybe a project management job is right for you.

MORE INFORMATION

**Association of Information
Technology Professionals**
330 N. Wabash Avenue, Suite 2000
Chicago, IL 60611
800.224.9371
www.aitp.org

**Network Professional
Association**
1401 Hermes Lane
San Diego, CA 92154
888.672.6720
www.npa.org

John Pritchard/Editor

Network & Computer Systems Administrator

Snapshot

Career Cluster(s): Business Administration; Information Technology

Interests: Computer programming, computer science, software development

Earnings (Yearly Average): $77,810

Employment & Outlook: Average Growth Expected

OVERVIEW

Sphere of Work

Network and computer systems administrators design, build, and maintain computer systems for businesses and organizations. In addition to constructing local area networks and wide area networks, systems administrators also support and maintain organizational internet systems and related infrastructure. Any computer problems or computer related questions posed by employees of a company are traditionally handed by system administrators or their staff.

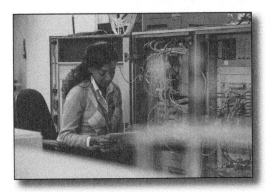

Network and computer systems administrators work closely

with computer security professionals and other senior administrative staff to ensure that the computing needs of a business or organization are in place and are functioning properly. They also assist fellow employees with computer-related projects and routine maintenance.

Work Environment

Network and computer systems administrators work predominantly in business, administrative, and office settings. They are employed by large companies often have their own workspaces adjacent to facilities that house computer servers and other hardware relevant to network systems. Network and computer systems administrators are often required to strike a balance between work conducted on their own and collaborative work with other staff members, which can include system maintenance, demonstrations of hardware and software capabilities, or developing and implementing new technologies with fellow staff.

Profile

Working Conditions: Work Indoors
Physical Strength: Light Work
Education Needs: Bachelor's Degree,
Licensure/Certification:
Recommended
Opportunities For Experience:
Military Service, Volunteer Work, Part Time Work
Holland Interest Score*: IRC

* See Appendix A

Occupation Interest

The field of computer administration traditionally attracts professionals with technological skills who have a lengthy history of involvement with and demonstrated passion for computing, be it through academic study, personal interest, or professional development. Most network and computer systems administrators develop an interest in working with and around computers at a young age and are intricately familiar with modern developments in personal and business computing. They may also enter the discipline through previous exposure to programming, software development, or any one of numerous disciplines related to computer science.

A Day in the Life—Duties and Responsibilities

Network and computer systems administrators divide their time between monitoring and maintaining existing computer systems, devising new computer and network technologies with other staff, and assisting different departments and fellow employees with their computing and networking needs through maintenance, troubleshooting, and conducting training seminars.

Network and computer system administrators are traditionally the primary individuals responsible for the configuration and maintenance of network e-mail systems. In addition to monitoring archival systems and implementing virus prevention programs, they are also called upon to set up network and mobile e-mail accounts for new employees or vendors.

In addition to e-mail systems, network and computer system administrators also maintain computer systems related to inventories, financial records, meeting logs, and other relevant data. They build, maintain, and monitor backup systems for archival data. They often work in concert with organizational computer security specialists to ensure that data can be recovered in the event of an unforeseen system failure.

Network and computer system administrators also spend a great deal of time troubleshooting and installing new programs on network computers, making updates to employee machines so productivity is not interrupted, or routing out any viruses or system malfunctions that are preventing them from accessing projects. They are traditionally in charge of the master computer and network systems from which all company computers are connected. They may be called upon to supervise access to particular network locations.

Duties and Responsibilities

- Managing and maintaining an organization's computer network, including all computer hardware and software
- Diagnosing and solving network problems
- Performing functions related to data security, virus protection and disaster recovery
- Monitoring network performance to determine current and future adjustments that need to be made
- Communicating with network users to understand and correct issues

OCCUPATION SPECIALTIES

Computer Security Specialists

Computer Security Specialists plan, coordinate and implement their organization's information security program.

WORK ENVIRONMENT

Transferable Skills and Abilities

Communication Skills
- Speaking effectively
- Writing concisely
- Listening attentively
- Reading well

Interpersonal/Social Skills
- Being able to work independently

Organization & Management Skills
- Paying attention to and handling details
- Performing duties that change frequently
- Managing time
- Managing equipment/materials
- Coordinating tasks
- Making decisions
- Handling challenging situations

Research & Planning Skills
- Identifying problems
- Determining alternatives
- Gathering information
- Solving problems

Physical Environment

Network and computer systems administrators work primarily in computer labs and office settings. They balance a workload that is performed at their own individual workstation and the workstations of other employees.

Network and computer systems administrators work in nearly every type of industry and organization, including local, state and federal governments; construction; medical research; publishing; education; and media.

Human Environment

Systems administration requires patience and collaboration and explanatory skills. Network and computer systems administrators normally interact with colleagues across various departments on a

- Defining needs
- Analyzing information
- Developing evaluation strategies

Technical Skills

- Performing scientific, mathematical and technical work
- Working with machines, tools or other objects
- Using technology to process information
- Understanding which technology is appropriate for a task
- Applying the technology to a task
- Maintaining and repairing technology

daily basis, including engineers, technicians, managers, directors, and executive staff.

Technological Environment

Network and computer systems administrators must be well versed in the entire gamut of contemporary computer systems technologies, ranging from circuitry, processors, and programming languages, and all computer hardware and software relevant to their industry of expertise, including applications and database platforms.

EDUCATION, TRAINING, AND ADVANCEMENT

High School/Secondary

High school students can best prepare for a career in network and computer systems administration by completing coursework in algebra, calculus, geometry, trigonometry, introductory computer science, and programming. Specialized seminars or advanced placement coursework related to computer topics are also recommended.

Many high school students supplement their course load by participating in volunteer programs and summer internships in which they can work directly with system administration fundamentals and its importance in the professional world.

Suggested High School Subjects

- Algebra
- Applied Communication
- Applied Math

- Business & Computer Technology
- Business Data Processing
- Calculus
- College Preparatory
- Computer Programming
- Computer Science
- English
- Geometry
- Keyboarding
- Mathematics
- Statistics
- Trigonometry

Famous First

The first client/server systems emerged in the late 1980s with the advent of Intel's 386 chip and IBM's OS/2 operating system. Now, dedicated machines (servers) could control and share computer files with others (clients) using Local Area Networks (LANs) and Wide Area Networks (WANs).

College/Postsecondary

Systems administration has evolved from a niche field to an academic and professional specialty widely studied across post-secondary institutions in the United States. Requirements for specific academic training in the field often vary from position to position and industry to industry, though a bachelor's degree in a related field is commonplace for most entry-level positions. Several certificate-level and undergraduate programs are available nationwide.

While graduate programs specifically related to systems administration are rare, applicants with master's-level accreditation in fields such as programming, computer science, and networking are often prime candidates for senior management positions related to network and systems administration in major companies, research institutes, and universities. Basic bachelor's degree coursework in systems administration programs includes topics such as system administration, network infrastructures, UNIX, business telecommunications, and information security.

Related College Majors

- Computer Installation & Repair
- Computer Maintenance Technology
- Computer Programming
- Computer Science
- Data Processing Technology
- Information Sciences & Systems
- Management Information Systems & Business Data Processing

Adult Job Seekers

Network and computer systems administrators are often employed by businesses and organizations of all size and scope. Senior-level positions at large organizations and companies are usually the domain of professionals with extensive academic and professional experience in computing. However, adult job seekers interested in a career change to the field can, with requisite training, acquire the skills necessary to become eligible for systems administrator positions at smaller organizations. Network and computer systems administrators traditionally work regular business hours.

Professional Certification and Licensure

The number of available and required certifications for network and computer systems administrators is complex and varied. Examples include Microsoft Certified IT Professional certification, Linux certification, and Accredited Systems Engineer certification.

Additional Requirements

Network and computer systems administrators must possess a constant desire to stay up to date with emerging developments in digital technology, networking, and database systems. Organizations rely on network and computer systems administrators to help their firms stay in tune with the technologies that can expand their production and profitability.

Fun Fact

According to a study by Radware, it takes e-commerce sites an average of 3.1 seconds to reach the point where consumers can interact with the site. Amazon. com was among the fastest, with an average speed of 1.8 seconds.

Source: https://www.internetretailer.com/2016/03/23/e-retailers-win-race-site-load-times

EARNINGS AND ADVANCEMENT

Median annual earnings of network and computer system administrators were $77,810 in 2014. The lowest ten percent earned less than $47,460, and the highest ten percent earned more than $124,090.

Network and computer system administrators may receive paid vacations, holidays and sick days; life and health insurance; and retirement benefits. These are usually paid by the employer.

Metropolitan Areas with the Highest Employment Level in this Occupation

Metropolitan area	Employment	Employment per thousand jobs	Annual mean wage
New York-Jersey City-White Plains, NY-NJ	19,000	2.93	$97,820
Washington-Arlington-Alexandria, DC-VA-MD-WV	17,190	7.11	$99,160
Dallas-Plano-Irving, TX	10,800	4.64	$86,800
Los Angeles-Long Beach-Glendale, CA	10,270	2.50	$84,820
Chicago-Naperville-Arlington Heights, IL	9,980	2.79	$84,690
Houston-The Woodlands-Sugar Land, TX	8,940	3.05	$94,480
Atlanta-Sandy Springs-Roswell, GA	8,440	3.40	$85,510
Denver-Aurora-Lakewood, CO	7,160	5.21	$85,660
Minneapolis-St. Paul-Bloomington, MN-WI	6,810	3.62	$86,250
Baltimore-Columbia-Towson, MD	6,670	5.08	$99,190

Source: Bureau of Labor Statistics

EMPLOYMENT AND OUTLOOK

Network and computer system administrators held about 380,000 jobs nationally in 2014. Employment of network and computer system administrators is expected to grow as fast as the average for all occupations through the year 2024, which means employment is projected to increase 5 percent to 10 percent. Almost every organization in today's workforce needs to keep a computer network running smoothly and secure from hackers, viruses and other attacks. The growth of security as a main concern for organizations will help to fuel the growth of network and computer system administrators.

In addition, the demand for organizations to have newer, faster and more mobile networks; the growth of the use of information technology in the healthcare field; and the growth of e-commerce will continue to create new jobs for network and computer systems administrators. This growth demands workers who can help their organizations use the internet and other technologies to communicate with employees, clients and customers.

Employment Trend, Projected 2014–24

Computer occupations: 12%

Network and computer systems administrators: 8%

Total, all occupations: 7%

Note: "All Occupations" includes all occupations in the U.S. Economy. Source: U.S. Bureau of Labor Statistics, Employment Projections Program.

Related Occupations

- Computer & Information Systems Manager
- Computer Engineer
- Computer Network Architect
- Computer Programmer
- Computer Support Specialist
- Computer Systems Analyst
- Database Administrator
- Information Security Analyst

- Software Developer
- Web Administrator
- Web Developer

Related Military Occupations

- Computer Programmer
- Computer Systems Officer
- Computer Systems Specialist

Conversation With . . .
DAMIAN DAVIS

Network Operations Engineer, G3 Technologies, Inc.
Chantilly, Virginia
Network administrator, 3 years

1. What was your individual career path in terms of education/training, entry-level job, or other significant opportunity?

I always wanted to do something sports-related, so my degree is in sports management with a minor in business administration. As an intern for the Washington Wizards, I got to be part of the process of evaluating a free agent. That was really cool. But those moments were few and far between, and most of the work seemed repetitive. The demand for jobs in that field was very high and, apart from trainers and deal-makers, the salaries were maybe $30,000 a year to start. Meantime, I had friends who were computer science majors asking for my help on projects.

I worked for Hertz Rent a Car for five years after graduating, but it's a high turnover industry and I realized I wasn't making enough money and wasn't seeing my family. I started looking at what fields would be a better fit. A customer worked in IT, and I already knew how to do some of the things he talked about needing to learn.

I took a full year out of work to study how to become a network engineer. I started by taking a course at a small IT school for the Cisco Certified Network Associate (CCNA) certification; it was too much to learn in a short period of time. After that class ended, I offered to volunteer at local IT firms and studied on my own. At one company in particular, the CEO and one of his directors spent an hour speaking with me. They couldn't let me volunteer due to contract specifications with clients, but the CEO saw a lot of himself in me. He picked up a huge stack of routers and switches and said, "We're about to throw these out. Why don't you take them? You can practice." That really helped me out. It pushed my development and learning, and I realized the limitations of software.

A year after making my career change, I was hired as a Junior IT Network Administrator for G3. Besides my CCNA certification, I am Network+ certified and am studying for the Cisco Certified Network Professional (CCNP) and Certified Ethical Hacker (CEH) certifications.

I love what I do.

2. What are the most important skills and/or qualities for someone in your profession?

Be willing to learn. Every day. What you learned last year is already obsolete. Also, I recommend that anyone taking an entry-level job work for a small- to mid-size company. The bigger companies will hire you for a specific duty and you'll learn how to do that very well, but not much else. Smaller companies need employees to fill a lot of shoes, so you'll have the opportunity to learn a lot very quickly. In just three years of working, I've learned SharePoint Administration, Active Directory, CyberSecurity, and Linux Ubuntu, in addition to my Cisco training and studies.

3. What do you wish you had known going into this profession?

I wish I had started with an easier certification because Cisco equipment is very difficult to learn. The A+ and Network+ certifications are foundational training—but easier—that you can always fall back on. By not starting with those certifications, I encountered situations in my first IT job that should've been easy to resolve but weren't, because I did not have the basics.

4. Are there many job opportunities in your profession? In what specific areas?

Many. The best areas for network engineers are in California, New York City, and Washington D.C.

5. How do you see your profession changing in the next five years, what role will technology play in those changes, and what skills will be required?

The way technology keeps advancing, network administrators will always be essential. More and more companies will seek out people with my skills and knowledge. A strong understanding of Windows and Linux OS, Microsoft Office, and networking principles will be essential.

6. What do you enjoy most about your job? What do you enjoy least about your job?

I most enjoy interacting with my co-workers. When I've resolved all outstanding trouble tickets, I go around the office and ask my colleagues how their day has been. This usually creates better work relationships and also can remind them of IT issues or concerns they've been having but have forgotten to tell me about. What I enjoy least is occasionally having to speak to a co-worker about inappropriate activities on their computer, like porn. It's never an easy conversation, and always awkward for all parties involved.

7. Can you suggest a valuable "try this" for students considering a career in your profession?

Apply for an internship before you graduate. You'll learn a lot of the foundational knowledge you'll need to be successful and, more importantly, you'll learn whether the career is really for you. If you're a hard worker and you like the work, chances are that company you're interning with will offer you a job.

MORE INFORMATION

League of Professional System Administrators
P.O. Box 5161
Trenton, NJ 08638-0161
202.567.7201
lopsa.org

National Association of System Administrators
3305 South IL Rte. 31
Crystal Lake, IL 60012
800.724.9692
www.nasasupport.com

National Workforce Center for Emerging Technologies
Bellevue College
3000 Landerholm Circle SE, N258
Bellevue, WA 98007-6484
425.564.4229
www.nwcet.org

John Pritchard/Editor

Robotics Technician

Snapshot

Career Cluster: Engineering; Manufacturing; Maintenance & Repair; Technology

Interests: Robotics technology, engineering, computer science, electrical systems, machinery

Earnings (Yearly Average): $54,160

Employment & Outlook: Slower than Average Growth Expected

OVERVIEW

Sphere of Work

Robotics technicians, also known as electromechanical technicians, build and repair robots and mechanical devices in a manufacturing setting. Drawing on their knowledge of electrical and computer systems, robotics technicians develop efficient robots and keep them in good working order. Some technicians assist at all levels of a robot's conception, production, and installation. Others are experts when it comes to the machines they are assigned to maintain.

Technicians install new systems and replace old ones. Some robotics

technicians work closely with engineers in development and design. Others spend their time inspecting sites and making repairs. Robotics technicians read and interpret manuals and instructions, but they also think critically to find solutions to unusual or difficult problems with machines.

Work Environment

Most robotics technicians work in factories or similar manufacturing settings. Using a number of technologies, ranging from sophisticated computer programs to hand tools, technicians test machines and look for problems. A technician's work can be dangerous, so it is important for technicians to take proper safety precautions and follow correct procedures.

Profile

Working Conditions: Work Indoors
Physical Strength: Light Work
Education Needs:
  Technical/Community College
Licensure/Certification:
  Recommended
Physical Abilities Not Required: No
  Heavy Labor
Opportunities For Experience:
  Internship
Holland Interest Score*: REC

* See Appendix A

Occupation Interest

A robotics technician should be interested in engineering. He or she should enjoy taking machines apart and putting them back together again. Technicians are meticulous, and they always double-check their work. A robotics technician plays an important role within the larger framework of a factory operation.

A Day in the Life—Duties and Responsibilities

Every day is different for robotics technicians. Their responsibilities include building and installing new robotic devices, replacing old or outdated parts and machines, testing robot performance, troubleshooting problems within a system, maintaining inventories of necessary parts and tools, and programming computers.

There are generally two types of robotics technicians: those who work with engineers to design and assemble robots and those who maintain and repair those robots. The first type thinks creatively to find a way for machines to simulate the work of humans. Robot manipulators, or robots that simulate the work of arms or hands, are common in industrial settings, particularly when the work is repetitive or performed in a dangerous environment. Technicians work with engineers to develop machines like manipulators that perform a very specialized task within the larger framework of the factory or plant.

The second kind of robotics technician monitors the use of these machines. After the robot has been tested and installed, a technician routinely inspects it for missing or malfunctioning parts. This work is largely preventative, as a broken or worn-down machine can stall production across the plant. When a machine does break down, robotics technicians have the knowledge and skill to repair them.

Technicians typically work a regular forty-hour week, though sometimes companies schedule repairs of robotic equipment during weekends or holidays. In this event, a technician might have to work overtime.

Duties and Responsibilities

- Assisting engineers in designing and applying robot systems
- Inspecting electronic components prior to robot assembly
- Inspecting and testing robots for defects after assembly
- Installing robots or robot systems at users' sites
- Providing start-up assistance to users, including fine tuning performance and accuracy of robots
- Training other technicians and skilled workers to operate, program, repair and service robots
- Keeping records of test procedures and results

WORK ENVIRONMENT

Physical Environment

Robotics technicians work in factories, plants, and other industrial settings.

Plant Environment

The plants and factories in which robotics technicians work are often dirty and loud. Technicians are often required to wear protective gear when performing their job. Working with large machines can be dangerous, so people must follow strict safety precautions.

Human Environment

Most robotics technicians work in teams that include other technicians, technologists, engineers, and machine operators. A robotics technician rarely works alone. Even minor repairs require assistance from or interaction with others.

Technological Environment

A robotics technician must be familiar with a range of technologies. In terms of computers and computer programming, most technicians use computer-aided design (CAD) software and industrial control software programs.

Relevant Skills and Abilities

Communication Skills
- Speaking effectively
- Writing concisely

Organization & Management Skills
- Paying attention to and handling details

Research & Planning Skills
- Analyzing information
- Developing evaluation strategies
- Using logical reasoning

Technical Skills
- Applying the technology to a task
- Performing scientific, mathematical and technical work
- Working with machines, tools or other objects
- Working with your hands

EDUCATION, TRAINING, AND ADVANCEMENT

High School/Secondary

Aspiring robotics technicians should enroll in courses focusing on mathematics, physics, computer science, and English. Shop classes and extracurricular activities related to robotics or simple machinery are also valuable. A robotics technician is familiar with various kinds of machines and understands why and how those machines work. They are comfortable using the scientific method and solving equations. They are also adept at reading manuals and diagrams and are able to explain complex instructions with ease. A job as a robotics technician requires a high school diploma or equivalent.

Suggested High School Subjects
- Algebra
- Applied Math
- Applied Physics
- Blueprint Reading
- Computer Science
- Electricity & Electronics
- English
- Geometry
- Machining Technology
- Mathematics

Famous First

The first Robot Olympics was the ROBOlympics (later renamed RoboGames) held in San Francisco in March 2004. Under the sponsorship of the Robotics Society of America, participants entered their robots in 31 events, including sumo, soccer, combat, and wrestling. The games have been held annually since then.

College/Postsecondary

Most robotics technician jobs require only two years of postsecondary training, culminating in an associate degree or certificate. Community colleges and technical schools offer degree programs in electromechanics, robotics technology, industrial maintenance, and computer-integrated manufacturing. Many of these programs are accredited by the Accreditation Board for Engineering and Technology (ABET) and include courses in trigonometry, algebra, science, and engineering specializations.

Similar fields of study, including electrical engineering technology and mechanical engineering technology, are available in four-year bachelor's degree programs, but most robotics technicians do not pursue this career path. Students who earn a bachelor's degree are much more likely to pursue a career as an engineering technologist.

Related College Majors
* Robotics Technology

Adult Job Seekers

Robotics technicians draw upon a number of transferrable skills, including those of an electrician, mechanic, and computer programmer. Adults who already work as industrial machine operators or simply work in a factory setting might pursue work as a robotics technician. However, they will most likely need to return to school to acquire the proper training; it is unusual for a robotics technician to learn his or her trade completely on the job, though many complete internships.

Professional Certification and Licensure

Robotics technicians are not required to seek certification or licensure in their field, but it is recommended. Some companies offers a number of certifications tailored to different careers in and principles of robotics. For example, one can take certification tests in categories such as application lifecycle management, business planning and alignment, complex and embedded systems, design and development, and enterprise modernization. Local robotics societies also offer workshops and seminars for professional development.

Additional Requirements

Robotics technicians must be efficient and precise. They should work well with others, appreciate the needs of organizations, and be able to execute their job in the fulfillment of those needs. They enjoy working with their hands but are also adept at working with computers. Technicians must be able to think both analytically and creatively. The creation and maintenance of robotic systems requires technicians to draw upon all of their talents and knowledge. Due to the noisy conditions common in factories and plants, it is important that robotics technicians be able to focus on their work despite distractions.

Fun Fact

One of the earliest uses of the word "robot" was in the 1920s play, *Rossum's Universal Robots*, by Czech writer Karel Capek. It comes from the Slavonic word "robota," which means servitude, drudgery, or forced labor. In the play, robots, which are produced to do the work humans prefer not to, eventually rise up in revolt.

Source: sciencefriday.com/segment/04/22/2011/science-diction-the-origin-of-the-word-robot.html

EARNINGS AND ADVANCEMENT

Earnings of robotics technicians depend on the type and size of the employer and the individual's education, experience and job responsibilities. Mean annual earnings of robotics technicians were $54,160 in 2013. The lowest ten percent earned less than $33,490, and the highest ten percent earned more than $80,070.

Robotics technicians may receive paid vacations, holidays, and sick days; life and health insurance; and retirement benefits. These are usually paid by the employer. Some employers have profit-sharing and/or tuition reimbursement plans and also reimburse job-related travel expenses.

Metropolitan Areas with the Highest
Employment Level in this Occupation

Metropolitan area	Employment [1]	Employment per thousand jobs	Hourly mean wage
San Jose-Sunnyvale-Santa Clara, CA	690	0.75	$25.11
Boston-Cambridge-Quincy, MA	670	0.38	$28.94
Phoenix-Mesa-Glendale, AZ	590	0.33	$24.77
Santa Ana-Anaheim-Irvine, CA	440	0.31	$22.10
Los Angeles-Long Beach-Glendale, CA	360	0.09	$26.67
San Diego-Carlsbad-San Marcos, CA	330	0.25	$28.42
Baltimore-Towson, MD	290	0.23	$32.47
Atlanta-Sandy Springs-Marietta, GA	290	0.13	$27.60
Chicago-Joliet-Naperville, IL	270	0.07	$32.01
Oklahoma City, OK	270	0.45	$18.53

[1]Does not include self-employ ed. Source: Bureau of Labor Statistics

EMPLOYMENT AND OUTLOOK

Nationally, there were approximately 17,500 electro-mechanical technicians, of which robotics technicians are a part, employed in 2012. Employment is expected to grow slower than the average for all occupations through the year 2022, which means employment is projected to increase 1 percent to 7 percent. Many job openings will result from the need to replace robotics technicians who transfer to other occupations or retire.

Employment Trend, Projected 2012–22

Total, All Occupations: 11%

Robotics Technicians: 4%

Engineering Technicians (All): 1%

Note: "All Occupations" includes all occupations in the U.S. Economy. Source: U.S. Bureau of Labor Statistics, Employment Projections Program

Related Occupations
- Computer Service Technician
- Computer-Control Machine Tool Operator
- Computer-Control Tool Programmer
- Electrical & Electronics Engineer
- Electrician
- Electromechanical Equipment Assembler
- Engineering Technician

Conversation With . . .
PAUL CARUSO

Robotics Technician
iRobot Corporation, Bedford, MA
Electronics & Robotics Professional, 33 years

1. What was your individual career path in terms of education/training, entry-level job, or other significant opportunity?

After graduating from James Madison High School in New York, I went on to earn a two-year degree from The College of Staten Island in electrical engineering and a one-year certificate in electronic technology at the PSI Institute. In the past, I worked as a technician for Tandy Corporation. I was a field technician for Circuit City for almost seven years before going to work for iRobot in 2006. Today, I'm a Senior Quality Engineering Technician with iRobot Corporation.

2. What are the most important skills and/or qualities for someone in your profession?

This position requires a lot of troubleshooting. Working in robotics, it's important to take a methodical approach to solving a problem—starting at one point and working step-by step until you solve the issue. That requires patience.

3. What do you wish you had known going into this profession?

If I had known what I know now, I would have continued with my studies to get my bachelor's degree, plus take other classes along the way to broaden my knowledge in areas outside of electronics and electrical engineering.

4. Are there many job opportunities in your profession? In what specif-ic areas?

Yes, there are many opportunities in robotics, including video conferencing/remote presence; medical electronics and telemedicine (which is the remote delivery of clinical information and health care services via the internet or satellite, etc.); home and elderly independent-living robotics; and many more.

Robotics technicians often find themselves working for a robotics company, such as iRobot, in a diagnostic lab environment. Since robots are such complicated machines, special parts and tools are required to service them that are not always accessible away from the lab. As robots become more pervasive in society, there will be a need for technicians to travel into the field for troubleshooting, updates, and repairs—particularly for larger robots installed in hospitals, manufacturing plants, and elderly care facilities that are not easily transportable.

5. How do you see your profession changing in the next five years? What role will technology play in those changes, and what skills will be required?

Constant breakthroughs in technology mean we will see advances in robotics that were impossible to consider only a few years ago. You will soon be able to buy cars that drive themselves. There will be robots working together to clean the house and ambidextrous robots helping the elderly with daily tasks. This will create a need for more technical people to design and maintain these robots. We will need people with mechanical, software and electrical engineering degrees who can work together to solve complicated problems.

6. What do you enjoy most about your job? What do you enjoy least about your job?

I truly enjoy working with my hands. And there's great satisfaction that comes with solving a difficult problem in a way that will help improve the quality of the product. What I don't enjoy? Of course, there's always paperwork involved with any job, which isn't quite as exciting.

7. Can you suggest a valuable "try this" for students considering a ca-reer in your profession?

I suggest that students attend electronic trade shows, where they can walk the show floor and get a glimpse at the latest technology hitting markets. Not only is it a great way to see cutting-edge technology, but it's also a great way to make connections with companies that may be hiring or seeking internship candidates. Internships are critical to breaking into a career in robotics.

SELECTED SCHOOLS

Many technical and community colleges offer programs in or related to robotics technology. Commercial trade schools are also an option. Students are advised to consult with their school guidance counselor or research area post-secondary schools to find the right program.

MORE INFORMATION

American Society for Engineering Education
1818 N Street NW, Suite 600
Washington, DC 20036-2479
202.331.3500
www.asee.org

Association for Unmanned Vehicle Systems International
2700 S. Quincy Street, Suite 400
Arlington, VA 22206
703.845.9671
www.auvsi.org

Institute of Electrical and Electronics Engineers
3 Park Avenue, 17th Floor
New York, NY 10016-5997
212.419.7900
www.ieee.org

National Robotics Training Center
1951 Pisgah Road
P.O. Box 100549
Florence, SC 29501-0549
800.228.5745
www.nrtcenter.com

Technology Student Association
1914 Association Drive
Reston, VA 20191-1540
703.860.9000
www.tsaweb.org

Molly Hagan/Editor

Software and/ or Mobile/Apps Developer

Snapshot

Career Cluster: Arts, A/V Technology & Communications, Information Technology

Interests: Computer Software Technology, Math, Science, Information Technology

Earnings (Yearly Average): $96,444

Employment & Outlook: Faster Than Average Growth Expected

OVERVIEW

Sphere of Work

Software developers design and write computer programs or computer applications for use in a variety of media, including computer games. They also modify existing programs to improve functionality or to meet client needs. On large-scale projects, software developers typically work with a team of professionals that includes software engineers, software architects, and computer programmers. In these cases, they might be primarily responsible for developing the functional or "front-end" user interface of the program to ensure that it is compatible

with an existing system and that it works reliably and securely. On smaller jobs, software designers might also handle the programming, engineering, and architecture of the program. In any case, they serve as the creative link between an abstract idea for a program or application and its realization as a functioning piece of software.

Work Environment

Many software developers are self-employed and work at home or in small businesses. Others work for the military, government agencies, or industries such as telecommunications, health care, aerospace, e-commerce, video games, and education. Software developers working for corporations typically work forty-hour weeks, while those who are self-employed may set their own hours. In either case, strict deadlines or unexpected problems may require software developers to work additional hours as needed. A typical workstation includes top-quality computer hardware and systems for designing and writing software.

Profile

Working Conditions: Work Indoors
Physical Strength: Light Work
Education Needs: Bachelor's Degree
Licensure/Certification:
  Recommended
Physical Abilities Not Required: No
  Heavy Labor
Opportunities For Experience:
  Internship, Apprenticeship, Military
  Service, Volunteer Work, Part-Time
  Work
Holland Interest Score*: AES, IRE

* See Appendix A

Occupation Interest

People who are attracted to software development careers are analytical and mathematically inclined, with strong problem-solving skills and an aptitude for learning programming languages. They are detail oriented, yet also able to envision the overall design and application of products. Software developers need good communication skills to interact with team members and convey their ideas. Leadership and organizational skills are also important, as is the desire to be knowledgeable about new developments in the industry.

A Day in the Life—Duties and Responsibilities

Most computer programs are born out of a need. Software developers first evaluate that need, usually in consultation with a client, and then conceive of a program to solve the problem. They design computer games, applications for mobile phones, and other highly visible types of software. They also design behind-the-scenes programs known as utilities, which may help users download content from the internet seamlessly, convert files to different formats, protect computers from malware, or free up computer disk space when needed. Some software developers design programs used in business, education, graphic arts, multimedia, web development, and many other fields, as well as programs intended just for other programmers.

Software developers are often responsible for planning a project within budget and time constraints. They must consider compatibility issues, determining the type of platform on which the software will operate and the oldest version on which it will work reliably. They also consider issues such as the maintainability of the software (how often it will need to be updated).

Software developers then devise a schematic of the program that shows its structure, often displayed as a hierarchy consisting of modules. They develop algorithms, which are sets of instructions or steps needed to solve the problems identified by each module. Developers program the code line by line, or supervise other programmers. They test the modules, locate and correct any errors, and then test the program repeatedly until it is secure, user-friendly, and reliable. They might also add graphics and multimedia components or hand that job over to a graphic designer.

Duties and Responsibilities

- Identifying the purpose and scope of new software
- Outlining new software components and functionality
- Providing detailed instructions for programmers
- Documenting each step necessary to create new software
- Testing to make sure steps are correct and will produce the desired results
- Rewriting programs if desired results are not produced
- Creating graphics, animation, and sound effects for software
- Monitoring maintenance needs and providing upgrades as necessary
- Staying abreast of trends in the industry

OCCUPATION SPECIALTIES

Application Software Developers

Application Software Developers design computer applications, such as word processors and games, for consumers. They may create custom software for a specific customer or commercial software to be sold to the general public. Some applications software developers create complex databases for organizations. They also create programs that people use over the internet and within a company's intranet.

Systems Software Developers

Systems Software Developers create the systems that keep computers functioning properly. These could be operating systems that are part of computers the general public buys or systems built specifically for an organization. Often, systems software developers also build the system's interface, which is what allows users to interact with the computer. Systems software developers create the operating systems that control most of the consumer electronics in use today, including those in phones or cars.

WORK ENVIRONMENT

Physical Environment

Software developers usually work in comfortable offices or from their homes, although some may also travel to meet with clients. Spaces are usually environmentally controlled. Given the nature of the work, developers may be at risk for developing carpel tunnel syndrome, back problems, and eyestrain owing to prolonged use of computers.

Human Environment

Software developers typically report to a project manager and are usually members of a development team, along with programmers, systems architects, quality assurance specialists, and others. The developer might also manage the team or oversee the work done by programmers. A high level of communication and cooperation is usually necessary for success. Many developers, however, work alone and are responsible only to their clients.

Relevant Skills and Abilities

Analytical Skills
- Identifying technical problems
- Using logical reasoning

Communication Skills
- Speaking and writing effectively
- Using diagrams and flowcharts

Interpersonal/Social Skills
- Being able to work independently and as a member of a team

Organization & Management Skills
- Organizing information or materials
- Paying attention to and handling details
- Performing routine work
- Supervising others as necessary

Planning & Research Skills
- Creating ideas
- Laying out a strategy

Technological Environment

Software developers use a variety of stationary and portable computers and computer devices, video game consoles, and related hardware. They use and interface with various operating systems and database management programs. While software developers do not necessarily do programming, they should be familiar with various computer and markup languages, including C++, Java, ColdFusion, and HTML, as well as related compilers and interpreters.

EDUCATION, TRAINING, AND ADVANCEMENT

High School/Secondary

Students should take a strong college-preparatory program that includes English, chemistry, physics, and four years of mathematics, including trigonometry, calculus, and statistics. Computer science or technology, engineering, and electronics courses are also important. Students interested primarily in designing video games or visual-heavy programs should take computer graphics and drawing courses.

Other potentially beneficial subjects include psychology, sociology, and business. Participation in technology clubs, science fairs, mathematics competitions, and other related extracurricular activities is encouraged, as is independent study and creation of programs.

Suggested High School Subjects
- Accounting
- Algebra
- Applied Communication
- Applied Math
- Bookkeeping
- Business & Computer Technology
- Business Data Processing
- Calculus
- College Preparatory
- Computer Programming
- Computer Science
- English
- Geometry
- Graphic Communications
- Keyboarding
- Mathematics
- Statistics
- Trigonometry

Famous First

The first software program to receive a patent was a program called Swift-Answer, designed in 1981 by Satya Pal Asija of St. Paul, Minn. The program searched a database in response to a query posed by a user. Since that time, applications for software patents have become so numerous that the U.S. Patent Office can barely keep up—and patent litigation (one person or firm suing another over allegations of patent infringement) has become a multibillion-dollar industry.

College/Postsecondary

Although some employers consider job applicants with an associate degree, most prefer to hire workers with a bachelor's degree or higher in computer science, computer engineering, or a related technical field. Prospective software developers must be familiar with different types of computers and operating systems, systems organization and architecture, data structures and algorithms, computation theory, and other related topics. Internships and independent projects are recommended.

Related College Majors
- Computer Engineering
- Computer Engineering Technology
- Computer Maintenance Technology
- Computer Programming
- Computer Science
- Design & Visual Communications
- Educational/Instructional Media Design
- Graphic Design, Commercial Art & Illustration
- Information Sciences & Systems
- Management Information Systems & Business Data Processing

Adult Job Seekers

Adults with a computer science or programming background who are returning to the field can update their skills and knowledge by taking continuing education courses offered by software vendors or colleges. Some courses are available online. Those with family obligations might want to consider self-employment, although regular full-time employment may offer more financial stability. Professional associations may provide networking opportunities, as well as job openings and connections to potential clients.

Advancement is partially dependent on the size of the company and the scale of projects. In large companies, software developers with leadership skills typically move into project management and higher-ranked positions as experience and education warrant. Experienced developers may also establish their own businesses, while developers with advanced degrees may move into college teaching.

Professional Certification and Licensure

There are no mandatory licenses or certifications needed for these positions, although voluntary certification from the Institute of Electrical and Electronics Engineers (IEEE), the Institute for Certification of Computing Professionals (ICCP), and other professional organizations can be especially advantageous for job hunting and networking. Software developers can be certified as Software Development Associates (CSDA) or Software Development Professionals (CSDP) through IEEE or as Computing Professionals (CCP) and Associate Computing Professionals (ACP) through ICCP. Software developers are encouraged to consult prospective employers and credible professional associations within the field as to the relevancy and value of any voluntary certification program.

Additional Requirements

Software developers must have excellent conceptual skills in addition to nuts-and-bolts programming skills. Although some developers may serve as the "creative genius" behind an important project, the first requirement is a combination of conceptual and logical skills.

Fun Fact

Portio Research estimates that 1.2 billion people worldwide were using mobile apps at the end of 2012, a figure estimated to grow at a 29.8 percent rate each year and reach 4.4 billion users by the end of 2017.

Source: socialmediatoday.com

EARNINGS AND ADVANCEMENT

Earnings for software developers vary depending on the size and location of the employer and the education, experience and certification of the employee. Median annual earnings of software developers were $96,444 in 2012. The lowest ten percent earned less than $61,162, and the highest ten percent earned more than $146,514.

Software developers may receive paid vacations, holidays, and sick days; life and health insurance; and retirement benefits. These are usually paid by the employer.

Metropolitan Areas with the Highest Employment Level in This Occupation (Applications Developer)

Metropolitan area	Employment[1]	Employment per thousand jobs	Hourly mean wage
Seattle-Bellevue-Everett, WA	35,650	25.29	$48.99
New York-White Plains-Wayne, NY-NJ	33,360	6.47	$50.86
Washington-Arlington-Alexandria, DC-VA-MD-WV	28,360	12.10	$50.56
San Jose-Sunnyvale-Santa Clara, CA	24,160	26.89	$56.06
Boston-Cambridge-Quincy, MA	19,950	11.66	$50.35

(1) Does not include self-employed. Source: Bureau of Labor Statistics, 2012

Metropolitan Areas with the Highest Employment Level in This Occupation (Systems Developer)

Metropolitan area	Employment[1]	Employment per thousand jobs	Hourly mean wage
Washington-Arlington-Alexandria, DC-VA-MD-WV	28,600	12.20	$54.88
San Jose-Sunnyvale-Santa Clara, CA	24,790	27.58	$61.13
Boston-Cambridge-Quincy, MA	19,430	11.35	$53.93
Seattle-Bellevue-Everett, WA	13,670	9.70	$51.01
Los Angeles-Long Beach-Glendale, CA	13,280	3.43	$54.80

(1) Does not include self-employed. Source: Bureau of Labor Statistics, 2012

EMPLOYMENT AND OUTLOOK

Software developers held about 978,000 jobs nationally in 2012. (586,000 were applications developers, and 392,000 were systems developers.) Employment of software developers is expected to grow much faster than the average for all occupations through the year 2020, which means employment is projected to increase 29 percent or more. The increasing uses of the internet, and mobile technology such as wireless internet, have created a demand for a wide variety of new products. In addition, information security concerns have created new software needs. Concerns over cyber security should result in businesses and government continuing to rely on security software that protects their networks from attack. The growth of this technology in the next ten years will lead to an increased need for these workers to design this type of software.

Employment Trend, Projected 2010–20

Software Developers, Systems Software: 32%

Software Developers: 30%

Software Developers, Applications: 28%

Total, All Occupations: 14%

Note: "All Occupations" includes all occupations in the U.S. Economy Source: U.S. Bureau of Labor Statistics, Employment Projections Program

Related Occupations
- Computer & Information Systems Manager
- Computer Engineer
- Computer Operator
- Computer Programmer
- Computer Security Specialist
- Computer Support Specialist

- Computer Systems Analyst
- Computer-Control Tool Programmer
- Information Technology Project Manager
- Multimedia Artist & Animator
- Network & Computer Systems Administrator
- Network Systems & Data Communications Analyst
- Web Administrator
- Website Designer

Related Military Occupations
- Computer Programmer
- Computer Systems Specialist
- Graphic Designer & Illustrator

Conversation With . . .
CRAIG KAHN

Software Developer, 34 years

1. What was your individual career path in terms of education, entry-level job, or other significant opportunity?

Although I have a bachelor of arts degree, my education did not include any courses in computer science. I wish it had and I certainly recommend taking as many courses in computer science as possible if one's desired profession is to write software code. My education in software programming was strictly "on the job" at first, although I did take classes eventually. My first foray into programming came out of necessity. I was at a company that ran ski trips, via bus, to ski resorts in New England. We were dealing with multiple groups on multiple buses going to multiple resorts utilizing multiple rooms and types of lodging. In addition, some individuals needed rentals and/or lessons. This was 1979 and we were keeping track of all of this information by hand. The PC hadn't been invented yet (MS-DOS, the first popular operating system, had yet to be developed) but the desktop computer existed. It was actually the size of a desktop. Our company bought a dual 8" floppy disk drive computer running the CPM operating system. I learned how to program using a database program called dBase II.

2. Are there many job opportunities in your profession? In what specific areas?

I get the sense that there is a significant demand for programmers who can do more than merely write code. People are looking for programmers who can develop, or help develop, a complete application, including designing the user interface and developing the logic necessary for the program to work. The pure "coding" work seems to be going overseas.

3. What do you wish you had known going into this profession?

I wish I had taken classes and was more informed – there would have been less trial and error and I would have been up to speed much more quickly.

4. How do you see your profession changing in the next five years?

This is a tough one to call. My niche is developing small- to medium-scale applications for clients that want to move from keeping track of things on paper to being able to enter, retrieve and report on that information via computer. I think this will pretty much stay the same.

5. What role will technology play in those changes, and what skills will be required?

It's difficult to predict how the computer programming profession will change in the next five years. A lot will depend on the economy and the political environment, especially in regards to outsourcing. The good news is that certain types of programming cannot be shipped overseas because they require a lot of face-to-face meetings to go over and revise specifications. Basically, any development that would be considered "Agile Software Development," where requirements and solutions evolve over time as a result of working with others, would most likely need to be local.

As technology evolves, different skill sets will be needed. For example, 10 years ago a programmer didn't need to know much about web programming. These days it is essential to know how to develop for the desktop and for the web. I suspect that as smartphones become more powerful, and as tablets become more common, a requirement may be for an application to work among all platforms.

6. Do you have any general advice or additional professional insights to share with someone interested in your profession?

The most important requirement for a software developer is to be aware of what is going on in the world of technology and embrace the advances and changes. Even if you don't deem it necessary to learn how to use the newest technology, you should at least know it's out there and be ready to absorb and learn at a moment's notice.

Also, one of the things clients look for is someone with good communication skills – including being a good listener. If the choice is between two equally good coders, the one who the client feels can "get it" – and can explain what he or she is doing – will get the job.

7. Can you suggest a valuable "try this" for students considering a career in your profession?

I would suggest coming up with an idea for a program and spending time developing it in one's language of choice. Make mistakes and learn on your own time instead of on the client's time. If a potential client wants to know what you've developed in the past, you'll have something to show them.

SELECTED SCHOOLS

Many colleges and universities have bachelor's degree programs in computer science; some have programs in software developments, specifically. The student may also gain initial training in programming at a community college. Below are listed some of the more prominent four-year institutions in this field.

California Institute of Technology
1200 E. California Boulevard
Pasadena, CA 91125
626.395.6811
www.caltech.edu

Carnegie Mellon University
5000 Forbes Avenue
Pittsburgh, PA 15213
412.268.2000
www.cmu.edu

Cornell University
401 Thurston Avenue
Ithaca, NY 14850
607.255.5241
www.cornell.edu

Georgia Institute of Technology
225 North Avenue NW
Atlanta, GA 30332
404.894.2000
www.gatech.edu

Massachusetts Institute of Technology
77 Massachusetts Avenue
Cambridge, MA 02139
617.253.1000
www.mit.edu

Stanford University
450 Serra Mall
Stanford, CA 94305
650.723.2300
www.stanford.edu

University of California, Berkeley
101 Sproul Hall
Berkeley, CA 94704
510.642.6000
www.berkeley.edu

University of Illinois, Urbana, Champaign
601 E. John Street
Champaign, IL 61820
217.333-1000
illinois.edu

University of Michigan, Ann Arbor
1031 Greene Street
Ann Arbor, MI 48109
734.764.1817
www.umich.edu

University of Texas, Austin
110 Inner Campus Drive
Austin, TX 78712
512.471.3434
www.utexas.edu

MORE INFORMATION

Association for Computing Machinery
2 Penn Plaza, Suite 701
New York, NY 10121-0701
800.342.6626
www.acm.org

Computing Research Association
1828 L Street NW, Suite 800
Washington, DC 20036
202.234.2111
www.cra.org

Institute for the Certification of Computer Professionals
2400 East Devon Avenue, Suite 281
Des Plaines, IL 60018-4610
800.843.8227
www.iccp.org

Institute of Electrical and Electronics Engineers (IEEE) Computer Society
2001 L Street, NW, Suite 700
Washington, DC 20036-4928
202.371.0101
www.computer.org

National Center for Women and Information Technology
University of Colorado
Campus Box 322 UCB
Boulder, CO 80308
303.735.6671
www.ncwit.org

Software & Information Industry Association
1090 Vermont Avenue NW, Sixth Fl.
Washington, DC 20005
202.289.7442
www.asiia.net

Sally Driscoll/Editor

Telecommunications Equipment Installer/ Repairer

Snapshot

Career Cluster: Electronics; Maintenance & Repair; Technology

Interests: Traveling, working with your hands, solving problems, working with tools

Earnings (Yearly Average): $54,030

Employment & Outlook: Slower than Average Growth Expected

OVERVIEW

Sphere of Work

Telecommunications equipment installers and repairers, also known as telecom technicians, set up, maintain, service, and repair networks and devices that carry communication signals, including internet connections. These signals are carried over telephone lines and fiber-optic cable. Telecom technicians perform their work in homes, commercial facilities, and office buildings. Technicians

may take devices that require significant work to a repair shop. Technicians also perform installations of telecom equipment.

Work Environment

Work environments for telecommunications equipment installers and repairers vary for each job. Offices, commercial facilities, and homes predominate. Depending on the job, workers may have to climb ladders or use trucks with lift buckets to reach telephone wires and rooftops. Technicians also work in communication centers, where telephone calls are routed. Job locations and repair shops are usually well lit. Field workers spend some time traveling to and from clients. Working high off the ground in utility trucks can be dangerous, and safety guidelines should be followed. Telecom technicians also work with electrical components that can pose safety risks.

Profile

Working Conditions: Work Indoors
Physical Strength: Light to Medium Work
Education Needs: On-The-Job Training, Technical/Community College
Licensure/Certification: Usually Not Required
Physical Abilities Not Required: No Heavy Labor
Opportunities For Experience: Military Service
Holland Interest Score*: REI, RES

* See Appendix A

Occupation Interest

Each day of work can present a telecommunications equipment installer and repairer with a different problem, so technicians must be able to apply skills and knowledge in varying circumstances. The profession typically attracts individuals who enjoy solving problems and working with their hands outside of an office environment. A telecommunications equipment installer and repairer must be willing to stay abreast of new technologies, tools, and repair methods. Driving to and from clients is often required, so a repairer should enjoy traveling.

A Day in the Life—Duties and Responsibilities

Telecom technicians repair and maintain telecommunications systems that keep the public connected. These systems include telephone networks, switchboards, computer equipment, and radios. Field repairers will travel to a client's location, which may be a home, office, or commercial building, to perform maintenance and repairs. Some technicians will work at the central offices of telephone companies and internet service providers.

When a client calls for a repair, a technician will travel to the location with tools and other necessary equipment. In order to help diagnose the problem, the worker will examine telephone wires both inside and outside the house, which may require him or her to inspect lines attached to telephone poles. For internet malfunctions, the worker will test the connection using basic troubleshooting techniques and electronic devices. Technicians who work with radio technology service both stationary equipment on transmission towers and mobile equipment in vehicles. If the worker decides that a repair cannot be performed on location, he or she will either call in more technicians or bring the equipment back to a repair shop for service.

Technicians who work at central offices maintain and service telephone exchanges. Exchanges are systems that connect telephone calls. Workers test connections on exchanges to ensure that the communication links are functioning correctly. These exchanges can sometimes feature complex digital components.

Duties and Responsibilities

- Installing, rearranging, replacing and removing the complex switching and dialing equipment used in central offices
- Testing, repairing and maintaining all types of local and toll switching equipment that automatically connects lines when customers dial numbers
- Locating problems by using testboards or by entering instructions into a computer terminal

OCCUPATION SPECIALTIES

Central Office Technicians

Central Office Technicians install, test, analyze defects and repair telecommunications circuits and equipment in central telecom company offices.

PBX Installers and Repairers

PBX Installers and Repairers install, analyze and repair defects in telecommunications switchboards, network systems, and Voice Over Internet applications.

Station Installers and Repairers

Station Installers and Repairers—also known as home installers and repairers—set up and repair telecommunications equipment in customers' homes and businesses. For example, they set up modems to install telephone, internet, or cable television services.

WORK ENVIRONMENT

Physical Environment

Telecom technicians typically work in repair shops and on site at the offices of telecom/telephone companies. Field repairers work at a variety of locations, including offices and homes, in all weather. Their duties can involve working off the ground on telephone poles, ladders, and lift trucks.

Human Environment

Telecommunications equipment installers and repairers collaborate with supervisors and colleagues. They also work closely with clients and often work to make sure clients have a clear understanding of how their telecommunications systems work.

Relevant Skills and Abilities

Communication Skills
- Speaking effectively

Interpersonal/Social Skills
- Being able to work independently
- Cooperating with others
- Working as a member of a team

Organization & Management Skills
- Making decisions
- Paying attention to and handling details
- Performing duties that change frequently

Research & Planning Skills
- Developing evaluation strategies
- Using logical reasoning

Technical Skills
- Performing technical work
- Working with machines, tools or other objects

Technological Environment

Telecom technicians work with a wide range of tools and technologies. Technicians use basic hand tools, including screwdrivers and wire cutters, as well as specialized equipment such as spectrum analyzers and polarity probes. Telecommunications equipment includes electronic components and color-coded wires. Those who work in the field also use vans, ladders, and lift trucks.

EDUCATION, TRAINING, AND ADVANCEMENT

High School/Secondary

Employers typically require applicants to have a high school diploma or an equivalent certificate. Any high school courses involving electronics, computers, or mathematics will give future telecommunications equipment repairers a good understanding of industry fundamentals.

Suggested High School Subjects
- Applied Communication
- Applied Math
- Blueprint Reading
- Computer Science
- Electricity & Electronics
- English
- Shop Math
- Shop Mechanics
- Welding

Famous First

The first radio telephone service for commercial use was launched in 1920, between Los Angeles and Santa Catalina Island, California. A radio link connected the two locations via telephone lines. The service ran for three years, when it was replaced by a cable in order to provide privacy to users. Operators of the original service pictured.

College/Postsecondary

Most employers require applicants to have completed relevant postsecondary training. Technicians who work at central offices are usually required to have a degree in a relevant field. Vocational, technical, and trade schools offer postsecondary training programs. Training programs in electronics repair, computer science, and communication technology will greatly benefit an aspiring telecommunications equipment repairer. Typically, these associate degree programs last two years, but an individual interested in more advanced work in the telecommunications industry may want to consider a four-year program.

Related College Majors
- Computer Engineering Technology
- lectrical, Electronic & Communications Engineering Technology
- Instrument Calibration & Repair
- Instrumentation Technology

Adult Job Seekers

Anyone interested in a profession in the telecommunication industry should build up a strong background of knowledge and skills. The best way to do this is through a formal associate degree training program at a technical, trade, or vocational school. For individuals with no experience in the trade, a formal training program is essential. Researching reputable schools is important before enrolling. Being a telecommunications equipment installer and repairer covers a wide range of knowledge and skills, so an individual should approach his or her training with a broad perspective. Since telecommunications technology is always developing, a technician needs to be willing to keep learning throughout his or her career.

Professional Certification and Licensure

Commonly, employers provide telecommunications equipment installers and repairers with on-the-job training. More experienced workers or supervisors train new hires. Training can last anywhere from a few weeks to several months. Some employers will send new hires and experienced workers alike to training sessions to learn about new technologies, products, and repair methods. Equipment manufacturers will sometimes send a representative to companies to train employees on new products.

Certification is required for individuals interested in performing more complex tasks and for specialization in a specific area of telecommunications. Employers dictate which employees need certification. Organizations like the Telecommunications Industry Association (TIA) offer certification programs for repairers in various areas, including telecommunications infrastructure standards and land mobile communications standards. Manufacturers also offer certification on equipment they produce.

Individuals interested in advancing their career should seek out certification. The more certifications an employee has, the greater his or her chance of higher pay and promotions.

Additional Requirements

Telecommunications equipment installers and repairers must possess great dexterity to handle the wires, cables, tools, and electronic components used in the industry. Since most telecommunication wires are color coded, workers must also be able to distinguish colors well. Those who plan to work in the field should be in good physical shape and able to endure climbing, kneeling, and long periods on their feet. Repairers should also have good communication skills in order to collaborate with colleagues, supervisors, and clients.

EARNINGS AND ADVANCEMENT

Earnings of telecommunications equipment repairers vary by employer and location. Median annual earnings of telecommunications equipment installers and repairers were $54,030 in 2013. The lowest ten percent earned less than $30,070, and the highest ten percent earned more than $75,690.

Union contracts determine paid holidays and vacations based on seniority. Other benefits include paid sick leave; group life, medical, and dental insurance; vision care; accidental benefits; educational benefits; retirement and disability pensions; a savings plan and an employee stock ownership plan.

Metropolitan Areas with the Highest
Employment Level in this Occupation

Metropolitan area	Employment [1]	Employment per thousand jobs	Hourly mean wage
New York-White Plains-Wayne, NY-NJ	7,930	1.51	$32.62
Chicago-Joliet-Naperville, IL	7,610	2.06	$26.62
Los Angeles-Long Beach-Glendale, CA	7,300	1.84	$26.69
Atlanta-Sandy Springs-Marietta, GA	6,880	2.98	$25.17
Dallas-Plano-Irving, TX	5,750	2.68	$23.49
Houston-Sugar Land-Baytown, TX	3,470	1.26	$23.23
Tampa-St. Petersburg-Clearwater, FL	3,130	2.72	$21.50
Fort Lauderdale-Pompano Beach-Deerfield Beach, FL	2,900	3.96	$26.67
Phoenix-Mesa-Glendale, AZ	2,870	1.61	$27.87
Washington-Arlington-Alexandria, DC-VA-MD-WV	2,800	1.18	$29.89

[1]Does not include self-employ ed. Source: Bureau of Labor Statistics

EMPLOYMENT AND OUTLOOK

Telecommunications equipment installers and repairers held about 217,000 jobs in 2012. Employment is expected to grow slower than the average for all occupations through the year 2022, which means employment is projected to increase 1 percent to 7 percent. Although the need for installation work will grow as companies seek to upgrade their telecommunications networks, there will be a declining need for maintenance work because of increasingly reliable equipment. Most job openings will occur as workers transfer to other occupations or leave the labor force.

Employment Trend, Projected 2012–22

Total, All Occupations: 11%

Installation, Maintenance, and Repair Occupations (All): 10%

Telecommunications Equipment Installers and Repairers: 4%

Note: "All Occupations" includes all occupations in the U.S. Economy. Source: U.S. Bureau of Labor Statistics, Employment Projections Program

Related Occupations
- Biomedical Equipment Technician
- Computer Service Technician
- Electrical Line Installer & Repairer
- Electrician
- Electronic Equipment Repairer
- Office Machine Repairer
- Telecommunications Line Installer/Repairer
- Telephone Installer & Repairer
- Television & Radio Repairer

Related Occupations
- Communications Equipment Repairer
- Communications Manager

Conversation With . . .
ROBERT H. PICKNELL, CETma

Senior Technician
Advanced Communications and Electronics, Inc.
Albuquerque, NM
In the industry, 20 years

1. What was your individual career path in terms of education/training, entry-level job, or other significant opportunity?

I've always had a fascination with electricity and electronics, but it wasn't until later in life that I had the discipline to educate myself and to see entry-level jobs as opportunities for advancement.

I started out as a volunteer at an easy listening and inspirational radio station in the Midwest and worked as an on-air announcer for a few hours every week. When the General Manager/Engineer found out I was interested in electronics, I started working with him. Upon his departure, I became the station's first paid part-time engineer.

That's when I started taking night classes for computer networking. I moved to another company and became an engineer for seven radio stations. That company held twice-annual conferences for their engineers, where I learned a lot by being around all those years of experience, as well as about the importance of networking. Having the ability to call other people for help and ideas was invaluable.

This eventually led me to the two-way radio and microwave communications field of electronics. For 11 years, I have worked for a company that handles about half of the 911 dispatch centers around the state of New Mexico. This job affords me the opportunity to work in various aspects of the electronics industry, including telecommunications, two-way radios, and microwave communications.

2. What are the most important skills and/or qualities for someone in your profession?

The ability to articulate, both verbally and in writing, what you need to say; the desire to want to learn more about your field; and the desire to work. When times are tough for a company, it's difficult to justify keeping an employee whose only apparent desire is to be paid top-dollar to play solitaire on a computer.

3. What do you wish you had known going into this profession?

That mentors are critical. People in this vast field of electronics are willing to be mentors to those willing to learn, and each mentor usually has one or two areas that they are strong in. If possible, find several.

That education is not static. You must be willing to continue your education throughout your entire life.

That education comes in many forms. Classroom education is good to build a foundation and to learn the fundamentals. But there's also on-the-job training; trade publications for keeping abreast of changes; manufacturer websites and training programs that help you stay current and relevant; and trade certifications and memberships.

4. Are there many job opportunities in your profession, in what specific areas?

With cell phones, home computers, and world communications, the electronics industry has exploded and the need for technicians has never been greater than it is today.

The electronics industry covers nearly all aspects of life and fields of interest. A few areas that are growing rapidly include telecommunications—cell phones, satellites, DSL, cable, broadcast communications, computers; automotive, and power—wind, solar, nuclear and gas and oil.

5. How do you see your profession changing in the next five years, what role will technology play in those changes, and what skills will be required?

If recent history is any measure of things to come, we can expect this industry to expand exponentially for the foreseeable future. A firm understanding of the fundamentals, and in this case of electricity and electronics, will be required if you wish to do more than just replace modules using an instruction manual.

6. What do you enjoy most about your job? What do you enjoy least about your job?

Variety is, without a doubt, the one thing I most like about my job. I seldom know exactly what I will be doing from day-to-day. I have to be able to "think outside the box" on a consistent basis.

I least enjoy dealing with customer support. It can be extremely frustrating, but I do have to say it has helped me tremendously to learn to deal with different types of people and attitudes.

7. **Can you suggest a valuable "try this" for students considering a career in your profession?**

Do an internship. When I was a teenager and wanted to be a truck driver, my parents got me to meet with a truck driver and his "rig." I spoke with him regarding his carrier choice, asked lots of questions, and got to ride in his truck. It didn't take me long to realize that while driving a truck across the county may be a great job for others, it was not for me. Take the time to research a career; it's much easier to change direction at 20 than it is at 40.

SELECTED SCHOOLS

Many technical and community colleges offer programs in telecommunications technology. Commercial trade schools are also an option. Students are advised to consult with their school guidance counselor or research area post-secondary schools to find the right program.

MORE INFORMATION

Communication Workers of America
501 3rd Street NW
Washington, DC 20001
202.434.1100
www.cwa-union.org

National Coalition for Telecommunications Education and Learning
www.nactel.org

Telecommunications Industry Association
2500 Wilson Boulevard, Suite 300
Arlington, VA 22201
703.907.7700
www.tiaonline.org

United States Telecom Association
607 14th Street, NW, Suite 400
Washington, DC 20005-2164
202.326.7300
www.usta.org

Patrick Cooper/Editor

UX Designer

Snapshot

Career Cluster(s): Information Technology
Interests: Computer technology, artistic expression, engineering, consumer psychology
Earnings (Yearly Average): $64,970
Employment & Outlook: Much faster than average growth expected

OVERVIEW

Sphere of Work

UX design is a relatively recent field that typically falls under the general heading of "web design" or "web development." UX designers specialize in creating interactive designs based on user preferences, ergonomics, and user psychology. When applied to web design, UX design typically involves looking at the way that users interact with websites and creating web sites and interactive user interfaces that capitalize on user tendencies and preferences. While often grouped under the category of web development, UX designers can work on a variety of projects including mobile and desktop apps,

software, and user interfaces for operating systems. In comparison to general web design or app development, UX designers may use a variety of specific analysis and metrics tools that help determine how users interact with various aspects of a product or website.

Work Environment

UX designers typically work in office environments, though at least 1 in 7 UX designers and web designers in general are self-employed and remote work is common in the field. Depending on whether the designer is self-employed or works for a company or design firm, UX design can either be a collaborative or largely independent activity. UX designers working for computer firms or design firms typically handle a specific aspect of the design process and will work with other designers, programmers, engineers, and project managers to complete a project.

Profile

Working Conditions: Work Indoors
Physical Strength: Light Work
Education Needs: Associate Degree, Bachelor's Degree
Licensure/Certification: Not Required
Opportunities For Experience: On-the-job training
Holland Interest Score*: CIR

* See Appendix A

Occupation Interest

UX design blends computer programming, graphic design, and user psychology and professionals in the field should have interest in each of these areas. UX designers also need to have strong communication skills, as designers often need to communicate with clients or users about the functionality of their designs. UX design is also an artistic process, and therefore appeals to individuals with interest in art, graphic design, and other creative disciplines.

A Day in the Life—Duties and Responsibilities

Daily activities for a UX designer depend largely on the specifics of the project that he or she is working on and whether the designer is working alone or as part of a design team. Design projects typically start with a client request or an idea for a new project. UX designers, therefore, might spend time meeting with clients or other members of a design team to share ideas and strategize about an upcoming project. Before production begins, designers may use software or physical tools to create a basic map of the project and to refine ideas about the types of programming, design, and software needed to complete the job.

During production, designers may spend time participating in programming or coding or may spend time using digital design tools to create and refine aspects of the user interface or visual design. Each design element, once created, must be tested for functionality and UX designers also typically run numerous rounds of tests on each project to evaluate the way that users interact with the product. The designer may also present prototypes or beta versions of a product to a client or managers in a corporation to get feedback before refining the completed design.

Duties and Responsibilities

- Use computer programs to illustrate and design various graphics
- Develop models of web, app, of software functionality and user interface systems
- Write, correct, and alter various types of coding involved in a web or software project.
- Work with clients, producers, project managers, or employees to complete a project
- Research emerging apps and programs for design, implementation, and user experience analysis
- Create and deliver proposals to clients, managers, and other members of a design team

OCCUPATION SPECIALTIES

UX Researcher

A UX or UI researcher is a specialist that conducts background research on UX design trends and existing products. Researchers run tests and analysis to determine how users interact with the product. UX researchers often use tools and programs designed to analyze user experience like user polls and surveys and automated systems that show how users interact with a site, app, or software program.

Lead Designer

A lead designer is a manager who oversees a design team that may include visual designers, graphic artists, analytics and metrics specialists, and programmers.

UI Developer

A UI developer is responsible for working on the design and programming behind user-interfaces. Typically, UI developers will work with front-end code like HTML and CSS, while also ensuring that products are compatible with multiple types of browsers and operating systems.

Visual Designer

A visual designer is a graphic artist responsible for determining the aesthetics of a digital product, typically an app or website. Designers focus on picking, creating, or modifying fonts, determining the use of colors, and the placement of objects.

Producers

Producers are administrators who oversee the production process. Producers can serve as project managers, or may have one or more project managers working under them. In Web design, producers often meet with clients, handle budgeting and cost management, and oversee programmers, analysts, and designers working on a specific project.

WORK ENVIRONMENT

Physical Environment

Game designers tend to work in office environments, or may work in a cubicle as part of a larger production department. Approximately 1 in 7 web developers were self-employed in 2014, and freelance web/UX designers can choose to work from home or from a private office.

Relevant Skills and Abilities

Communication Skills
- Creating and giving presentations to clients.
- Being able to interpret user requests and needs.

Interpersonal/Social Skills
- Participating in design and development meetings.
- Understanding emotional and personal needs of clients.

Organization & Management Skills
- Time management and the ability to meet deadlines

Research & Planning Skills
- Researching developments in programming and new web design software
- Creating detailed models of web functions for clients.

Technical Skills
- Performing technical work
- Working with computers, programming languages, and hardware
- Skill with drawing, painting, drafting, and modeling

Human Environment

Many web developers work independently and may work from home, while others, working in design firms, may collaborate with other designers, engineers, and human factors specialists to create a finished design. Whether working alone or as part of a team, UX designers should be comfortable meeting with clients and should be comfortable discussing and analyzing designs conversationally to ensure that the finished product meets the client's needs.

Technological Environment

UX design is a highly technical field involving advanced web design techniques. Applicants should have familiarity with HTML programming, including the latest HTML 5 release, and will also benefit from knowledge of database management software like Teradata, Apache Hadoop, and Amazon Kinesis. Developmental software like Apache Maven, C, and C++ is also an recommended, in addition to familiarity with various operating systems like Macintosh OS, Microsoft Windows, and UNIX. In addition, there are a wide variety of apps and programs specifically useful to those interested in UX design. For instance, for the purposes of user testing, the Wufoo online survey system allows designers to poll clients about their user experience, while programs like Verify App provide developers with a way to upload and test website design elements. For longer term analytics there are programs like Crazyegg that provide a "heatmap" of a website, demonstrating the way that users navigate through a page.

EDUCATION, TRAINING, AND ADVANCEMENT

High School/Secondary

Individuals interested in pursuing careers in UX design should take preparatory classes in computer science and graphic/industrial arts. Students are advised to study computer science and, where available, basic programming, but should also study visual art, including graphic design, drawing, and drafting. Individuals should also study English composition and technical writing as UX design often involves writing web copy used in certain projects.

Suggested High School Subjects
- Computer Science
- English
- Graphic Design
- Drafting
- Industrial Arts
- Computer Programming
- Applied Mathematics
- Engineering
- Physics
- Creative Writing

Famous First

Donald "Don" Norman, a cognitive psychologist and designer who became director of the design lab at the University of California, San Diego, is a pioneer in UX design. Norman is credited with coining the term "user experience" to describe his pioneering experiments in user-centered design at Apple Inc. in the mid-1990s. Norman's application of user-centered engineering to computer and web design was based on earlier pioneering theories in user-oriented machine design, such as the development of the first "mouse and pointer" GUI system at Xerox Parc in the 1970s. Norman is widely known for his bestselling book *The Design of Everyday Things*, in 1988, which dealt with consumer psychology and the premise of designing according to user preference.

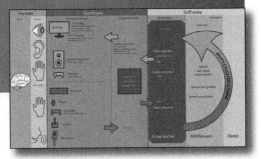

College/Postsecondary

A variety of specific college and postsecondary degrees are available for individuals interested in web development and UX design. Purdue Polytechnic University, for instance, offers a bachelor's degree in "Human Centered Design and Development," that includes specific instruction in front-end development, web development, and user-experience design for products. More generally, individuals interested in a career in UX design can seek out degrees in computer programming, graphic design, or software development and can then develop a specialization in UX design through work experience.

Related College Majors
- Graphic Design
- Web Design
- 3D Design
- Computer Programming
- IT Project Management
- Software Development

Adult Job Seekers

Individuals with experience in web design can apply for positions as UX designers, though companies hiring in the field may have specific requirements, including job experience and knowledge of various programming languages or techniques.

Professional Certification and Licensure

There are not specific licensing requirements for UX designers, though candidates with a background in web design may complete an associate degree in web design and may seek out additional certification in various types of web design or programming languages. Most web design professionals train in HTML programming, and may seek out additional certification in programming languages like JavaScript or SQL. Training in multimedia publishing programs, like Flash is also helpful for those in the field.

Additional Requirements

UX designers need to be keep updated on the latest technology, techniques, and trends for web and software design. Individuals looking to become web or UX designers should be detail oriented as the job often requires writing long sequences of code where minor mistakes can interrupt the functionality of the entire program. In addition, UX designers need to be creative as they are also responsible for designing the appearance of websites or user systems and are also frequently called upon to develop creative solutions to user problems or requests.

Fun Fact

Attention to detail, a focus on immersion, and the desire constantly improve his products made Walt Disney one of the earliest designers of user experience.

Source: https://uxmag.com/articles/walt-disney-the-worlds-first-ux-designer

EARNINGS AND ADVANCEMENT

According to the BLS, the mean hourly wage for web developers was $33.97, though some earned as high as $50-56 an hour. The median salary for web specialists was estimated at $64,970, with the lowest paid 10 percent earning less than $34,770 annually and the highest-paid 10 percent earning in excess of $116,620 per year.

Metropolitan Areas with the Highest Employment Level in this Occupation

Metropolitan area	Employment	Employment per thousand jobs	Hourly mean wage
New York-Jersey City-White Plains, NY-NJ	8,600	1.33	$39.77
Los Angeles-Long Beach-Glendale, CA	5,370	1.31	$33.85
Washington-Arlington-Alexandria, DC-VA-MD-WV	4,310	1.78	$41.75
San Francisco-Redwood City-South San Francisco, CA	3,640	3.57	$46.83
Chicago-Naperville-Arlington Heights, IL	3,630	1.02	$38.01
Seattle-Bellevue-Everett, WA	3,480	2.26	$44.11
Dallas-Plano-Irving, TX	2,950	1.27	$35.06
San Jose-Sunnyvale-Santa Clara, CA	2,930	2.89	$51.68
Minneapolis-St. Paul-Bloomington, MN-WI	2,900	1.54	$33.44
Boston-Cambridge-Newton, MA	2,590	1.47	$38.83

Source: Bureau of Labor Statistics

EMPLOYMENT AND OUTLOOK

Thanks to the continued proliferation of web development in corporations, the web design industry was growing at a rate of 27 percent annually, which is more than three times the average of 7 percent across all occupational categories. The BLS estimated there could be as many as 39,500 job opportunities in the field between 2014 and 2024. UX designers and other web designers who have completed a Bachelor's degree or higher may be more likely to be offered managerial positions, such as becoming a lead designer or team leader.

Related Occupations
- Computer and Information Systems Managers
- Computer Programmers
- Computer Systems Analysts
- Database Administrators
- Software Developers
- Multimedia Artists and Animators
- Graphic Designers

Related Occupations
- Army IT Systems Administrator

Conversation With . . .
JOHNNY CHEW

Director/Animator, Self-employed, johnnychew.com
Los Angeles, California
Multimedia Artist and Animator, 10 years

1. What was your individual career path in terms of education/training, entry-level job, or other significant opportunity?

I've always loved and been fascinated by animation. In high school, I taught myself how to use Adobe Flash, doing some simple animations. At the end of high school, an art teacher connected me with a small studio outside of Boston where I began interning two days a week. That eventually turned into a full-time position and I ended up working there for two years. After that I attended the Massachusetts College of Art and Design, where I really got interested in multimedia art and doing less traditional animation.

Once I graduated, I worked at another studio in Boston for a year before deciding that the studio life wasn't for me. I quit that job and did freelance work and ended up teaching animation at my alma mater for a year. I got connected to a director's rep and made the move out to Los Angeles. I'm now doing freelance work ranging from editing and post-effects to directing and animating. I've worked for Nintendo, Toyota, Cinemax, Capitol Records, PBS, Audi and lots of various record labels doing lyric videos and editing. I've worked on television commercials, music videos, title sequences, documentaries and video games.

2. What are the most important skills and/or qualities for someone in your profession?

I think the most important skill to have in animation and multimedia art is to be creative within limitations. Time, budget, and facilities are all limitations that you'll face constantly. The ability to work creatively and to work around problems and issues within those limits is a difficult but important skill set to learn. Being able to design a project with a three-day turn around and still make something striking and something that is your own has been invaluable in my experience.

3. What do you wish you had known going into this profession?

That there is no singular path to follow to success. Going into this field, a lot of my friends and I thought there was some sort of checklist of steps to follow in order to "break in." That couldn't be further from the truth. There is no one way to go about it besides trying things out and trusting your gut. Your path may be different from your friend's path and that's OK.

4. **Are there many job opportunities in your profession? In what specific areas?**

There are tons of job opportunities in multimedia art. Most projects involve lots of people, so there are many positions that open up with each new project. It's also a field that's constantly growing, so even when one studio closes, another will pop up to take its place. It's a newer form of content that the internet has made very popular, so there are lots of people and companies looking to do it.

5. **How do you see your profession changing in the next five years? What role will technology play in those changes, and what skills will be required?**

I think the internet will continue to change the way multimedia art is consumed and distributed. It's going to keep moving towards alternative forms of distribution like Netflix or Hulu, creating much more opportunity for a wide variety of work to be created and seen. I think that because of these newer channels for distribution, we're going to see a wider range of style and content of work being shown. A good web presence and a unique, individual style of work is going to be invaluable going forward.

6. **What do you enjoy most about your job? What do you enjoy least about your job?**

The novelty of making an image or video from scratch still hasn't worn off for me. Animating something moving and then going back and watching it still feels like magic to me. The least favorite part of the job is how little the outside world knows about what goes into it. You'll have to spend more time than you'd imagine trying to communicate why something can or cannot be done.

7. **Can you suggest a valuable "try this" for students considering a career in your profession?**

The best thing you can do if you're thinking about getting into multimedia art or animation is to find free or trial animation software, or just get a ton of paper and dive in head first. There's certainly a learning curve to the software and traditional animation, but the big test is whether you enjoy sitting and drawing or creating frame after frame for hours only to end up with five seconds of footage after a full day's worth of work. Don't worry about learning all the ins and outs before you start creating; just go for it and focus on whether or not you're having fun while you're doing it. If you are, this might be the right field for you.

MORE INFORMATION

IEEE Computer Society
2001 L Street NW, Suite 700
Washington, DC 20036-4928
202-371-0101
www.computer.org

CompTIA
3500 Lacey Road, Suite 100
Downers Grove, IL, 60515
866-835-8020
www.comptia.org

Computer Research Association
1828 L Street, NW, Suite 800
Washington, D.C. 20036-4632
202-234-2111
www.cra.org

Association for Computing Machinery (ACM)
2 Penn Plaza, Suite 701
New York, NY 10121-0701
800-342-6626
www.acm.org

National Center for Women & Information Technology (NCWIT)
University of Colorado
Campus Box 417 UCB
Boulder, CO 80309-0322
303-735-6671
www.ncwit.org

Micah Issitt/Editor

Web Administrator

OVERVIEW

Sphere of Work

Web administrators build, maintain, and monitor web-based information and communications systems. Businesses and organizations employ web administrators to manage their day-to-day computing and networking needs, including server management, e-mail functionality, data storage, and intranet systems. Web administrators oversee all network security measures, apply computer-system updates, back up system data in case of emergency or disaster, and work with staff members to implement new systems and improve usability. In addition to staying abreast of staff

and organizational computing needs, web administrators must be knowledgeable of emerging trends in software and hardware and of potential threats such as viruses and malware.

Work Environment

Web administrators work primarily indoors in administrative settings. While interaction with other staff members is a major facet of the job, much of the work of web administrators is done alone, either at a traditional desk setting with one or more computer monitors or in rooms that house servers and other network equipment. Web administrators are often required to travel to different places within an organization or on a business campus to troubleshoot problems and answer computer-related questions.

Profile

Working Conditions: Work Indoors
Physical Strength: Light Work
Education Needs: Junior/
 Technical/Community College,
 Bachelor's Degree
Licensure/Certification:
 Recommended
Opportunities For Experience:
 Internship, Volunteer Work
Holland Interest Score*: CIR

* See Appendix A

Occupation Interest

Web administration traditionally attracts technologically savvy professionals who have had a lifelong passion for computing. In addition to possessing an extensive background in computers, web administrators also come from academic and professional backgrounds pertaining to communications, media, electronics, customer service, and business administration. Web administration requires deft reasoning, critical analysis, and active listening skills.

A Day in the Life—Duties and Responsibilities

The day-to-day responsibilities of web administrators include tasks related to preventing and correcting system errors, troubleshooting user problems, detecting and reporting security breaches, and developing new network technologies for use within their particular organization.

Business, educational, and organizational computer networks run a constant risk of being impaired, observed, or damaged by outside threats such as viruses, hackers, and other malicious parties. Web administrators combat these threats by doing a daily surveillance of network systems and regularly testing and monitoring system backup plans and security software. If a network's security or infrastructure is compromised, it is the role of the web administrator to minimize the damage and eliminate threats as soon as possible. Administrators must be equally vigilant about looking for breakdowns in hardware systems that can occur from long-term use.

Web administrators also use their extensive knowledge of contemporary networking-systems technology to work with other professionals within their organization to develop new web-based technologies. Such projects traditionally entail adapting network technologies and computerized systems to the specific needs of an organization in order to expand employee interaction, improve

Duties and Responsibilities

- Analyzing log files to collect information about site usage
- Correcting website or server problems quickly
- Updating website content
- Monitoring and backing up applications in the event of a security breach or if disaster recovery is required
- Encrypting data and erecting firewalls to protect confidential information
- Consulting with web developers to discuss and solve site issues
- Incorporating site upgrades and updates as necessary
- Performing site tests to ensure that all recovery plans and security measures are functioning properly
- Staying up to date with the latest technology

WORK ENVIRONMENT

Transferable Skills and Abilities

Communication Skills
- Speaking effectively
- Writing concisely
- Listening attentively
- Reading Well

Interpersonal/Social Skills
- Being able to work independently

Organization & Management Skills
- Paying attention to and handling details
- Performing duties that change frequently
- Managing time
- Managing equipment/materials
- Coordinating tasks
- Making decisions
- Handling challenging situations

Research & Planning Skills
- Identifying problems
- Determining alternatives
- Gathering information
- Solving problems
- Defining needs
- Analyzing information
- Developing evaluation strategies

Technical Skills
- Performing scientific, mathematical and technical work
- Working with machines, tools or other objects
- Working with data or numbers
- Using technology to process information (SCANS Workplace Competency – Information)

customer communication, or create an online database of company projects, training, or sales data.

Physical Environment

Office and administrative settings predominate. Web administrators work in businesses, nonprofit organizations, colleges and universities, and governments.

Human Environment

Self-discipline is required, given the large number of tasks that web administrators must complete individually or with small teams. Patience, listening skills, and the ability to explain complex technological concepts are also beneficial.

Technological Environment

Web administration involves an array of complex computerized technology, from data-communication systems to servers, intranets, software, and wireless technology. Web administrators

- Understanding which technology is appropriate for a task
- Applying the technology to a task
- Maintaining and repairing technology

EDUCATION, TRAINING, AND ADVANCEMENT

are traditionally well versed in several computer-programming languages.

High School/Secondary

High school students can best prepare for a career in web administration by completing as many computer-science courses as possible, including introductory programming, networking, desktop publishing, and word processing. Studying algebra, calculus, and trigonometry is also beneficial. Advanced-placement (AP) classes in computer-related subjects are especially recommended. Summer volunteer programs or internships in relevant fields can help students attain hands-on experience that will bolster their college applications.

Suggested High School Subjects
- Algebra
- Applied Communication
- Applied Math
- Business & Computer Technology
- Business Data Processing
- Calculus
- College Preparatory
- Computer Programming
- Computer Science
- English
- Geometry
- Keyboarding
- Mathematics

Famous First

The first web browser was developed by Tim Berners-Lee in 1990; it led to the World Wide Web protocol on the internet. Early web browsers included Mosaic, Netscape Navigator, and Internet Explorer.

- Statistics
- Trigonometry

College/Postsecondary

Postsecondary course work exclusively dedicated to web administration is an emerging academic discipline. Few colleges and universities offer degree programs specifically in web administration, so aspiring web administrators usually complete postsecondary education in another computer-related field. While a bachelor's degree is customary for most administrator jobs, positions in smaller companies may only require the applicant to have completed relevant certificate-level course work.

Network-security professionals customarily complete courses in telecommunications, software and web security, server administration, and computer-operating-system management. Many of these topics are covered in programs offering associates degrees and professional certificates in web administration.

More advanced course work, such as that required for a bachelor's degree in computer science, traditionally entails classes in project management, business security, wireless-systems administration, and financial-systems management. Additional course work in rhetorical communication, project management, and technical writing can also be beneficial to postsecondary students interested in a career in web administration.

Related College Majors
- Computer Installation & Repair
- Computer Maintenance Technology
- Computer Programming

- Computer Science
- Data Processing Technology
- Information Sciences & Systems
- Management Information Systems & Business Data Processing

Adult Job Seekers

Web administration requires an extensive education in computers and networking, though not all education must be attained in a formal setting. Some web administrators are self-taught. Adult job seekers with an extensive background in computer science as a hobby may be able to transition to the field with ease. Other job seekers interested in switching careers to become a web administrator can become viable candidates for positions in smaller organizations by completing associate- or certificate-level course work.

Professional Certification and Licensure

Although certification is not typically required, product vendors and software firms offer certification and recommend that professionals who work with their products be certified. Voluntary certification is also available through various organizations associated with computer specialists.

Additional Requirements

One of the most difficult parts of being a professional web administrator is explaining network systems and various other computer programs and hardware to users who may not understand the complex technology. This part of the role requires deft interpersonal and instructional communication skills and patience.

Fun Fact

The maximum length of a domain name is 63 characters. While a number of sites claim to have been the first to have the longest domain name, the shortest isn't in dispute:. www.g.cn was purchased by Google to help Chinese users locate Google more easily.

Source: http://easily.co.uk/10-Things-You-Really-Didnt-Know-About-Domain-Names.html

EARNINGS AND ADVANCEMENT

According to the Robert Half Technology Salary Guide, median annual earnings of web administrators were $79,625 in 2014. The lowest ten percent earned less than $63,500, and the highest ten percent earned more than $95,750.

Web administrators may receive paid vacations, holidays, and sick days; life and health insurance and retirement benefits. These are usually paid by the employer.

EMPLOYMENT AND OUTLOOK

Web administrators held about 180,000 jobs nationally in 2014. Employment of web administrators is expected to grow as fast as the average for all occupations through the year 2024, which means employment is projected to increase 8 percent or more. Job demand will result from the continued increasing levels of data being sent over the internet, in addition to the continual growth of internet users and of goods and services being provided online.

Employment Trend, Projected 2014–24

Computer occupations: 12%

Web administrators and other network support specialists: 8%

Total, all occupations: 7%

Note: "All Occupations" includes all occupations in the U.S. Economy. Source: U.S. Bureau of Labor Statistics, Employment Projections Program

Related Occupations
- Computer & Information Systems Manager
- Computer Engineer
- Computer Network Architect
- Computer Programmer
- Computer Support Specialist
- Computer Systems Analyst
- Database Administrator
- Electronic Commerce Specialist
- Information Security Analyst
- Network & Computer Systems Administrator
- Software Developer
- Web Developer

Related Occupations
- Computer Programmer
- Computer Systems Officer
- Computer Systems Specialist

MORE INFORMATION

International Webmasters Association
119 E. Union Street, Suite A
Pasadena, CA 91103
626.449.3709
www.iwanet.org

League of Professional System Administrators
15000 Commerce Parkway, Suite C
Mount Laurel, NJ 08054
800.285.2141
lopsa.org

National Workforce Center for Emerging Technologies
Bellevue College
3000 Landerholm Circle SE, N258
Bellevue, WA 98007-6484
425.564.4229
www.nwcet.org

World Organization of Webmasters
P.O. Box 1743
Folsom, CA 95630
916.989.2933
www.webprofessionals.org

John Pritchard/Editor

Web Developer

Snapshot

Career Cluster(s): Information Technology
Interests: Web Design, Computer languages, Computers, Art, Marketing
Earnings (Yearly Average): $64,970
Employment & Outlook: Much Faster Than Average Growth Expected

OVERVIEW

Sphere of Work

Web developers generate the final look of a website according to the client's wishes and needs and the principles of the overarching design theme. These developers create the public appearance, organizing functionality, and design principles, or interface, of websites. Website developers brainstorm the creative and technical design of websites. They design a basic webpage structure, or architecture, and select fonts, colors, graphics, and other visual elements, to apply creatively to that architecture.

Work Environment

Having a company or organizational website has become nearly universal. Web developers work in many settings, including software or graphic design firms, advertising agencies, and large and small corporations. They may also be employed in government, hospitals, schools, and colleges, and a multitude of different types of organizations. Some are self-employed. In larger firms or departments, the website developer is part of a team of creative and technical professionals who share responsibility for websites. They spend their days working on computers. The forty-hour work week is most prevalent, although sometimes developers must work long hours to meet deadlines.

Profile

Working Conditions: Work Indoors
Physical Strength: Light Work
Education Needs: On-The-Job Training, Junior/Technical/Community College
Licensure/Certification: Recommended
Opportunities For Experience: Internship, Apprenticeship, Military Service, Part Time Work
Holland Interest Score*: AES

* See Appendix A

Occupation Interest

Designing websites requires creativity, color and design skills, technical knowledge about computer code languages and software, and strong organizational skills. Developers must also communicate effectively with team members and clients. They must keep up with technology and trends and be willing to update websites as necessary. They are fast, creative problem-solvers who understand the needs of business and their clients. Many also enjoy the competition inherent in their industry.

A Day in the Life—Duties and Responsibilities

Sometimes Web developers begin work with the acquisition of a domain name and a suitable website host provider. Other projects might consist of updating an existing website. These and other details are usually worked out during meetings with clients and may also be discussed with colleagues.

One of the most important steps in designing a new site is planning its structure, or architecture. Before beginning work on the actual page, the developer compiles a list of all the necessary components, including databases, shopping carts, calendars, and directories. He or she then decides how each element will best fit into the overall structure of the website.

The website developer next creates an attractive layout for individual pages. This might involve coding a cascading style sheet (CSS), which allows colors, fonts, and other aesthetic elements to be automatically applied to all pages. The developer imports files, such as the company logo, graphics, and navigational buttons, to the website and arranges them in the layout. Sometimes the website developer creates these graphics files.

The website developer might then add coding language to make the page dynamic, mapping out illustrations, adding hyperlinks to text, and so on. Alternatively, he or she might create the site in a WYSIWYG (what you see is what you get) editor that requires less technical knowledge. The website developer ensures that links work properly and that the site displays correctly on various monitors and with different browsers. When the developer is satisfied with the work and the client has approved it, the developer publishes the website on the internet. In some situations, the website developer or administrator executes all of the technical aspects of building the page; this frees the website developer to spend more time on design and creative considerations and the creation of original graphics or multimedia displays. Additional responsibilities of a website developer sometimes include website maintenance, depending on the client's expectations.

Duties and Responsibilities

- Working with customers to determine the content of the website
- Determining the look and feel of the website based on the customer's needs
- Determining the website page structure
- Creating the website pages using various tools and languages including HTML, XML, CGI, PERL and Java
- Creating visually appealing graphics and animation for the website
- Documenting the website
- Loading the web pages to the web server
- Maintaining and updating the website at the customer's request

WORK ENVIRONMENT

Physical Environment

Web developers typically work in offices or studios, either alone or with other developers and programmers. They spend long hours working at a computer. Self-employed web developers frequently work out of home offices.

Human Environment

Most web developers either report to art directors or technical managers. They may supervise part-time staff or interns. In many cases, they work on teams that include illustrators, photographers, videographers, copywriters, and programmers. Web developers who work for a large company or organization may interact with marketing and advertising specialists and the many different people who are responsible for web content. Self-employed web developers necessarily are the sole point of contact for clients.

Technological Environment

Web developers should be familiar with HTML, CSS, WYSIWYG editors, and other basic website design programming languages and tools. They should be comfortable using art creation and graphic design programs, basic office software, and various operating systems, browsers, and displays. Developers must use scanners, printers, digital cameras, smartphones, and other electronic equipment. Those who do more substantive programming should learn more specialized skills in other programs. Some

Transferable Skills and Abilities

Communication Skills
- Speaking effectively
- Writing concisely

Interpersonal/Social Skills
- Being able to work independently
- Working as a member of a team

Organization & Management Skills
- Organizing information or materials
- Paying attention to and handling details
- Performing duties that change frequently
- Performing routine work

Research & Planning Skills
- Creating ideas
- Identifying problems
- Solving problems
- Using logical reasoning

developers need to be familiar with web analytics while others may need to know computer animation and modeling programs.

EDUCATION, TRAINING, AND ADVANCEMENT

High School/Secondary

Aspiring web developers may benefit from taking a college preparatory program with an emphasis in English, mathematics, speech communication, and computer science, and additional electives in graphic design, fine art, photography, video, and other subjects that develop the imagination. Learning new techniques and computer programs outside of school hours is essential. Prospective web developers should consider volunteer or part-time work designing websites for local individuals and businesses.

Suggested High School Subjects
- Accounting
- Algebra
- Applied Communication
- Applied Math
- Bookkeeping
- Business & Computer Technology
- Business Data Processing
- Calculus
- College Preparatory
- Computer Programming
- Computer Science
- English
- Geometry
- Graphic Communications
- Keyboarding
- Mathematics
- Statistics
- Trigonometry

Famous First

The first web pages in the early and mid-1990s were simple, static pages (little interactivity) written in HTML (Hyper Text Markup Language). Eventually, developers employed new techniques and technologies to make pages more dynamic, thereby allowing users to interact with files, input data (such as personal information), and so on.

```
<!DOCTYPE html>
<html>
<!--
Created 16-10-2014
-->
<head>
<title>Sample</title>
</head>
<body>
<p>Sample text</p>
</body>
</html>
```

The HTML code above produces the following below

```
← → C  🗋 file:///\                              .html
Sample text
```

College/Postsecondary

There is no specific postsecondary degree or certificate required by all employers; however, most employers prefer some type of certification. Building a professional portfolio is vital. There are many different learning opportunities that will meet individual employment needs and provide the education needed to prepare an attractive portfolio. Programs in web design are offered through college continuing education programs and in business, technical and commercial art schools.

Students may opt instead for an associate's or bachelor's degree program in graphic design with an emphasis in web design. They can also pursue an undergraduate degree in computer science or information technology, with additional courses in art and design. Disciplines such as business or marketing can also be advantageous areas of study for aspiring web developers. Independent study in website design, internships, workshops offered by software developers, and distance education courses are other options.

Related College Majors
- Computer Engineering
- Computer Engineering Technology
- Computer Maintenance Technology
- Computer Programming
- Computer Science
- Design & Visual Communications
- Educational/Instructional Media Design
- Graphic Design, Commercial Art & Illustration
- Information Sciences & Systems

- Management Information Systems & Business Data Processing

Adult Job Seekers

Web design can be an attractive occupation for adults, especially those with some design or computer aptitude and an interest in working from home. Those who need to update their skills or learn new techniques can choose from many courses offered in the evenings, weekends, or online.

Advancement is dependent upon experience, education, and talent. Developers who acquire more specialized software skills may be given more sophisticated, prestigious jobs or additional responsibilities, such as programming or creating multimedia content. Some developers may move into supervisory positions or start their own design firms.

Professional Certification and Licensure

There are no mandatory licenses or standardized certificates; however, individual schools, vendors, and professional associations offer various certificates. Some of these meet the standards set for the Certified Web Professional (CWP) program established by the World Organization of Webmasters (WOW).

Additional Requirements

Web developers must be internet savvy and enjoy keeping up with the latest trends in web design and technology. They should be creative, detail-oriented individuals capable of learning various software languages, programs, and computer operating systems relatively quickly, often without formal training. Web developers need strong communication and business skills, and they must work well independently or in teams on deadline-oriented projects. Those who wish to establish their own design firms should also have business acumen and strong marketing skills.

Fun Fact

The first domain every registered online—www.symbolics.com—belonged to a now-defunct computer manufacturer.

Source: http://symbolics.com/about-symbolics/

EARNINGS AND ADVANCEMENT

Earnings greatly depend on whether a website developer works for an organization or is self-employed. Earnings for self-employed web developers depend on the number of clients. Median annual earnings of web developers were $64,970 in 2014 and could range from about $35,000 a year to over $115,000 per year.

Metropolitan Areas with the Highest
Employment Level in this Occupation

Metropolitan area	Employment	Employment per thousand jobs	Annual mean wage
New York-Jersey City-White Plains, NY-NJ	8,600	1.33	$82,710
Los Angeles-Long Beach-Glendale, CA	5,370	1.31	$70,410
Washington-Arlington-Alexandria, DC-VA-MD-WV	4,310	1.78	$86,840
San Francisco-Redwood City-South San Francisco, CA	3,640	3.57	$97,400
Chicago-Naperville-Arlington Heights, IL	3,630	1.02	$79,070
Seattle-Bellevue-Everett, WA	3,480	2.26	$91,740
Dallas-Plano-Irving, TX	2,950	1.27	$72,920
San Jose-Sunnyvale-Santa Clara, CA	2,930	2.89	$107,500
Minneapolis-St. Paul-Bloomington, MN-WI	2,900	1.54	$69,560
Boston-Cambridge-Newton, MA	2,590	1.47	$80,760

Source: Bureau of Labor Statistics

EMPLOYMENT AND OUTLOOK

Web developers held about 150,000 jobs nationally in 2014. Employment is expected to grow much faster than the average for all occupations through the year 2024, which means employment is projected to increase 25 percent or more. The large number of businesses and other organizations that require their own website will continue to create demand for this occupation for many years to come.

Employment Trend, Projected 2014–24

Web developers: 27%

Computer occupations: 12%

Total, all occupations: 7%

Note: "All Occupations" includes all occupations in the U.S. Economy. Source: U.S. Bureau of Labor Statistics, Employment Projections Program

Related Occupations
- Commercial Artist
- Computer & Information Systems Manager
- Computer Engineer
- Computer Operator
- Computer Programmer
- Computer Security Specialist
- Computer Support Specialist
- Computer Systems Analyst
- Computer-Control Tool Programmer
- Developer
- Electronic Commerce Specialist
- Graphic Developer
- Information Technology Project Manager
- Network & Computer Systems Administrator
- Network Systems & Data Communications Analyst
- Online Merchant
- Software Developer
- Web Administrator

Related Occupations
- Computer Programmer
- Computer Systems Specialist
- Graphic Developer & Illustrator

Conversation With . . .
REBECCA BLAKE

Design Director, Optimum Design & Consulting
New York
Web developer, 26 years

1. What was your individual career path in terms of education/training, entry-level job, or other significant opportunity?

I graduated from Mount Holyoke College in Massachusetts with a degree in biology. I thought I wanted to go to med school, and got a job at a really good research lab. But I wasn't happy, so I took a drawing class at the Brooklyn Museum to cheer myself up.

The teacher influenced me to keep studying art. My older sister is a designer and she said, "You like words and problem solving—why don't you look at design?" So I took a graphic design class and fell in love. I spent my days working in a research lab and every penny I made on design classes at the School of Visual Arts' night school. I built a portfolio.

In 1990, I became a staff designer at a small non-profit organization and designed their magazine, logos, educational programs, and annual reports. I also got involved with the Graphic Artists Design Guild, a trade union. One of their local committees was run by a dynamic young woman who had lots of cool ideas. She announced she was looking for a design director, hired me, and I've been with her ever since.

My first task was to redesign the website. This was in 1996. I had to learn web design and worked with our company's internet services department, which helped us with this new idea of the web. I learned basic HTML coding. In some ways, it was easier because websites were static, not responsive as they are now.

What I do is now is called front-end web development. The bulk of our sites are in WordPress, although we also design sites where we work with a back-end development team that creates a custom content management system for our clients.

Even though I took a circuitous path to become a web designer and developer, having a varied background and a lot of interests helps. As a designer, you bring everything you've got to the game.

2. **What are the most important skills and/or qualities for someone in your profession?**

Attention to detail. Web design can drive you nuts because stuff will go wrong and you have to spend hours figuring out why something isn't working. That's why you should learn HTML—mess around and have fun with it—as well as a content management system (CMS) like WordPress, which is fun and easy to learn. While you're at it, learn PHP— the engine that controls a lot of the functionality—and cascading style sheets. They'll allow you to customize your site. If you tap into the fun element, that will carry you through the frustration.

Learn traditional design skills. Learn what layout is. Learn typography. Learn how colors work. Pay attention to code if you're a designer. Design and code have to work together.

If you design for clients, you have to learn it's not about you; it's about the client. As a student, you're driven by your passion. If you actually want to earn a living, you have to learn to channel that passion to your clients, and what they need.

3. **What do you wish you had known going into this profession?**

I have become much more involved with design on a policy level. Early on, I didn't understand that designers are absolutely needed because they understand the technology, and they are problem solvers.

4. **Are there many job opportunities in your profession? In what specific areas?**

There are job opportunities, but we're increasingly finding companies want to hire web developers as contract workers at low wages. They're expected to do print, web design, and asset management. You've got to make sure you've got your skills— HTML, CMS and the like—and meld that with traditional design skills. It's rare to find a web developer who has both of those skill sets, and that's going to be valuable to a company.

5. **How do you see your profession changing in the next five years, what role will technology play in those changes, and what skills will be required?**

Companies are now being sued for not having accessible sites, and there's a movement to bring our accessibility standards up to international standards. We have a movement toward inclusivity, as well as an aging population, which will require thinking about things like: "How can somebody who can't see well use this website?"

I think we're going to see more being done with virtual reality, but I don't know how it will tie in with web development.

6. What do you enjoy most about your job? What do you enjoy least about your job?

I enjoy making things that work. It's really satisfying. I least enjoy clients who expect magic and don't understand there is a discipline and thought process behind what designers do.

7. Can you suggest a valuable "try this" for students considering a career in your profession?

Build your own website in straight HTML. Build a WordPress site. Experiment. Chances are you will crash everything, but that's good because it will teach you why your site isn't working. Also, internships are great.

MORE INFORMATION

American Institute of Graphic Arts
164 Fifth Avenue
New York, NY 10010
212.807.1990
www.aiga.org

Association for Computing Machinery
2 Penn Plaza, Suite 701
New York, NY 10121-0701
800.342.6626
acmhelp@acm.org
www.acm.org

Sponsors scholarships for female students to attend conferences:
women.acm.org/participate/scholarship/index.cfm

Graphic Artists Guild
32 Broadway, Suite 1114
New York, NY 10004
212.791.3400
communications@gag.org
www.graphicartistsguild.org

IEEE Computer Society
2001 L Street, NW, Suite 700
Washington, DC 20036-4928
202.371.0101
www.computer.org

Institute for the Certification of Computer Professionals
2400 East Devon Avenue, Suite 281
Des Plaines, IL 60018-4610
800.843.8227
www.iccp.org

International Webmasters Association (IWA)
119 East Union Street, Suite F
Pasadena, California 91103
626.449.3709
www.iwanet.org

Offers online courses:
www.iwanet.org/en/profdevel/62

World Organization of Webmasters (WOW)
P.O. Box 1743
Folsom, CA 95630
916.989.2933
www.webprofessionals.org

Certifies web developers at the apprentice, associate and professional levels:
www.webprofessionals.org/certification

Sponsors National Web Design Contest for high school and college students:
www.webdesigncontest.org/overview

Sally Driscoll/Editor

What Are Your Career Interests?

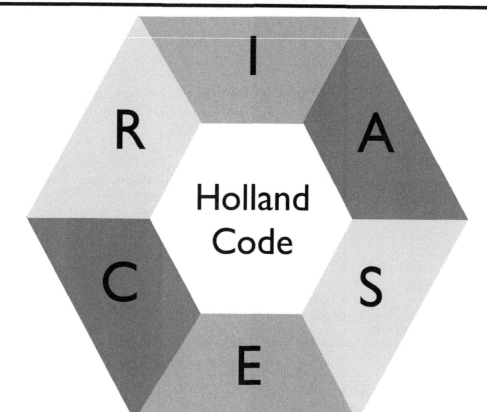

This is based on Dr. John Holland's theory that people and work environments can be loosely classified into six different groups. Each of the letters above corresponds to one of the six groups described in the following pages.

Different people's personalities may find different environments more to their liking. While you may have some interests in and similarities to several of the six groups, you may be attracted primarily to two or three of the areas. These two or three letters are your "Holland Code." For example, with a code of "RES" you would most resemble the Realistic type, somewhat less resemble the Enterprising type, and resemble the Social type even less. The types that are not in your code are the types you resemble least of all.

Most people, and most jobs, are best represented by some combination of two or three of the Holland interest areas. In addition, most people are most satisfied if there is some degree of fit between their personality and their work environment.

The rest of the pages in this booklet further explain each type and provide some examples of career possibilities, areas of study at MU, and co-curricular activities for each code. To take a more in-depth look at your Holland Code, take a self-assessment such as the SDS, Discover, or a card sort at the MU Career Center with a Career Specialist.

This hexagonal model of RIASEC occupations is the copyrighted work of Dr. John Holland, and is used with his permission. The Holland Game is adapted from Richard Bolles' "Quick Job Hunting Map." Copyright 1995, 1998 by the MU Career Center, University of Missouri-Columbia.

Realistic (*Doers*)

People who have athletic ability, prefer to work with objects, machines, tools, plants or animals, or to be outdoors.

Are you?
practical
straightforward/frank
mechanically inclined
stable
concrete
reserved
self-controlled

independent
ambitious
systematic

Can you?
fix electrical things
solve electrical problems
pitch a tent
play a sport
read a blueprint
plant a garden
operate tools and machine

Like to?
tinker with machines/vehicles
work outdoors
be physically active
use your hands
build things
tend/train animals
work on electronic equipment

Career Possibilities
(Holland Code):

Air Traffic Controller (SER)
Archaeologist (IRE)
Athletic Trainer (SRE)
Cartographer (IRE)
Commercial Airline Pilot (RIE)
Commercial Drafter (IRE)
Corrections Officer (SER)

Dental Technician (REI)
Farm Manager (ESR)
Fish and Game Warden (RES)
Floral Designer (RAE)
Forester (RIS)
Geodetic Surveyor (IRE)
Industrial Arts Teacher (IER)

Laboratory Technician (RIE)
Landscape Architect (AIR)
Mechanical Engineer (RIS)
Optician (REI)
Petroleum Geologist (RIE)
Police Officer (SER)
Practical Nurse (SER)

Property Manager (ESR)
Recreation Manager (SER)
Service Manager (ERS)
Software Technician (RCI)
Ultrasound Technologist (RSI)
Vocational Rehabilitation
  Consultant (ESR)

Investigative (*Thinkers*)

People who like to observe, learn, investigate, analyze, evaluate, or solve problems.

Are you?
inquisitive
analytical
scientific
observant/precise
scholarly
cautious

intellectually self-confident
Independent
logical
complex
Curious

Can you?
think abstractly
solve math problems
understand scientific theories
do complex calculations
use a microscope or computer
interpret formulas

Like to?
explore a variety of ideas
work independently
perform lab experiments
deal with abstractions
do research
be challenged

Career Possibilities
(Holland Code):

Actuary (ISE)
Agronomist (IRS)
Anesthesiologist (IRS)
Anthropologist (IRE)
Archaeologist (IRE)
Biochemist (IRS)
Biologist (ISR)

Chemical Engineer (IRE)
Chemist (IRE)
Computer Systems Analyst (IER)
Dentist (ISR)
Ecologist (IRE)
Economist (IAS)
Electrical Engineer (IRE)

Geologist (IRE)
Horticulturist (IRS)
Mathematician (IER)
Medical Technologist (ISA)
Meteorologist (IRS)
Nurse Practitioner (ISA)
Pharmacist (IES)

Physician, General Practice (ISE)
Psychologist (IES)
Research Analyst (IRC)
Statistician (IRE)
Surgeon (IRA)
Technical Writer (IRS)
Veterinarian (IRS)

<u>A</u>rtistic *(Creators)*

People who have artistic, innovating, or intuitional abilities and like to work in unstructured situations using their imagination and creativity.

<u>Are you?</u>
creative
imaginative
innovative
unconventional
emotional
independent
Expressive

original
introspective
impulsive
sensitive
courageous
complicated
idealistic
nonconforming

Can you?
sketch, draw, paint
play a musical instrument
write stories, poetry, music
sing, act, dance
design fashions or interiors

Like to?
attend concerts, theatre, art
  exhibits
read fiction, plays, and poetry
work on crafts
take photography
express yourself creatively
deal with ambiguous ideas

Career Possibilities
(Holland Code):

Actor (AES)
Advertising Art Director (AES)
Advertising Manager (ASE)
Architect (AIR)
Art Teacher (ASE)
Artist (ASI)

Copy Writer (ASI)
Dance Instructor (AER)
Drama Coach (ASE)
English Teacher (ASE)
Entertainer/Performer (AES)
Fashion Illustrator (ASR)

Interior Designer (AES)
Intelligence Research Specialist
  (AEI)
Journalist/Reporter (ASE)
Landscape Architect (AIR)
Librarian (SAI)

Medical Illustrator (AIE)
Museum Curator (AES)
Music Teacher (ASI)
Photographer (AES)
Writer (ASI)
Graphic Designer (AES)

<u>S</u>ocial *(Helpers)*

People who like to work with people to enlighten, inform, help, train, or cure them, or are skilled with words.

Are you?
friendly
helpful
idealistic
insightful
outgoing
understanding

cooperative
generous
responsible
forgiving
patient
kind

Can you?
teach/train others
express yourself clearly
lead a group discussion
mediate disputes
plan and supervise an activity
cooperate well with others

Like to?
work in groups
help people with problems
do volunteer work
work with young people
serve others

Career Possibilities
(Holland Code):

City Manager (SEC)
Clinical Dietitian (SIE)
College/University Faculty (SEI)
Community Org. Director
  (SEA)
Consumer Affairs Director
  (SER)Counselor/Therapist
  (SAE)

Historian (SEI)
Hospital Administrator (SER)
Psychologist (SEI)
Insurance Claims Examiner
  (SIE)
Librarian (SAI)
Medical Assistant (SCR)
Minister/Priest/Rabbi (SAI)
Paralegal (SCE)

Park Naturalist (SEI)
Physical Therapist (SIE)
Police Officer (SER)
Probation and Parole Officer
  (SEC)
Real Estate Appraiser (SCE)
Recreation Director (SER)
Registered Nurse (SIA)

Teacher (SAE)
Social Worker (SEA)
Speech Pathologist (SAI)
Vocational-Rehab. Counselor
  (SEC)
Volunteer Services Director
  (SEC)

Enterprising *(Persuaders)*

People who like to work with people, influencing, persuading, leading or managing for organizational goals or economic gain.

Are you?
self-confident
assertive
persuasive
energetic
adventurous
popular

ambitious
agreeable
talkative
extroverted
spontaneous
optimistic

Can you?
initiate projects
convince people to do things
 your way
sell things
give talks or speeches
organize activities
lead a group
persuade others

Like to?
make decisions
be elected to office
start your own business
campaign politically
meet important people
have power or status

Career Possibilities
(Holland Code):

Advertising Executive (ESA)
Advertising Sales Rep (ESR)
Banker/Financial Planner (ESR)
Branch Manager (ESA)
Business Manager (ESC)
Buyer (ESA)
Chamber of Commerce Exec
 (ESA)

Credit Analyst (EAS)
Customer Service Manager
 (ESA)
Education & Training Manager
 (EIS)
Emergency Medical Technician
 (ESI)
Entrepreneur (ESA)

Foreign Service Officer (ESA)
Funeral Director (ESR)
Insurance Manager (ESC)
Interpreter (ESA)
Lawyer/Attorney (ESA)
Lobbyist (ESA)
Office Manager (ESR)
Personnel Recruiter (ESR)

Politician (ESA)
Public Relations Rep (EAS)
Retail Store Manager (ESR)
Sales Manager (ESA)
Sales Representative (ERS)
Social Service Director (ESA)
Stockbroker (ESI)
Tax Accountant (ECS)

Conventional *(Organizers)*

People who like to work with data, have clerical or numerical ability, carry out tasks in detail, or follow through on others' instructions.

Are you?
well-organized
accurate
numerically inclined
methodical
conscientious
efficient
conforming

practical
thrifty
systematic
structured
polite
ambitious
obedient
persistent

Can you?
work well within a system
do a lot of paper work in a short
 time
keep accurate records
use a computer terminal
write effective business letters

Like to?
follow clearly defined
 procedures
use data processing equipment
work with numbers
type or take shorthand
be responsible for details
collect or organize things

Career Possibilities
(Holland Code):

Abstractor (CSI)
Accountant (CSE)
Administrative Assistant (ESC)
Budget Analyst (CER)
Business Manager (ESC)
Business Programmer (CRI)
Business Teacher (CSE)
Catalog Librarian (CSE)

Claims Adjuster (SEC)
Computer Operator (CSR)
Congressional-District Aide (CES)
Cost Accountant (CES)
Court Reporter (CSE)
Credit Manager (ESC)
Customs Inspector (CEI)
Editorial Assistant (CSI)

Elementary School Teacher
 (SEC)
Financial Analyst (CSI)
Insurance Manager (ESC)
Insurance Underwriter (CSE)
Internal Auditor (ICR)
Kindergarten Teacher (ESC)

Medical Records Technician
 (CSE)
Museum Registrar (CSE)
Paralegal (SCE)
Safety Inspector (RCS)
Tax Accountant (ECS)
Tax Consultant (CES)
Travel Agent (ECS)

BIBLIOGRAPHY

Alpern, Naomi, et al. *IT Career JumpStart: An Introduction to PC Hardware, Software, and Networking*. Indianapolis, IN: Sybex/Wiley, 2012.

Chatham, Robina. *The Art of IT Management: Practical Tools, Techniques and People Skills*. Swindon, UK: BCS, 2015.

Chou, Wushow. *Fast-Tracking Your Career: Soft Skills for Engineering and IT Professionals*. Hoboken, NJ: Wiley, 2013.

Enelow, Wendy S. and Louise M. Kursmark. *Expert Resumes for Computer and Web Jobs*. Indianapolis, IN: JIST Works, 2011.

Erickson, Aaron. *The Nomadic Developer: Surviving and Thriving in a World of Technology Consulting*. Upper Saddle River, NJ: Addison-Wesley, 2009.

Fox, Richard. *Information Technology: An Introduction for Today's Digital World*. Boca Raton, FL: CRC Press, 2013.

Grossman, Kevin. *Tech Job Hunt Handbook: Career Management for Technical Professionals*. New York: Apress, 2012.

Heller, Steven and Veronique Vienne. *Becoming a Graphic & Digital Designer: A Guide to Careers in Design*. Hoboken, NJ: Wiley, 2015.

Lester, Andy. *Land the Tech Job You Love*. Raleigh, NC: Pragmatic Bookshelf, 2009.

Lopp, Michael. *Being Geek: The Software Developer's Career Handbook*. Sebastapol, CA: O'Reilly, 2010.

McDowell, Gayle Laakmann. *Cracking the Tech Career: Insider Advice on Landing a Job at Google, Microsoft, Apple, or Any Top Tech Company*. Hoboken, NJ: Wiley, 2014.

Moran, Matthew. *Building Your IT Career: A Complete Toolkit for a Dynamic Career in Any Economy*. n.p.: Pearson Certification, 2012.

Stanton, Jeffrey M., et al. *Information Nation: Education and Career in the Emerging Information Professions*. Medford, NJ: Information Today, 2011.

Van Vlack, Tarah Wheeler. *Women in Tech: Take Your Career to the Next Level With Practical Advice and Inspiring Stories*. Seattle: Sasquatch Books, 2016.

Vault.com. *Vault Guide to Information Technology Jobs*. New York: Vault.com, 2014.

INDEX

L

lead designer 180, 185, 274, 280
League of Professional System Administrators 149, 229, 293
Level designers 179
Librarian 24
Lithographer 158

M

Machinery 13, 28, 29, 38, 57, 69, 83, 95, 123, 149, 256, 283, 307
Machine Technologist 35
Machining Technology 34, 154, 234
Machinist 38
Management Analyst & Consultant 118
Management Information Systems 63, 76, 114, 141, 195, 209, 221, 248, 290, 300
Manufacturing 29, 43, 230
Marill, Thomas 63
Marketing Management & Research 169
Market Research Analyst 172
Massachusetts Institute of Technology 56, 255
Master's Degree 2, 15, 43, 111, 183, 204
Masters of Business Administration 7
Mathematician 79, 118
MBA 20, 173
Mechanical Drawing 88
Medical Records Administrator 24, 211
Merchandising 168
Metal/Plastic Working Machine Operator 38
Military Service 15, 43, 59, 71, 97, 111, 125, 137, 191, 204, 216, 243, 258, 295
Millwright 38
MIS 114, 141
Mobile Gaming 183
Multimedia Artist & Animator 252

N

National Association of Colleges and Employers 49
National Association of Programmers 83
National Association of Schools of Art and Design 162
National Association of System Administrators 229

National Business Education Association 135
National Center for Women & Information Technology 283
National Coalition for Telecommunications Education and Learning 270
National Institute for Metalworking Skills 35, 41
National Institute of Standards and Technology 202, 213
National Robotics Training Center 241
National Security Agency 201, 202
National Tooling and Machining Association 41
National Workforce Center for Emerging Technologies 69, 229, 293
NCWIT 283
Network architects 58, 59, 60, 61
Network & Computer Systems Administrator 24, 52, 66, 79, 106, 119, 145, 211, 215, 252, 292, 303
Network Professional Association 69, 149, 214
Network Systems & Data Communications Analyst 252, 303
NIMS 35
Norman, Donald "Don" 277
Northeastern University 201
Numerical Control Drill-Press Operators 32
Numerical Control Jig-Boring Machine Operators 32
Numerical Control Milling-Machine Operators 32
Numerical Control Router Set-Up Operators 32

O

Office Machine Operator 131
Office Machine Repairer 91, 266
Online Merchant 172, 303
Operations Research Analyst 24, 52, 79, 119, 211
Operations specialties managers 23, 211

P

Part Time Work 15, 59, 71, 85, 97, 111, 137, 204, 216, 295
PBX Installers and Repairers 260